Soundings and the Politics of Sociolinguistic Listening for Transnational Space

Contemporary Studies in Linguistics

Series Editor: Li Wei

The *Contemporary Studies in Linguistics* series presents state-of-the-art accounts of current research in all areas of linguistics. Written by internationally renowned linguists, the volumes provide a selection of the best scholarship in each area. Each of the chapters appears on the basis of its importance to the field, but also with regard to its wider significance either in terms of methodology, practical application or conclusions. The result is a stimulating contemporary snapshot of the field and a vibrant reader for each of the areas covered the in series.

Titles published in the series:
Applied Linguistics and Politics, edited by Christian W. Chun
Applying Linguistics in Illness and Healthcare Contexts, edited by Zsófia Demjén
Diversifying Family Language Policy, edited by Lyn Wright and Christina Higgins
Contemporary Applied Linguistics Volume 1, edited by Vivian Cook and Li Wei
Contemporary Applied Linguistics Volume 2, edited by Li Wei and Vivian Cook
Contemporary Computer-Assisted Language Learning, edited by Michael Thomas, Hayo Reinders and Mark Warschauer
Contemporary Corpus Linguistics, edited by Paul Baker
Contemporary Critical Discourse Studies, edited by Christopher Hart and Piotr Cap
Contemporary Linguistic Parameters, edited by Antonio Fabregas, Jaume Mateu and Michael Putnam
Contemporary Media Stylistics, edited by Helen Ringrow and Stephen Pihlaja
Contemporary Task-Based Language Teaching in Asia, edited by Michael Thomas and Hayo Reinders
Contemporary Stylistics, edited by Marina Lambrou and Peter Stockwell

Soundings and the Politics of Sociolinguistic Listening for Transnational Space

Kinga Koźmińska

BLOOMSBURY ACADEMIC
LONDON • NEW YORK • OXFORD • NEW DELHI • SYDNEY

BLOOMSBURY ACADEMIC

Bloomsbury Publishing Plc, 50 Bedford Square, London, WC1B 3DP, UK
Bloomsbury Publishing Inc, 1385 Broadway, New York, NY 10018, USA
Bloomsbury Publishing Ireland, 29 Earlsfort Terrace, Dublin 2, D02 AY28, Ireland

BLOOMSBURY, BLOOMSBURY ACADEMIC and the Diana logo are trademarks of Bloomsbury Publishing Plc

First published in Great Britain 2024
Paperback edition published 2025

Copyright © Kinga Koźmińska, 2024, 2025

Kinga Koźmińska has asserted her right under the Copyright, Designs and Patents Act, 1988, to be identified as Author of this work.

For legal purposes the Acknowledgements on p. x constitute an extension of this copyright page.

Cover design: Elena Durey

All rights reserved. No part of this publication may be: i) reproduced or transmitted in any form, electronic or mechanical, including photocopying, recording or by means of any information storage or retrieval system without prior permission in writing from the publishers; or ii) used or reproduced in any way for the training, development or operation of artificial intelligence (AI) technologies, including generative AI technologies. The rights holders expressly reserve this publication from the text and data mining exception as per Article 4(3) of the Digital Single Market Directive (EU) 2019/790.

Bloomsbury Publishing Plc does not have any control over, or responsibility for, any third-party websites referred to or in this book. All internet addresses given in this book were correct at the time of going to press. The author and publisher regret any inconvenience caused if addresses have changed or sites have ceased to exist, but can accept no responsibility for any such changes.

A catalogue record for this book is available from the British Library.

A catalog record for this book is available from the Library of Congress.

ISBN: HB: 978-1-3503-3130-3
PB: 978-1-3503-3134-1
ePDF: 978-1-3503-3131-0
eBook: 978-1-3503-3132-7

Series: Contemporary Studies in Linguistics

Typeset by Deanta Global Publishing Services, Chennai, India

For product safety related questions contact productsafety@bloomsbury.com.

To find out more about our authors and books visit www.bloomsbury.com and sign up for our newsletters.

To my parents and sister Ula

Wierzę, że nasze życie jest nie tylko sumą zdarzeń, lecz skomplikowanym splotem sensów, które tym zdarzeniom przypisujemy. Owe sensy tworzą cudowną tkaninę opowieści, pojęć, idei i można ją uznać za jeden z żywiołów – jak powietrze, ziemia, ogień i woda – które fizycznie determinują nasze istnienie i nas kształtują.

I believe that our life is not only the sum of events, but also the complex interweaving of meanings that we ascribe to those events. Those meanings create a marvelous fabric of stories, concepts, ideas, and can be considered one of the elements – like air, earth, fire, and water – that physically determine our existence and shape us as organisms.

Olga Tokarczuk, *Czuły Narrator [The tender narrator]*, originally published in Polish by Wydawnictwo Literackie and translated by Jennifer Croft for *Words without Borders*.

Contents

List of Figures	viii
List of Tables	ix
Acknowledgements	x
Transcription Conventions	xi

1	Unsettling Systems of Domination	1
2	Politics of Sounding Out and Being Heard	41
3	Weaving Webs of Material–Semiotic Practices in a Community of Movement	83
4	Juxtaposing Dominant Images of Time-Space-Personhood	119
5	Redefining Sociolinguistic Listening	177

Notes	193
References	195
Index	217

Figures

3.1 Measurement of VOT for a word-medial /t/ in *wymarzyłam sobie Wielką BryTAnię*, uttered by a Polish Pole (P9) — 112
3.2 Measurement of VOT for a word-medtial /t/ in *dyskusji politycznej w Wielkiej Brytanii* uttered by a cosmopolitan (C1) — 112
3.3 An intonational phrase, *wymarzyłam sobie właśnie Wielką Brytanię*, 'I dreamt precisely of Great Britain', produced by P9 — 114
3.4 An intonational phrase, *jesteśmy Polakami*, 'we are Poles', ending with a fall produced by Adam (P1) — 116
3.5 An intonational phrase, *nie mam pojęcia skąd jesteś*, 'I have no idea where you're from', ending with a rise produced by Daria (I4) — 117
3.6 An intonational phrase, *nie pokazują swojej niechęci*, 'they don't show their aversion', produced by Natalia (C7) — 117

Tables

3.1	Network scores for all speakers based on contacts other than kinship in descending order of the score	104
3.2	Reported VOTs for Polish and English	109
4.1	Variables used in statistical analysis	120
4.2	Mean VOT(ms), standard deviations and number of all stops for fifteen women ($N=1408$)	122
4.3	Results for significant fixed effects for all stops ($N=1408$)	123
4.4	Distribution of all intonation patterns (fall, rise, fall-rise) for all fifteen women	124
4.5	Distribution of fall-rises across fifteen women according to discursive function	125

Acknowledgements

This book would not be possible without support of many fantastic people that I have met on my way. First of all, it would not come into being without the people I love or loved, who have been my guiding light for years. Special thanks to my parents, Iza and Zbyszek Koźmińscy, and sister Ula: I am the luckiest person on Earth to have you in my life. Thank you for always believing in me, pushing me to see the world and listening to my stories in transnational space. To my relatives in Poland, the United States, the United Kingdom, France, Belgium or elsewhere: you continue to be an inspiration to me, and it is the greatest honour to be part of this crowd. Special thanks to my late grandfather, Tadeusz Kalbarczyk, for teaching me how to walk and talk to *everyone*.

Many thanks to the series editor, Prof Li Wei, for giving me an opportunity to turn these thoughts into my first book. Special thanks to Prof Zhu Hua for sharing comments on one of the chapters and being a wonderful friend. The book would not be possible without my DPhil supervisor, Dr Rosalind Temple, and the continuous support of Prof Deborah Cameron as well as the Faculty of Linguistics, Philology and Phonetics at the University of Oxford, Somerville College, Language and Society Research Group and my college advisor, Prof Aditi Lahiri. The book would not be in its current shape also without discussions at Birkbeck, University of London, where I shared my thoughts with Dr Jackie Lou, Prof Bojana Petric, Prof Jean-Marc Dewaele, Prof Marjorie Lorch, Dr Lisa McAntee-Atalianis and was encouraged by many other colleagues. I want to thank audiences of many seminars and conferences in the United Kingdom, the United States, Europe and elsewhere, where I shaped my ideas. Finally, special thanks to the participants of my projects; and all my students: I always learn so much from you, thank you.

Thanks for comments on selected parts of the book and support to Prof Raluca Soreanou, Sahra Abdhullahi and Dr Sara Young. Thanks for wonderful friendships and helping me when I needed it the most to: Reut Barak-Smith, Dr Ola Hekselman, Kate Jarvis, Ola McLees, Bartłomiej Trochowicz, Dr Leonie Schulte, Julia Szyndzielorz, Dr Kristina Valendinova, Dr Marta Wojnowska, Dr Annette Zimmermann. I left a piece of my heart in various places, but two cities deserve special acknowledgements: the phoenix city of my upbringing, Warsaw, for teaching me about aesthetics and renewal; and London, for empowering me to be even more outspoken and for sharing its magical galleries with me every week.

Transcription Conventions

An inventory of transcript symbols; based on Jefferson 2004, Atkinson and Heritage 1986, Gumperz and Berenz (1993).

Symbol	Meaning
____	Nuclear accent
\	Fall
/	Rise
\/	Fall-Rise
=	No break/gap
(0.0)	Break in tenths of seconds
(.)	Brief pause
.hhh	Inbreath
-	Truncated phrase
[	Overlap onset
]	Overlap end
(h)	Simultaneous laughter, crying, breathlessness
( )	Transcriber did not understand the part of talk
((comment))	Transcriber's comments
:	Lengthening of the sound before the colon (the more colons, the longer the lengthening)
WORD	Loud sounds relative to the surrounding talk
°word°	Softer relative to the surrounding talk
> <	Talk speeded up in comparison to the surrounding talk
< >	Talk slowed down in comparison to the surrounding talk
(ms)	VOT in ms (aspiration)
ʲ	palatalized
ɫ	dark l

1

Unsettling Systems of Domination

Beginning the conversation

This book is a story made of situated research actions, communication and knowledge production in transnational space at times of radical change and contestation of authentic category reproduction. It focuses on connections between research practices, a spoken mode of discourse, objects of thought, forms of life and figures of community (Rancière 2013). In the pages that follow, I juxtapose ethnographic observations from my own engagement with variously positioned Polish-speaking migrants in the UK over the last decade with sociological, anthropological and linguistic literature and discourse analysis of recorded interview extracts. I do so to contribute to debates on modes of transformation, conditions of intelligibility and emerging regimes of politics, 'based on the indetermination of identities, delegitimization of positions of speech and deregulation of partitions of space and time' (Rancière 2013) in the globalized world. Moving away from colonial definitions both of culture and language, I focus on continuous and recursive processes of chaining of sounded signs to flesh out how 'time- and place-making processes are indexically linked to subject creation' (Faudree 2012) and how sonic recontextualization may contribute to emerging 'epistemologies of purification'. Examining mechanisms that link sounded signs to objects of thought, context and perceiving selves, I focus on the performance of embodied memory to empirically and ethnographically locate modalities of signification (French 2012) and flesh out processes that shape cartographies of communicability (Briggs 2007).

Drawing on arguments in sociolinguistics of globalization, linguistic anthropology and anthropology of the sound, my text hence urges the reader to follow calls for a holistic study of discourse and its embedding in the 'historical emergence of particular recording techniques, the ways in which they are implicated in particular politics of modernity and their implications for notions of authenticity' (Faudree 2012). The reader can hence expect a close examination of the internal dynamics of discourse production and research practices as well as a focus on the materiality of speech as physical events 'circulating in social worlds and phenomenally accessible to the senses' (Faudree 2012: 521). As the story unfolds, I try to convince the reader that surface representations of signs of migration rely on a certain 'distribution of the sensible' (Rancière 2013), that is, 'the system of self-evident facts of sense perception that simultaneously discloses the existence of something in common and the delimitations that define the respective parts and positions within it' (Rancière 2013). Situating this story in relation to a particular distribution of times, spaces and forms of engagement, I intend to show how various individuals play a part in this distribution, what they do with what is common to the community and how they establish their relations with otherness and the self in situated encounters in transnational timespace. I focus on the sonic dimension of discourse to move away from regimes of visibility on which the hierarchical imagination of the community is built, and to flesh out processes that transform discursive performances of collective memory. It is hence a story that centres upon possibilities conditioned by particular connections in the globalized world and the ways in which 'words make themselves understood' (Lefebvre 2014) in the context of formation of collective transnational actors and capitalist value. It is in the end a story that makes a radical call against the separation of discourse from materiality and the sensorium as a way to understand imbalances of power and transformations of lived realities in contemporary transnational space.

This story began in 2012 when I came to the UK to start my DPhil programme at Oxford, which focused on emerging linguistic practices among members of the UK Polish-speaking community. In late October, after calling various Polish organizations and talking to community organizers in London on the phone, I decided to make my first visit to one of them. I took an Oxford Tube bus, which became my frequent means of transportation in the next two years. I decided to meet with a community organizer in Shepherd's Bush, an area in West London. I didn't know this area of London extremely well at the time, although I had spent my late teens with Zadie Smith's novels, enjoyed music from London sound collectives and spent a few summers in London as a teenager and later a BA student learning about the English language and literature in various parts of the city. What I did know about West London was that it had an old Polish settlement. My own father would often recall his stays at a family friend's house in West London during his studies as one of the most exciting periods of his twenties. Additionally, Shepherd's Bush is located in the borough of Hammersmith and

Fulham, which, as I had already known, hosted, among others, the eldest and most well-known Polish cultural centre in the UK, POSK. I frequented it quite often throughout the years, especially after settling in London later on.

Polish presence in the area was immediately noticeable to me. Being a city walker, I started strolling along Uxbridge Road, noticing the eldest of the Mleczko chain delicatessen. Its white and red colours made it impossible for me to miss it. As I still had some time before my meeting and as I had been hanging out in the Polish shop in Oxford for the past few weeks, I decided to check out the shop. Similarly to the Oxford shop and many other Polish shops that I have visited in the following years, it was a strikingly Polish space to me. The voice of a Polish radio host from one of the major radio stations in Poland was introducing the next song as I started wandering around the shop's aisles. Various Polish products ranging from home-made bread through ordinary milk from Poland to fancy chocolate bars were available, some with no English translations. Well-known Polish weekly magazines and publications were piled in the press section. Shop assistants addressed most customers in Polish. After spending the last three and a half months before moving to the UK in Cambodia, I happily grabbed a Wedel chocolate wafer, which I associated with Warsaw, where the chocolate brand originates from and where I was born and raised. I walked around, eavesdropped and examined the products carefully. I heard various 'melodies' of the Polish language. Apart from 'the standard', some of them resembled regional and rural ways of speaking that I was familiar with from Poland. I delved into the sounds and was struck by the fact that in Warsaw, which had always been a hub for internal migrations within Poland, dominant rhythms of the language would be slightly different. As I reached the till, I observed the shop assistant addressing most customers in Polish, but somehow she switched to English when I was about to pay. Quite surprised, I answered in Polish, but the shop assistant just uttered: 'Thanks, bye', perhaps not recognizing me as a regular visitor. I found the exchange unexpected, which admittedly made me feel slightly strange, but I had no time: I had to rush to the meeting a few buildings down the road.

The person that had agreed to meet with me turned out to be a man who looked over forty to me. He greeted me in Polish and cordially invited me to his office. As we started chatting, I introduced myself and my project again, speaking in quite a formal register that I associated with public encounters from Poland. Carefully selecting his words, the man started sharing his life story with me. Speaking at a fairly slow pace, he told me that he was born in Cardiff to Polish parents who similarly to Władysław Mleczko, the founder of the Polish delicatessen that I had just visited, settled in the UK after the Second World War.

When one visits Mleczko's website, a few references to his family's service in the Polish army and deportation to Soviet gulags (Davis 2015) can be found. We learn that Mleczko spent his childhood in Siberia and then travelled through Iran to the UK. Similar references were made by my interlocutor. He told me that his parents had fought with 1 Polish Army Corps under General Maczek and settled in Cardiff after the war. We spent some time talking about their path, but I didn't reveal where my understanding of the story came from as I chose not to offer personal details in the first encounter. My father's family shared this experience, and I was continually reminded of it throughout the duration of the project as I was visiting my family in the north of England.

The significance of the references to the post-war migration became apparent when, similarly to other post-war organizers I had talked to, my interlocutor repeated them again and again to differentiate between Polish migrants in today's Britain. He told me that most Polish migrants at the time were from the post-communist Poland, and that it was a very different migration. He recalled that in 2004, when the UK opened its borders to Polish citizens, 'we [post-war Polish organisers] had to put out many fires', which included among other interventions to support the homeless and 'economic migrants' living at Victoria Station in London (https://poranny.pl/polacy-z-dworca-victoria/ar/5028138). Finally, he told me that the difference between the post-war and post-EU-enlargement migrants was, 'it's [like] AK [the Home Army] vs. PRL [Polish People's Republic]'. He also compared linguistic practices, reporting that he and his sibling grew up speaking Polish at home, and were immersed in English education outside the house, while the knowledge of English of the newcomers varied. We talked about Polish Saturday schools and the importance of language maintenance for identification in the UK. At one point, he turned to me and said in Polish: 'I'll tell you what, it'll be best to conduct a study to show the correlation between hours spent at a Polish school and proficiency.' I thanked him for his advice, we chatted about the schools more, and not long afterwards I left. As I was conducting this preliminary fieldwork also to establish what projects were needed, I made a note of yet another interest that particular institutional bodies and members of the community wanted me to represent in my project. I noticed the heterogeneity of concerns that would have to be addressed in a longer period than the three years I had ahead of me, perhaps by someone else. I left the man's office, not telling him that I had just started sitting in at a Polish Saturday school in Oxford, and was considering looking at multilingual practices among kids and teenagers. However, as I was walking towards my bus stop, I felt increasingly confused. On the way back, I wondered how he read me to make the comment about 'AK vs. PRL'. Was the immediate listener important at all? Or should I in fact see myself as equated with the whole People's Republic of Poland, disregarding the fact that being born in 1986 I lived in it for only three years of my life? How come was the Home Army only in the UK? Why was this the most relevant point to repeat today?

Upon reflection, these comments are no surprise in the light of the history of Polish presence in the UK. It can be dated back to the eighteenth century (Korys 2004), with migration in the nineteenth century being large enough to establish the first complementary school in Manchester. As Korys (2004) notes, in the second half of the eighteenth century and throughout the nineteenth century, Polish migrants were usually political refugees, whereas in the twentieth century they were frequently described as more economically motivated migrants. Thousands of Polish migrants also came to the UK after the First World War, with most settling in London and some going back to Poland once peace was restored. During the Second World War, the British government made a decision to allow Polish soldiers to demobilize and settle (Zubrzycki 1956) as well as to permit people from the labour camps in Europe to fill labour shortages in Britain (Tannahill 1958). Therefore, large Polish groups did not settle in Britain until the introduction of the first mass immigration law for people from outside the Empire – the 1947 Polish Resettlement Act. This is when my interlocutor, Mr Mleczko, and my grandmother's family stayed in the UK. This was also the first time that Britain acquired a significant Polish diaspora of approximately 160,000 members (Burrell 2006), some of whom later moved to North America or Australia (Waniek-Klimczak 2009). Second World War Polish combatants established an anti-communist Polish government-in-exile (Triandafyllidou 2006). Later, during the Cold War, the UK, like many Western states, allowed Polish citizens to come and settle if they expressed the will to do so (Triandafyllidou 2006), which usually meant not being able to go back. During the following forty-five years, official emigration from Poland remained low (Kępińska 2004) and highly controlled (Garapich 2016).

In the UK, most post–Second World War Polish migrants worked in manual occupations, for example, in the building industry, agriculture, mining. Some of the professionals who had been trained in Poland managed to find employment as doctors, dentists, pharmacists, engineers, lawyers, artists or clergy (Waniek-Klimczak 2009). Most people coming from Poland had little or no knowledge of English. Typically, they began their lives in the British Isles as unqualified workers, but moved up the economic ladder after a significant period of time. Reportedly, adapting to the new way of living was difficult for members of the

Polish intelligentsia. Polish workers were usually described as reliable, hard-working, ambitious, but also clannish, sticking with each other and not easily mixing with non-Polish colleagues (Waniek-Klimczak 2009), descriptors also used to describe other immigrant communities. During this period, various ethnic Polish organizations were established, for example, the already mentioned POSK. In fact, most of the powerful Polish organizations operating in Britain today were set up in the post-war period and are run by post-war migrants or their offspring who, like my interlocutor, still regulate access to the UK diasporic infrastructure for the newcomers. Many have reported 'nationalist' attitudes (Sales et al. 2008) among post-war community organizers and a negative stance towards those born in the People's Republic of Poland (Sword 1994). During the Cold War, Second World War settlers rejected the Warsaw regime, and in Britain compensated for their fall in status through insistence on ethnic prestige.

After coming back to Oxford and sharing my observations at a supervision meeting, one of my supervisors suggested that maybe I could devote my thesis to the study of language ideologies focusing on the post-war vs. post-EU-enlargement migrants. I admitted that such a project could be interesting, but felt slightly overwhelmed by the heterogeneity of ethnic experiences that I was encountering and possible factors that needed to be taken into account to conduct such a project. We both knew that the vast majority of those classified as 'Polish' by official measures at the time came after the 2004 EU enlargement, that is, when Britain granted full access to its labour market to such Eastern European[1] states as the Czech Republic, Estonia, Hungary, Latvia, Lithuania, Poland, Slovakia and Slovenia. According to *Migration to and from the UK* by John Salt (2011), in 2007, Poles took over the first position as the largest national group working and living in the UK, preceding the Irish and Indians. On the basis of the number of registered workers, the Office for National Statistics estimated that the most common non-UK nationality in England and Wales in 2011 was Polish with 558,000 residents (Office for National Statistics 2011), after the 'home nations'. People born in Poland accounted for 14 per cent of recent arrivals, with half of them coming between 2004 and 2006. According to the 2011 census, Poland, Ireland and India were the top three countries in terms of the number of foreign-born people in England and Wales. Importantly, the census also noted that the Polish language was the second most spoken language in the British Isles, scoring similarly to those who reported any knowledge of Welsh (https://gov.wales/sites/default/files/statistics-and-research/2019-03/121211sb1182012en.pdf). This increase in the number of Polish migrants living and working in the UK was rapid, which was also relatively new in the history of British society and migration to the UK. The 2011 census shows that nearly all (92 per cent) Polish-born usual residents had arrived since 2001. Later, in 2016, the House of Commons estimated that the number of Polish migrants living in the UK exceeded 900,000. Due to difficulties with estimates of migrant populations, the Home Office provided both numbers of nationals of a country and people born in a country. For Polish migrants, both numbers exceeded 900,000. Finally, some unofficial reports talked about up to two million people.

Based on my knowledge of Poland and the Polish diaspora, the sheer number suggested heterogeneity. Geographically, those classified as 'Polish' in today's Britain spread across rural, metropolitan and inner-city localities (Hall 2015), with the largest numbers reported for London, the South-east and North-west (House of Commons 2016). While the Polish have often been portrayed as a fairly homogeneous ethnic group in the British press (e.g. Garapich 2008), they are in fact heterogeneous in terms of multiple migration motivations, various interests and differing sociocultural capital. Those migrating after the EU enlargement in 2004 were more highly educated individuals, but subsequent arrival of less educated workers was also reported (Okólski and Salt 2014). Post-1989, unofficially, many single men came for work (Young 2018), but after 2004 the main demographic changed to families with children (Ryan et al. 2009). Statistics from 2016, when I finished my programme, showed that 646,000 people born in Poland were employed in a range of occupations, both low-paid and high-paid (House of Commons 2016). While, despite fairly high levels of education, the exploitation and deskilling of Polish and Eastern European migrants have been widespread (e.g. Rzepnikowska 2018), the statistics suggested that the population is socio-economically stratified. Importantly for my language interests, the data also pointed to various levels of knowledge of the English language (Błasiak 2011).

At the time, I was not sure whether comparing post-war and post-EU-enlargement migrants was what I had the means to investigate thoroughly. Garapich (2016) later showed in detail how old migrants often claimed separateness and portrayed their presence in Britain as permanent, sedentary and integrated into British society and values, and framed the newcomers as 'Soviet' temporary migrants who were 'stained mentally and morally by being born and brought up in Polish People's Republic' (Garapich 2016: 287). Although the two migration waves were often contrasted, Garapich (2016) argued that the groups were in fact tightly interconnected and engaged in the politics of ethnic representation in relational terms. Drawing on his ethnographic work in Polish organizations in London, he demonstrated that discourse of 'right' Poles with 'true and patriotic values' (Garapich 2016) had mediated the post-war organizers' contact with post-EU accession migrants, often relying on the image of Polonia, the Polish diaspora as a symbol of return to the community, and 'the sacred imagined source of moral national spine' (277).

In 2021, after working on a multi-method project on family linguistic practices in UK Polish, Chinese and Somali communities, among others with Prof Zhu Hua, we eventually returned to this idea. Based on my own two-year-long ethnographic fieldwork in London's Polish organizations, we noted that the nationalistic attitudes of old migrants together with the diasporic infrastructure have allowed the dominant UK Polish ethnic community representation to be defined and differentiated in terms of two waves of migration. We claimed, however, that it was through their orientation to the standard language and preference for linguistic purity that the organizers united and erased observed historical, class and regional differences. We argued that by doing so, they aimed to create a representation of a timeless unified Polish community in line with the static framework of the European nation-state that promotes linguistic, cultural and racial purity.

In the months following my first trip to London, I attended various 'Polish' spaces, and participated in 'Polish' events and activities; talked to differently positioned migrants in person, online or by phone; watched documentaries on Polish migration produced in the UK next to those produced in Poland and conducted internet research about various Polish organizations. I established that there was an active large network of self-labelled UK Polish organizations. These were both post-war organizations and post-EU-accession ones, ranging from cultural centres, sports clubs, churches, Saturday schools, community centres to other need-based organizations (for an overview refer to Kozminska and Zhu Hua 2021). Some of them also belonged to wider networks of global Polish organizations. While conducting this research, I noted that the Polish state was an active actor in Polish diasporic life, which was also later shown by Garapich (2016). Additionally, I established that people migrating from Poland may access media targeting both the UK Polish population and the general Polish population in Poland and other diasporic contexts. As we reported in 2021 (Kozminska and Zhu Hua 2021), there were at least two Polish radio channels operating in London and three Polish radio channels located in Poland available in Britain. Apart from a local UK newspaper, *Tygodnik Polski*, disseminated since 1959 and now available online, two Poland-based digital media sites were among the top ten British media sites in terms of page views in 2017 (SimilarWeb 2017), which suggests that speakers of Polish made frequent use of non-UK resources. Finally, we also noted that there were online sites where children and teenagers may access education in Polish, for example, online Polish schools in London and Poland.

Despite the heterogeneity of UK-based Polish resources, talking to some community organizers I learned that not all Polish-speaking migrants actively participated in the community life. As we reported in 2021,[2] only one in four children classified by census measures as Polish in the UK attended Polish Saturday schools. Polish playgroups in London that I observed for the Family Language Policy project between 2017 and 2019 were attended by between a few and thirty mothers with children weekly. Interviews with the Polish Catholic mission together with participant observations in selected Polish churches in London in 2018 allowed me to confirm my initial observations of fairly low attendance from 2012 to 2014: in 2018, 50752 attended 90 Polish Catholic parishes in which mass is usually conducted in Polish. The emerging picture made the tensions, multiplicity of participation and variety of ethnic experiences increasingly difficult to miss. At the same time, the low participation and engagement in public life were no surprise to me as they resembled norms of civic social capital (Zukowski and Theiss 2014) reported for Polish society that I, as a person who spent twenty-three years of my life mostly in Poland, was quite familiar with. In 2017, Kordasiewicz and Sadura (2017) also corroborated such norms for the UK Polish community by reporting fairly low civic and political participation, as well as a greater sense of alienation from the institutional order among Polish migrants, especially youth, in Lewisham, London. At the time, it was often argued that active participation in Poland tended to be limited to private and informal family and friendship networks rather than the public domain due to the legacy of state socialism (Zukowski and Theiss 2014).

In autumn 2012, I also attended various meetings of a Polish society at Oxford University. At one of the meetings organized to celebrate the anniversary of Polish independence in one of the colleges in November, I found myself talking to two students. Similarly to many of my encounters with Polish-speaking migrants over the next decade, at the beginning we greeted each other cordially and introduced ourselves in Polish with informal register and forms of address. Suddenly, one of the students asked about our places of origin. While doing that, he first asserted that he was from Silesia. I took the next turn and replied that I came from Warsaw, but the third interlocutor just uttered, 'Oh, I'm from nowhere'. The other student urged him to state what that meant, and we learnt that the student grew up in a middle-sized city in north-eastern Poland and Lviv, and attended the last year of his high school in the UK. The conversation continued as we talked about our studies, reasons for coming to the UK and observations about the event and community more broadly. The students asked me about my project and immediately started sharing their observations about linguistic practices and changes that they had observed among Polish-speaking migrants in the UK. Suddenly, the student 'from nowhere' turned to me and asked, 'Do I have different p's and t's?' Intrigued by his question, I asked for an explanation. He recalled being frequently commented on his *p*'s and *t*'s by others since moving to the UK. I listened, while the other student looked at him and intervened: 'Oh, there are those who do that, but I don't.' The conversation continued and similarly to some of his peers with whom I had already conversed I noticed that the stops of the student 'from nowhere' were in fact occasionally more aspirated than those of the other student.

Intrigued by the variety of sounded experiences that I was encountering, and noticing that in sociolinguistics of globalization little attention had been paid to the soundings of transnational timespace, I eventually decided on a project that would focus on members of this particular group, UK-university-educated Polish-speaking young adults. At the time, most newcomers from Poland were also below thirty-five years of age. I noticed that this group was perhaps talked about, but rarely given voice in Poland or abroad at the time, although it happened to be important for the history of migrations from Poland. It was the first generation of Polish citizens who did not have to choose between Poland and the West as their parents and grandparents did, but who, like other Europeans, could move within the European Union. This was also the first generation in the history of Poland who, after more than forty years of state socialism, were raised and began their lives in a transforming, capitalist system.

I started by attending various events and chatting with various Polish-speaking young adults who were living and working in South-east England, whom I kept interviewing and, where possible, observing in the next two years. I noted that particular sounds, that is stops, fricatives and an occasional use of dark *l* were often linked to changing 'melodies' of the Polish language in metadiscourse and used to differentiate between peers in the UK. This was visible when I met with Renata in 2013, who asked me to come to Stratford, from where she took me to the flat she was renting with a friend in East London. At the time, she was working in an accountancy firm in London. When referring to the new ways of speaking, she suggested that they had to do with gendered differences. The comments linking some women to the 'new' ways of speaking were repeated by various women that I talked to, often being mentioned in relation to networks or international partners. The awareness of these associations sometimes popped up during my encounters with the interviewed men, but it seemed that their engagement with the meaningfulness of the new ways of speaking was less pronounced. I observed increased metalinguistic awareness among many people I talked to, which was only more noticeable during my later ethnographic work with Polish-speaking families and community organizations in London and South-east England in 2017–19.

I initially intended to conduct participant observations among a community of practice[3] that I have been put in touch with through some Oxford graduate students and alumni as this is where I studied for my DPhil degree. I saw it as an opportunity to investigate these emerging ways of speaking that I kept hearing and hearing about. As suggested earlier, I quickly realized that I was dealing with a community of movement[4] that relied on digital, often written communication and meetings in various places in transnational space, from gatherings in Oxford or London, and individual encounters, to UK-graduates' meetings in Warsaw that I attended. As I was listening to the dominant patterns among members of the Oxford community of practice, I also noticed that they were mostly similar to what at the time, I would hear as 'standard' Polish pronunciation.

Intrigued by these observations, I also registered the emerging tensions that made diaspora-oriented speakers usually reflect negatively upon new practices. As I quickly established, next to organized diasporic activities, which were mostly attended by Poland-oriented individuals, informal networks linked young adults in online spaces and dynamic encounters in South-east England and Poland. In addition to looking at Polish-speaking young adults who had ties to the Oxford group I was observing, so as not to skew my results only to those who usually relied on standard pronunciation, I sent out an announcement in Polish and English to local online networks, and got in touch with some people who were in South-east England and whom I knew from Poland. The limitations of my PhD programme would not allow me to follow all speakers to the same degree. To quote John Akomfrah, the founder of Black British Audio Film Collective, whose artistic work about Black communities and migrations to the UK continued to be an inspiration for me in the coming years, I had to 'quickly become comfortable with the idea of fragments, that discrete elements overlap'. I therefore decided to collect situated accounts of migration and investigate politics of production of perspectives on norms and practices. Between 2012 and 2014, I recorded forty-two interviews in the Greater London area and Oxford, and met in person with some thirty more individuals who had finished their studies at UK universities and stayed to work in South-east England.

Rather than imagining my project as either objectivist or relativist, or relying on static definitions that could lead to epistemic violence, with these accounts, at the time, I wanted to begin a conversation about emerging differences and see how situated perspectives and practices are embedded in relation to my own and others' practices of domination and unequal positions in transnational space. Over the years, I have searched for language to describe what I have been doing, and my language to talk about these observations has changed with further observations, projects and experiences. However, the project began with a strong conviction that subjectivities are always multidimensional, partial, multiple, unfinished, complex and contradictory (Haraway 1988). It also rested on a premise that situated accounts are not objective, but rather provide 'perspectives on events' (Ochs and Capps 2001: 45).

My participants also continually reminded me of this when I began collecting the accounts. For example, Adam, who at the time strongly aligned himself with Polish culture and language and embraced the logic of the state formation as the dominant frame to present himself as a Polish Pole in his interview with me, noted that his ways of seeing himself and practices in the UK and transnational space had changed.

> *na początku dla mnie to nie miałem tak dużej potrzeby, ponieważ dla mnie to było doświadczenie, ja chciałem się jak najlepiej nauczyć języka, zintegrować, zrozumieć perspektywę innych ludzi i priorytetem nie było, że tak powiem dla mnie spotkanie się z Polakami [. . .] ale z czasem perspektywa się zmieniała, ponieważ z trybu studiów zmieniło się to w tryb życia w Anglii więc, teraz to można powiedzieć, że jakieś malutkie korzenie zapuściliśmy [on i jego żona], więc teraz szukamy tego właściwego balansu, to już nie jest kwestia tylko eksploracji czy próby ciągłej nauki, tylko teraz już jest to próba znalezienia balansu w życiu*

> (at the beginning for me, I didn't need to, because for me it was an experience, I wanted to learn the language as well as I could, integrate, understand other people's perspectives and the priority was not for me to meet with Poles [. . .] but the perspectives changed with time because being a student changed into living a life in the UK, so now you can say that we have put down little roots [we = he and his Polish wife], so we are now looking for a right balance, it's no longer only a matter of exploration or an attempt to constantly learn, but now it is an attempt to find a balance in life)

I must confess that my recognition of the changing and multiple nature of public subjectivity was also linked to my own dissatisfaction with objective scientific accounts where the male, White, Western, heteronormative and human voice has continuously rendered other voices as subjective or invalid and therefore not deserving to be heard. At the same time, it is also motivated by observed limitations of relativist positions, where all perspectives are seen as equal and where all claims to objectivity are erased. The book therefore draws on Haraway's concept of *situated* knowledges, which stresses that perspectives and vision are always partial, but they are also embodied and accountable, hence enabled by semiotic–material circumstances. This in turn does not allow us to erase claims to objectivity and present views purely as 'a matter of opinion', but rather as a result of encounters in an active world of power relations where particular knowledges are sounded out and heard and get to be institutionalized in academic projects.

To understand disparate orientations and rhythms that sat momentarily with one another to form emerging Polish-sounding stories in the UK, observed and studied in this research project, I chose to collect situated accounts of transnational experiences among middle-class UK-educated Polish-speaking young adults in the British state. Relying on my own linguistic skills and making another conscious choice to redirect sociolinguistic discussions to non-dominant linguistic resources in the British state, I decided to explore how sociolinguistic tools may be used to disrupt sociolinguistic imagination and, by focusing on the materiality of the code, bring us closer to emerging embodied transnational cultures and projects. Following calls for radical openness (Deumert et al. 2020), in this book, I think with the audio-recorded data, in order to understand what we can learn from the transience of diasporic soundings today and why it matters for our understanding of transnational space. I turn to emergent public subjectivities (Agha 2007b) and ways in which frames of performance were linked to frames of representation in these situated encounters, which reveals that despite common background, social location and shared experiences, my participants oriented themselves to historically contingent multitudes of centres of linguistic authority: from authentic 'Polish Poles' aligning with collective state-level political formations in sociohistorical timespace through evolving private 'in-between' selves moving through relatively unchanging timespaces to globalist private 'cosmopolitan' selves in the here-and-now. By bringing the emerging three ideological orientations into dialogue with one another and unpacking meanings behind my participants' self-presentations in detail later on, I intend to show how in transnational space, they were assembling self and collective images through 'felt' vibrations, modalities, resonances and tonalities (LaBelle 2018). I look at the ways in which through explorations of sociolinguistic possibilities and movements, new situated knowledges were being formed.

In line with Collins's (2015) call for no blind research methodologies, I quickly saw how the fact that both my Polish-speaking participants and I were situated within a matrix of domination in particular ways impacted our embodied knowledge production. First of all, I was aware that being citizens of the largest and most populous state in East-Central Europe from which post-EU accession migrants had been coming to the UK, 'Polish migrants' had been often targeted by the British press (e.g. Anderson and Blinder 2019, Fomina and Frelak 2008, Spigelman 2013) and were treated as an emblem of Eastern European migrants in Britain (e.g. Dorling and Tomlinson 2019), at the same time being entangled in Eastern European hierarchies, a point I unpack in the last section of this chapter. With this project, I therefore also made a conscious decision to begin the discussion about Eastern European experiences in transnational space from a sounded perspective. Rather than following purely nationalistic paradigms observed in the studies of Eastern European migrations (e.g. discussed in White et al. 2018), however, I turn to sounded experiences as a way to understand emerging collective desires among those on the move, and work through contradictions and complexities, to think about 'an emancipation of language and old ways of thinking' (Kelley 2002: 9).

Importantly, applying an intersectional (Collins 2019) lens, this project therefore makes a particular claim about transnational space: that is that it operates within interlocking systems of domination and oppression, where various forms of privilege linked to race, ethnicity, gender, class, sexuality, age or ability (Collins 2015) do not exist independently of each other. Rather, they are interconnected and cannot be fully understood without referring to other systems, which share 'a belief in domination and belief in the notions of superior and inferior, which are components of all of those systems' (bell hooks 2015). By foregrounding the sounded perspective, I make, however, a further claim that 'standard' languages are part of those systems. I demonstrate how particular ideas about language and culture are related to the logic of capitalism, patriarchy and the nation-state (Collins 2015), how emerging soundings create epistemic and affective effects, and shape processes of value attribution in transnational space. Putting emerging situated ideological orientations in dialogue with one another, I highlight how discourse reinforces and challenges the borders of recognized bodies and power regimes. By doing so, I aim to show that the focus on embodied material enactments may lead us to reflexive collective practice and a better understanding of specific operations of globalization, unsettling systems of domination and the legacy of colonial history.

Making sense of open European borders: Selected stories of Polish-speaking migrants in the UK

While my participants operated in transnational space, my encounters took place in the British state, where they spent most of their time working and living. To better understand the mode of articulation between forms of discourse and possible ways of thinking about emerging relations, one must therefore start with subject-creating dimensions in the UK. It is worth noting that the area where I conducted my fieldwork had traditionally been associated with most wealth in Britain, the South-east of England. The local market economy was organized through a particular class structure, which, as Skeggs (2016) points out, remained strong and whose emergence can be traced back to W. Petty's (1665) calculations of 'the value of "people of England" in 17th Century'. A long process of consolidation of class divisions in the UK has been often linked to, among others, the nineteenth-century 'rise of the bourgeoisie who needed to legitimise their colonial trade and emergent interests' (Skeggs 2016) as well as the importance of political representation. Strathern (1992) argues that class structure remains crucial for the circulating concepts of 'individuality' and personhood, which historically developed in opposition to the working-class masses. Skeggs notes that 'individuals' in England were most often seen as 'the respectable, the moral, the worthy, the English, the White and the non-working class' (Skeggs 1997).

In the 2010s, income inequalities were rising, with 'the best-off 1 per cent [taking] fifteen times the average income' (Dorling 2019: ix) in 2014. In contrast, food insecurity among those at the other end of the income spectrum almost doubled between 2004 and 2016 (Dorling 2019). Such inequalities have only worsened due to economic meltdown in the 2020s. Being central to understanding the unequal distribution of value and wealth in British society (Skeggs 2016) and today's high-income inequality (Dorling and Tomlinson 2019, Massey 2007), class remains an axis of polarization in the selective higher education sector as well (https://blogs.lse.ac.uk/politicsandpolicy/british-education-still-selecting-and-rejecting-in-order-to-rear-an-elite/). Although some projects suggest that based on family background, today most British citizens identify themselves as working class regardless of occupation or education, with just under half doing so in middle-class occupations (https://www.ox.ac.uk/news/2016-06-30-most-people-britain-today-regard-themselves-working-class), similarly to other contexts, implementation and reproduction of social hierarchies are linked to the education system. This was important for my project as my participants went through the university system in Britain. Thanks to the opening of the UK borders after the EU accession, they met the same financial conditions as British citizens and could 'initiate, continue or resume education there along with being employed' (Okólski and Salt 2014: 17). They could also qualify for the student loan that covers tuition fees, which rose up to 9,000 GBP per year, but not the cost of living. They belonged to the 30,000 Polish students enrolled at British universities between 2004 and 2013 (HESA 2014).

During one of my encounters, I met Tomasz, with whom I had been put in contact through the Oxford community of practice that I had been observing face-to-face. Tomasz was twenty-six years old, came from Silesia and had a partner originally also from Poland with whom he studied at Oxford. After his studies, thanks to his Oxford BA degree, among other credentials, he found employment in the corporate sector in London. His current economic, symbolic and sociocultural capital (Bourdieu 1989) easily made him a representative of the so-called international elite and could be associated with a fairly privileged class position in a Western capitalist political economy. However, like many of my interlocutors, in the interview, Tomasz also positioned himself towards discourses of class in England and mentioned the difference in material conditions, pointing to family difficulties and repeating '*i też miałem trochę problemy pie- z pieniędzmi . . . no finansowo po prostu miałem problem*' ('and I also had problems with mo- with money . . . so financially I just had a problem)'.

First, Tomasz's reflections must be understood within the context of economic political subordination in contemporary European space. Since the opening of the European borders, many researchers have examined economic reasons why Eastern Europeans, including Polish citizens, have been coming to the UK. The rapidity and size of the recent arrivals were explained in the light of the restructuring of the Polish economy, including low wages, youth unemployment and limited opportunities in Poland, particularly for women (Okólski and Salt 2014). Attention has been drawn to the high unemployment levels in Poland, which reached 20 per cent in 2003 (Drinkwater et al. 2006). Compared to the UK (http://ec.europa.eu/eurostat/statistics-explained/index.php/Earnings_statistics), in 2010, Polish median gross hourly earnings were also much lower: for the UK it was 12.6 euros, while for Poland 4.0 euros (average in Europe: 11.9 euros). This discrepancy was also maintained for people with higher education: in Poland, median gross hourly earnings were 6.9 euros, whereas in the UK they were 16.4 euros (European average: 16.3 euros). Compared to other countries in Eastern Europe which exhibited the lowest median gross hourly earnings in Europe, Poland was doing a bit better. However, it has been argued that the difference between the UK and Poland still remained substantial enough to influence Polish citizens' decisions for migrating. It must be also noted that at the same time, non-economic factors were widely discussed. These included demographic and sociopolitical changes in the two countries, for example, growing numbers of individuals with improved sociocultural capital, increased knowledge of English, understanding of European citizenship in Poland and reluctance to perform low-paid jobs by British workers. As the majority – 81 per cent – of the newcomers from Poland were under thirty-five years of age (Błasiak 2011), some proposed that for some migrants the stay in the UK was akin to 'a gap year' (Fabiszak 2007), enabled by the availability of budget airlines, not available to previous generations (Burrell 2006). According to Eade et al. (2007), many of the young migrants were 'searchers' who moved also for new experiences and skills, and finally, a growing cosmopolitanism among young Polish citizens living in London had also been observed (Datta 2007).

To fully understand Tomasz's reflections, however, it must also be noted that the neoliberal logic of the British state was not the only one shaping his understanding of the 'dynamic development in which values, inscriptions and institutionalization are central to how [he] learn[t] to recognise' (Skeggs 2016: 6) class relations. Like all my participants, he was also born and raised in the Polish state, where capitalism was fairly recent, income inequality lower than in Britain and various levels of class consciousness had been reported (Domański 2015). Despite that, he operated within a history of class relations that had a much longer history (Domański 2015, Leder 2014) and real-life consequences (Gdula and Sadura 2012). Some even argued that 'the persistence of class divisions was one of the People's Republic's biggest failures' (Pyzik 2016: 90). In order to understand Tomasz's positioning, one therefore needs to be reminded of the history of twentieth-century Poland.

In his book *Sleepwalking the Revolution: An Exercise in Historical Logic*, Leder (2014) shows that this cannot be understood without reference to the Nazi extermination of Jews and Soviet-led destruction of the domination of Polish nobility between 1939 and 1956. The author traces the emergence of middle classes among those classified as ethnic Poles to the revolution 'done with the hands of others' or 'experienced transpassively' by Polish society; a revolution that started the transformation of a predominantly agrarian Polish society into a modern, capitalist and urban one. Before the Second World War, the vast majority of the Polish population (70 per cent) consisted of peasantry, who depended on the cultural and political hegemony (Gramsci 1971) of the then nobility (Leder 2014). Despite strong political peasant movements, the peasantry remained socio-economically and politically disadvantaged and exploited, and the dominant and powerful position was held by the nobility. At the same time, in the pre–Second World War Polish state, 60–80 per cent of the petty bourgeoisie in cities could be classified as Jewish. Leder argues that after the Nazi extermination of Jews, their 'ploughing through' Polish society resulted in its restructuring that involved changing relations to property and means of production and the emergence of the middle classes in the post–Second World War Polish state. This was only reinforced by the Soviet Army, a consequent agrarian revolution between 1946 and 1956, and the exile of the nobility. Apart from changes in law, which guaranteed property rights, the exile of the nobility who represented the previous symbolic field and social imaginary resulted in the emergence of a new, revolutionary discourse (Leder 2014). However, as the author argues, haunted by the recent war and reigning politics of terror of the immediate post-war period, most experienced the agrarian revolution as 'something external'(146).

At the same time, the years immediately following the Second World War were characterized by the most radical population movements within and into the Polish state. Between 1945 and 1950, 4.7 million people were resettled to western and northern Polish territories with more than half from central and south-eastern Polish territories, 1.5 million from the USSR, 50,000 from France, 44,000 from Germany and the rest from other states or of unknown origin (Słabek 2009). In parallel to changing material realities, for many, the previous dominant feudal universe did not disappear, but rather travelled to new locations and the relevance of the Holocaust in the restructuring of Polish society was not fully recognized in the symbolic field (Leder 2014). However, the dominant social imaginary was also changing with new experiences, traumas and fears, and it was also reinforced by the 'levelling' of social structure in the new shortage economy (Domański 2015; Leder 2014).

Domański (2015) argues that in the People's Republic of Poland, the question of power remained the most polarizing factor for social divisions. The symbolic vacuum resulting from the destruction of the Polish nobility, who, if still present in Poland, became workers or 'people like others', was supplanted by new notables. Among those were the new party members and *nomenklatura* (party appointees), who by many were seen as owners of the means of production operating in opposition to other social classes, with most evident opposition in the intelligentsia (Domański 2015). At the same time, doctors, teachers, priests, policemen were also entering the symbolic field along with *nomenklatura* (Leder 2014), and social inequalities did not disappear despite improving material standards of living of the working classes (Domański 2015). The accelerated industrialization and urbanization also contributed to *awans społeczny* (social mobility) of *robotnicy* (workers) and *chłopi* (peasants) (Domański 2015; Fidelis 2020). A place in the social structure was hence no longer associated with hereditary wealth and birth, and class conflicts between social classes other than the powerful party elite became less vivid (Leder 2014). Leder argues that the revolution in Poland ended in 1989 (2014: 30), bringing rapid and radical changes to its symbolic order, relations between people and mass disruption of previous relations to property. He also notes that historically the role of elites remained important for shaping collective imaginaries by granting legitimacy to selected facts and events in the symbolic field.

The discourses of elites also became polarizing for the changes and divisions after 1989, and this group's dominant role was reinforced by the transformation of the system (Gdula and Sadura 2012). In Poland, both counter-elites of the final years of the People's Republic of Poland and the representatives of its authorities, *nomenklatura*, with increased sociocultural capital got to occupy the highest positions in transforming capitalist society. After 1989, the position of communist *funkcjonariusze* (senior public officials), who were economically privileged in the 1980s, quickly deteriorated, enabling both previous party and opposition intelligentsia to be in charge of the process of transformation and, thus, access economic capital which increased with foreign capital investments whose peak came in 1995 (Leyk and Wawrzyniak 2020).

Gdula and Sadura (2012) argue that the importance of sociocultural capital for transformation to neoliberal capitalism had to do both with the history of the region and the global division into centre and peripheries. Despite the fact that the post-communist criterion remained decisive for divisions in the political scene till approximately 2005 (Gdula and Sadura 2012), high sociocultural capital quickly became associated with modernization and, in this case, westernization that symbolize 'higher civilization and economic prosperity'. It must, however, be noted that the domination of pro-Western elites did not remain unquestioned and the cosmopolitan-traditionalist divide of the late 2000s echoed democratic divides in the current phase of capitalism in other European states (Gdula and Sadura 2012).

From the 1990s onward, increased foreign capital investments and inclusion of the Polish state in the capitalist market and OECD were accompanied by the privatization which involved further changes in relations to property and transformation of the state and public services into private ones. The transforming relations also resulted in new social inequalities and increased the precarious position of some groups. For example, the fast processes of privatization together with restructuring of organization of work relations resulted in faster deindustrialization and weakening of the industrial working class (Leyk and Wawrzyniak 2020): between 1980 and 1993 the number of workers in the industry sector fell from over 5 million to 3.5 million. Some of the workers began working for external businesses or became self-employed, but many stopped working in industry altogether. The growing unemployment in the 1990s also resulted in the decomposition of the industrial working class (Leyk and Wawrzyniak 2020). The changes of the transformation era have often been explained through two main narratives (Leyk and Wawrzyniak 2020) operating both in opposition and parallel to each other: the 'neoliberal narrative of modernization', where progress to modernity explains necessary radical restructuring and reductions, and that of the 'moral economy', where transformation is portrayed as destroying social bonds and the sense of community and bringing uncertainty and competition.

In contrast, one of the groups whose members have sometimes been portrayed as beneficiaries of the transformation in the 1990s was younger people. During the early years of transformation, older workers were often considered 'stained' by socialist habits and lacking foreign language skills (Leyk and Wawrzyniak 2020), which resulted in a tendency to make them redundant. In contrast, younger people were often seen as more adaptable to the demands of the capitalist system. In the following decades, compared to older generations, they grew to be perceived as mobile people who manage their time in new ways (Pańków 2012), which resulted in perceptions of the young being advantageous and uncertain at the same time.

Contrary to circulating social images of the young, while looking at official statistics, I noticed that overall, young people's share in unemployment in Poland has historically been higher than for other groups (Ministerstwo Pracy i Polityki Społecznej 2013). After the 2004 EU enlargement, in line with overall trends for unemployment in Europe and Poland, a rapid decrease in their unemployment rates was observed from 2004 to 2007. However, when most of my participants were studying or making their decisions to study in the UK, the economic crisis of 2008 severely hit young people in particular across the European Union (http://ec.europa.eu/europe2020/pdf/themes/2016/youth_employment_201605.pdf), and Poland was no exception. In Poland, the crisis resulted in a rapid downturn and steady increase in unemployment rates for the young, but not for the whole population. The peak of the unemployment among 15–24-year-olds came in 2013 (http://ec.europa.eu/europe2020/pdf/themes/2016/youth_employment_201605.pdf), reaching 27.3 per cent (10.3 per cent for all age groups). The Central Statistical Office reported that in 2010, 44.4 per cent of individuals aged 15–29 years old were employed (49.5 per cent male, 39.2 per cent female) with Poles being most economically active between the ages of thirty and forty-nine. Apart from the crisis in 2008, the worsening situation of the labour market for the young in Poland has been often explained in the context of changes in collective and individual work relations resulting from the crisis in the 1970s and 1980s onwards, the emergence of flexible contracts without typical social benefits, new segmentation of the job market and liberalization of legal provisions concerning employment (Pańków 2012). The references to exploitation post-university were also often made by my participants, where the UK experience was imagined to secure well-paid employment upon return among male Polish Poles, who were the only ones to explicitly talk about a return in the near future at the time, a point I come back to in Chapter 4.

Statistics for the EU indicate that at the time, the transition from education to employment was difficult all over Europe. According to Eurostat, 'male, youth and long-term unemployment appear to be more susceptible to cyclical economic changes than overall unemployment' (http://ec.europa.eu/eurostat), which is corroborated by the fact that youth unemployment rates worsened after the economic crisis in 2008 both in Europe and Poland. High youth unemployment rates were also indicative of the difficulties that the young were facing upon entering the job market (http://ec.europa.eu/eurostat), which in the case of young people in Poland might constitute a motivation to migrate/stay abroad. However, it has to be borne in mind that statistics for the young are usually much higher than for all ages as some members of this age group study full time. The pace at which the employment of young people was decreasing after the crisis was reported to be faster relative to other countries in the EU (Pańków 2012), with lower levels of employment reported for women; this was in line with a trend in Europe for women not to be in employment, education or training (NEET) more often than for men. In 2010 in Poland, 18- to 24-year-olds made less than 15 per cent of NEETs, with the percentage higher for 25- to 29-year-olds (2 per cent above the average for the EU), the women's percentage almost doubling that of men's. Overall the Polish share in NEETs was similar to the average in the EU.

Limited opportunities for women in the Polish state have been listed as one of the reasons for migrations after 2004 (Okólski and Salt 2014), although they do not constitute the dominant reason for all contemporary Polish migrations (White 2016). Gendered differences in life strategies and attitudes towards British society also emerged as a theme across the accounts that I collected between 2013 and 2014. In contrast to the interviewed men, women were more likely to have international partners and more international networks than men (more in Chapter 3). The ideological orientations towards the Polish diaspora and culture were also reflected along gendered lines. Despite recruitment efforts, the vast majority of the men that I met presented themselves as 'Polish Poles', an orientation which relied on a strong affiliation with Polish culture and language. In contrast, women presented themselves in three ways with the same degree of likelihood. Overall, the tendencies for interviewed women to be more oriented towards their life in the UK were shared and expressed in most accounts produced by women that I collected.

For example, when we met with Iza, a film documentary course graduate and social media employee in one of the cafés in Central London in 2013, not long into the interview she began discussing gendered differences and sociocultural expectations in Britain and Poland as one of the reasons for her staying in the UK. As discussed in more detail in Chapter 4, Iza repeatedly aligned with *inny koncept życia* 'a different concept of life', and, making generalized claims about all women and men in the two states, she quickly positioned herself towards opportunities and lifestyles that London in particular enabled women to have. While Iza distanced herself from the Polish diaspora, aligned with multicultural practices of London and expressed what I discuss further as a 'cosmopolitan' orientation, references to opportunities that Britain offered were also mentioned by other women, including 'Polish Poles'. This, for example, was the case with Maria, who unlike Iza had a history of being an active organizer in Polish organizations at her university, shared her life with a partner also originally from Poland, and worked in the corporate sector in London. Despite her clear alignment with Polish culture and diaspora, in the interview she stated that unlike her partner, she enjoyed her life, networks and opportunities in the UK. As the quote shows, while asserting it, she compared the two states, and pointed to hurdles one experiences in Poland.

> *takie małe rzeczy, które ułatwiają życie tutaj sprawiły, że co raz mniej mam ochotę wrócić, bo jak wraca się do Polski, to po prostu na każdym kroku czuje się jakby kłody ci ktoś pod nogi rzucał, a tu, a tu jest łatwiej, tak, raczej na stałe tak, on chciałby wrócić, natomiast nie natychmiast, chciałby wrócić tak właśnie może za dziesięć lat, ale na pewno, ja mówię, że może, a on mówi, że na pewno, także taką mamy debatę*

[. . .] bo on się chyba dużo gorzej zasymilował tutaj z Brytyjczykami, y to też wynika chyba z tego, co się dzieje u niego w pracy, on pracuje w takiej firmie międzynarodowej, więc z samymi Brytyjczykami ma niewiele do czynienia, ja pracuję w firmie, gdzie właściwie dziewięćdziesiąt procent to Brytyjczycy, i się bardzo dobrze z nimi dogaduję, więc jakoś dla mnie to już jest naturalne tutaj być, i z nimi się dogadywać i z nimi żyć

(such small things that make life easier here made me feel less like going back because when you go back to Poland you can feel that they put skids under everything you do and here it's easier, yes, probably forever, yes [i.e. staying in the UK], he would like to go back, but not yet, he wants to go back in ten years, but for sure, and I'm saying maybe and he's saying for sure, so we're having a debate like this [. . .] because he probably hasn't assimilated that well with the Brits and it's a result of what is happening in his international company, he doesn't have to do with the Brits that much, I work in a company where in fact 90 per cent are British and I get along with them very well, so for me it's natural to be here and get along with them and live with them)

The gendered differences in the participants' strategies for life in the UK observed in my project must be explained within the history of patriarchy in Poland (Graff 2001, 2008; Środa 2012), which was shaped differently from patriarchy in classic liberal welfare states (Gal and Kligman 2000). Importantly, state socialism brought both revolutionary discourses of equality and continued conservative discourses on reproduction (Fidelis 2020: 37). Unlike in Western liberal societies, after WWII in Eastern Europe, women's relation to the state did not rely on relationships with 'private' men. Apart from the social mobility of the working classes discussed before, which as Leder (2014) argues would not have been possible without the radical transformation of feudal hierarchy and its imaginary, the new system brought mass employment for women. As a result, equality before the law and the mass presence of women in factories and other workplaces after 1945 triggered a revolution of everyday life, state politics, understanding of gendered roles and social relations (Kenney 1997). In comparison to Western states, after the war access to education, training and employment for all women increased. In 1956, abortion was allowed with the permission of a doctor, when the pregnancy was a result of a crime or when the mother's life conditions were difficult. After the Stalinist years that brought radical societal changes, most often built on violence and repressions, the workplace became increasingly more marked by gender inequalities, for example, in terms of women's possibilities of promotion or visible gendered segregation (Fidelis 2020). Importantly, while similarities across the Soviet-influenced region have been observed (e.g. Gal and Kligman 2000), scholars also point to the significance of specificities of negotiation of gender relations in particular nation-states and localities. For example, similarly to Hungary, but not to other states in the region, in Poland it was also difficult to dismantle old workers' traditions that relied on well-established gender hierarchies (Fidelis 2020: 38). Therefore, it was more common for men to hold more prestigious jobs, and interwar right-wing politics regarding the family continued.

Crucially, the communist modernity was built on an ideal of a modern woman who could combine family and work life with engagement in public life. This ideal echoed wider developments in gender relations in post-war Europe, but as Fidelis reminds us, unlike in capitalist societies, in theory, it was not aimed for profit, but 'educational and moral' values. Scholars note that access to education and employment enabled peasant women, for example, to break with their centuries-old subordination to men perpetuated through both psychological matriarchy of the home, and societal patriarchy (Szpakowska 2003). However, at the same time, in order to boost birth rates, the communist regime still promoted motherhood as women's primary responsibility (Gal and Kligman 2000). In wider society, women were often portrayed as superwomen, but in the seemingly 'apolitical' sphere of consumption, the household was still portrayed as a feminized space which associated women with private rather than public life and propagated stereotypes of reasonable, sensitive and caring women (Bren 2012). In comparison, images of man included dominant leaders in the workplace as well as 'big children' in the family (Gal and Kligman 2000).

While it has been often argued that there was a radical backlash against gender ideals and relations formed in the state-socialist era after 1989 which has supposedly pushed Eastern Europe to a growing societal conservatism, the historical perspective rather suggests that there was a continual complex process of linking women with the home and family life (Fidelis 2020). However, the transformation to a capitalist system additionally made employment of many women unstable and part-time. Women were also paid less than men. At the same time, growing nationalistic and religious movements, crucial for the public life in post-state-socialist Eastern Europe, led to anti-women policies, for example, Poland's anti-abortion law of 1993, which was to remain one of the most restrictive in the EU in the 2010s, was backed by the Catholic Church. As a result, femininity was being linked even more to the romanticized private, as masculinity was to competition and leadership of the public.

In the 2000s and 2010s, more women worked and were being educated than in the past in Poland (Central Statistical Office 2007). At the same time, they were also expected to perform their roles as mothers and wives slightly earlier than in Britain, which was often echoed in Polish public discourse by right-wing parties and the Catholic Church. Femininity was hence often assigned symbolic maternal significance and equated with the Holy Mary/Mother-Pole/Poland (Graff 2008: 15). In contrast, in the 2010s, images of hegemonic masculinity included not only traditional breadwinners and rational leaders in the workplace (Wojnicka 2011), but also strongmen and mother's sons. Images of men fighting for gender equality and the deconstruction of hegemonic masculinity remained less popular (Wojnicka 2011). In the same decade, an observable anti-gender movement also gained its momentum, which reportedly aimed to 'restore the authority of men' globally (Graff and Karolczuk 2022), culminating after my fieldwork when the openly anti-gender Law and Justice (PIS) party came to power. The anti-gender rhetoric demonized 'gender', contrasted it with traditional Polish values and ended in radical anti-women policies such as the 2020 ruling of the Constitutional Tribunal that banned abortions due to foetal abnormalities (Graff and Karolczuk 2022). These in turn radically divided Polish society with frequent statewide and diasporic women's strikes, which at its peak in 2020 made almost half a million, mostly younger people, take 'to the streets of over 600 Polish cities and villages in what appears to be the biggest street protests since the Solidarity upheaval' (Graff and Karolczuk 2022: 2).

The divisions surrounding gendered expectations in the 2010s and 2020s have been also accompanied by strong anti-LGBTQ+ rhetoric (Pakuła 2021), which has historically lumped sexual minorities together with women demanding equal rights and framed them as competition. While some projects later reported 'a persistent move towards acceptance over the last ten years', other studies claimed that 'acceptance has recently fallen' (https://www.greeneuropeanjournal.eu/gender-ideology-and-the-crisis-of-care-in-poland/?fbclid=IwAR07QpywzFstSwNq0ux5weKsM9GtJNrmBrycX72oEaDDDbhZ85WYIbfLnKk). In 2016, the UN criticized Poland for lack of protection of LGBTQ+ citizens and decreasing initiatives in sex education, while the Law and Justice representatives as well as the Catholic Church continued to make public attacks on the LGBTQ+ community. When I was collecting my accounts of migration experiences, I talked to self-identified LGBTQ+ participants, but the recorded sample was too small to make any claims about sexuality and language at this point. In my next project on family linguistic practices conducted with Prof Zhu Hua, we came back to the topic of sexuality and language in family language data showing how it may impact ideological orientation and linguistic practices among those classified as Polish in the UK. I briefly discuss this point in Chapter 5.

When compared to gender relations reported for the UK, gender relations in the Polish state described so far have historically been shaped differently, which in turn may have an impact on the ways in which gendered subject positions are 'occupied, negotiated and resisted' (Skeggs 1997). In contrast to state-socialist gendered stereotypes and relations forming in Eastern Europe after the Second World War, in Britain women's position in society has historically depended more on private relationships with men and class relations built on hereditary wealth and birthplace. These have significantly changed over the course of the last two centuries, when as Cameron (2018) describes, experiences of women's subordination stopped being restricted by legal arrangements that required women to obey their husbands. After the Second World War, more women remained in employment than in the 1930s, and the Beveridge report transformed Britain into a welfare state, which provided a range of social provisions and secured minimal subsistence for all. The report paved the way to establishing British citizenship in social, civil and political rights. However, the creation of the welfare state also 'turned on assumptions about the gendered nature of home and work' (Kent 1999: 317), making married women financially reliant on men and linking them more to the home, which in turn was embedded in class hierarchies. The ideal of middle- and upper-class women has historically been developed in strong opposition to working-class women (Skeggs 1997). Skeggs argues that representations of working-class women changed in different historical periods, but working-class women have been 'massified' and 'othered' in British public discourse, where portrayals of working classes are usually negatively framed and 'pathologized'.

Similarly to other countries in the global North and West, in the 1970s critique and contestation of dominant narratives on femininity and masculinity were propagated by strong feminist movements which supported women's equality in the workplace and the home, as well as sexual liberation. In Britain, in 1967, abortion was decriminalized, although initially it had to be certified by two doctors (Cameron 2018). With time, as Cameron argues, most women have found employment outside the home, and have been able to choose to marry. Experiences of subordination of women did not, however, disappear, but rather depend less on private relationships with men and more on 'their public roles as citizens and employees' (Cameron 2018: 24). Women have been observed to more often perform low-paid and low-status jobs, and, in line with a worldwide trend, have been responsible for 'unpaid care work at home'.

In more recent decades, counter-movements and images undermining feminist solidarities have been also emerging. These include, for example, images of 'female triumphalism' (McRobbie 2009) often built on the rhetoric of individualism, which has been linked both to the Protestant concept of 'free individual will' and subsequent attempts to eradicate socialism through media campaigns and policies propagated in the 1980s. McRobbie has also argued that media portrayals of women and men themselves remain entangled in class and gender assumptions underlying the programmes. The social images of 'female success' and 'empowerment' are hence accompanied by more traditional romantic motherhood and female 'vulnerability' (McRobbie 2009). Images of men are also varied with traditional rational, objective, and unemotional images of masculinity circulating in parallel with body-conscious metrosexual and technosexual as well as 'aggressive' and tough images of man. Finally, similarly to Poland, heterosexuality of the dominant images is visible (McRobbie 2009), but the UK's LGBTQ+ community enjoys more visibility and a wide range of rights, including the right to form families since 2002 and the right to marry since 2013.

These social images of women and men in Britain have also for a long time been built on 'British whiteness', despite the fact that colonial history and globalization have made the UK one of the most diverse states in Europe. With 'whiteness' understood as a 'historical and contemporary subject position that can be situationally inhabited both by individuals recognized as white and nonwhite' (Rosa and Flores 2017: 628), after Bryan et al. (2018 [1985]), I noted that experiences and voices of women of colour were mostly absent from the dominant discussions on gender relations till the 1980s. Discussing Black women's experiences of working in the NHS, a key aspect of the welfare state, they demonstrated however that the state had heavily relied on Black women's labour, a point only emphasized during the Covid-19 pandemic (https://www.england.nhs.uk/blog/covid-19-and-race-equality-lessons-to-learn/). The lack of representation of Black and migrant communities in dominant discourses was countered by subsequent accounts of scholars of colour, who also uncovered the workings of 'racism of employers and workers alike' (Bryan et al. (2018 [1985]): 23), and highlighted qualitative differences of experiences of women and men with links to places as diverse as the Caribbean, Asia, Ireland or southern Europe. The insider/outsider status of migrant communities was also embedded in Britain's historically colonial understanding of difference and migrations. I had to therefore think about contemporary 'other White' Polish and Eastern European migrations in relation to other communities and the principle of whiteness that has governed dominant understandings of ethno-racialized divisions and governance for a long time (Patel 2021).

Situating post–Cold War migrations and contemporary politicization of movement in time and space

As the previous section shows, the local perspective helped me identify important commonalities and differences for processes of authentication in the context of unsettling interlocking systems of domination in the globalized world. The state is the space where 'global care claims are assembled, where reproductive labour is negotiated and costs of austerity and lack of public infrastructure felt most acutely' (Gago 2020: 198). The local perspective also enabled me to see that contemporary class, age and gender relations are still entangled in the history and institutionalized practices of particular state bodies that grant legitimacy to particular ways of being, acting and seeing associated with the state's citizens. However, while important, I also noticed that it relied on dominant sedentary understandings of national and ethnic identities, easily erasing the history of changing borders, transnational participation and population movements. This in turn may erase transborder efforts and a history of international cooperation in which 'constellations of struggles [. . .] empower each other' (Gago 2020), such as international women's strikes, digital workshops and platforms for discriminated migrants or indigenous populations, or global anti-racist protests and initiatives.

Following the state logic, when examined in isolation, one might also consider the size and speed of contemporary Polish migrations to the UK a historical aberration, perhaps a reason for the UK's decision to leave the EU in 2016. After the 'Vote Leave, take control' campaign, 33.6 million British citizens participated in the EU referendum, when 51.9 per cent voted to leave the EU, and 48.1 per cent voted to remain. Some 13 million of those registered to vote did not cast their vote, and 7 million were not registered. Those most likely not to vote were either poorer or younger citizens (Dorling and Tomlinson 2019), while those most likely to vote to remain in the EU were based in Scotland, Northern Ireland and London; and were young, especially in the age range between thirty-five and forty-four. Older citizens were reported to be in favour of Brexit, with a substantial middle-class leave constituency in South-east England and the relationship between deprivation and the leave vote being non-linear (Dorling and Tomlinson 2019). In the following four years, the negotiations with the EU resulted in the UK formally leaving the EU in January 2021, and EU citizens being asked to secure settled/pre-settled status to stay to work legally in the UK. At the time of my project, however, unlike other non-EU migrants in the UK, my participants enjoyed full rights that came with the EU citizenship, which included work permit, right to vote in local elections, access to healthcare and not being subjected to immigration control (Anderson and Blinder 2019) when entering the UK.

I knew however that Polish and Eastern European migrants were frequently singled out in the British media during the pre-Brexit-vote campaign in line with tendencies observed in preceding years (e.g. Spigelman 2013), and negatively framed (Moore and Ramsay 2017). In fact, it was noted that the Leave campaign had been built around issues of migration, with the press coverage of the topic more than tripling before the referendum (Moore and Ramsay 2017). Some sought to explain the references to migration together with the common questioning of the key principle of the European project – the freedom of movement – in the pre-Brexit-vote debate, by claiming that the vote had little to do with racism and discrimination as EU migrants were 'White' (for detailed discussion refer to Rzepnikowska 2018). I noted that similarly to previous trends during the pre-referendum campaign, migration had continued to be presented as an economic threat across political parties (Rzepnikowska 2018), with many pointing out that it is apparently 'against the interests of the working-class Brits'. New migrants also continued to be portrayed as contributing to overall decline (e.g. Garner 2009). Finally, when considering the result of the Brexit referendum, I had to also note that it coincided in time with the so-called 'migrant crisis' in Europe in 2015 and 2016, when refugees and migrants mostly from the Middle East were fleeing war and persecution (https://www.unrefugees.org/emergencies/refugee-crisis-in-europe/). This in turn boosted anti-migration sentiments across the continent (https://ec.europa.eu/migrant-integration/sites/default/files/2017-05/shadowreport_2015x2016_long_low_res.pdf).

As a result, even if the focus of the project depicted in this book is indeed on participants who predominantly lived first in the Polish state, and then in the British state, the points that I make in the book must be considered in a larger temporal and spatial context. It must accordingly be highlighted that 'the management of mobilities under post-slavery and postcolonial regimes in the liberal West is fundamental to the making of classed, racial, sexual, able-bodied, gendered, citizen and non-citizen subjects' (Sheller 2018: 18). Mignolo (2020) argues that in the current phase of global migrations, economic differentials result in, on the one hand, movements 'from underdeveloped to developed centers', and, on the other, movements to former colonial metropoles. Their current directionality is still embedded in modern/colonial power differentials. It depends on 'racial classification and hierarchy that structures the colonial matrix of power' (Mignolo 2020), which remains fundamental for images of humanity assumed by the nation-state, a model of governance adopted worldwide. I was aware that migrations remained politicized around the globe as states and international agencies were engaging in bordering practices that limit 'uneven patterns of capitalist development', continuously assigning value to moving bodies in transnational space. I also knew that politicization of migrations was not a new development worldwide. The UN reports for example on Western anxieties surrounding the influx of migrants after the collapse of the Soviet Union, fears of invasion among old EU member states about arrivals from the new EU member states in the 2000s, discussions of the role of migrants in South-east Asian economic crisis or US anti-immigration policies after 9/11 (https://www.un.org/sites/un2.un.org/files/wmr_2020.pdf).

It must be remembered that 'mobility is an inherent characteristic of all populations unless specific policies or other factors are in place that limit or control that mobility' (https://www.un.org/sites/un2.un.org/files/wmr_2020.pdf). However, in 2020, globally 272 million people were considered international migrants, which made only 3.5 per cent of the whole global population with most migrating to larger economies such as the United States, France, Russian Federation, United Arab Emirates or Saudi Arabia. These numbers captured both coerced and voluntary migrations. The 2020 estimates already surpassed predictions for 2050 and today, migrations are not likely to stop. By 2020, major displacements had been triggered by conflict (e.g. Syria, Yemen), violence (e.g. Rohingyas' movement to Bangladesh), lack of political and economic stability (e.g. Venezuela), or climate change (e.g. Mozambique, China, India, the United States). The increase of migrants has been widely debated and politicization of movement continues worldwide.

I noticed that discourses of high inequality were often mentioned in discussions about the reasons for the outcome of the 2016 referendum in Britain, but so were rising imperialist sentiments within the British state. It must therefore be noted that in the case of the British state, the state perspective also takes the focus away from its imperial past and colonial legacy, which have also shaped today's politicization of movement. Discussions surrounding post-EU accession Polish and Eastern European communities also operated within the context of historical discourses on migration in the UK. These in turn involved multiple locations, people and trajectories of migration that interacted with one another in complex ways. Patel argued that the image of immigration in Britain had traditionally also been 'a byword for race and for ideas about who is and who is not native to the nation – or [. . .] native to the imperial heartland' (2021: 2). Global movements of people from and to the British Isles cannot therefore be understood without reference to the Empire, imperialism and colonialism, discourses of 'civilizing' indigenous populations (Cowen 2021) or financial assistance and policies promoting White settlements in the 'new' world (Patel 2021). It must be also noted that while the presence of non-White people in Britain has been reported for centuries (Cowan 2021), the dangers of immigration started being widely discussed mostly after the Second World War. Patel posited that the ways in which migration had been portrayed in the UK must be linked to 'the primary domestic encounter of British political elites with questions of race' in the 1960s (2021: 2). He reminded me that the number of non-White people in the UK rose from 30,000 in 1945 to 1 million in 1973, and 5 million in 2001 (Spencer 1997). The changing demographics in Britain had to do, among other factors, with the worsening economic situation in the (former) colonies (e.g. Bryan et al. 2018). They were also motivated by Britain's labour shortages after the Second World War, which were also supplanted by Polish migrants settling in the UK thanks to the already mentioned Polish Resettlement Act of 1947, the first act to grant permission for settlement to people from outside the Empire.

Most newcomers were, however, coming from the post-war Commonwealth. While the formal British Empire ended by the mid-1960s, the Commonwealth of Nations continued without decolonization of British nationality and citizenship till 1981. This was influenced by legal changes in definitions of citizenship which were introduced by the British Nationality Act of 1948. With an aim to retain and rearticulate British subjecthood and imperial understanding of British nationality after the Second World War, the act granted citizenship of the UK and Colonies to people from the Commonwealth. It hence extended the idea of the 'British subject' to the 'Commonwealth citizen'. However, in political discourse in the following decades, the non-White British citizens were first politically and then legally redefined as 'immigrants'. This was also accompanied by continued public discourse linking 'coloured immigration' to 'social unrest', social and administrative hostility and violence, and subsequent racially discriminatory immigration laws. Legal changes began with the 1962 Commonwealth Immigrants Act, which started limiting the right to enter Britain to those born in the UK. Later acts made further distinctions and restrictions, culminating in the new 1981 British Nationality Act. This act restricted citizenship to those born and whose parents were also born in the UK. The legal changes hence did not fully consider that between 1966 and 2005 'every year, the pace at which people with British nationality have left Britain has outstripped those with British nationality coming into Britain by almost 70,000' (Patel 2021: 53). They rather echoed earlier imperial principles built on 'transnational white solidarity of settler colonialism' (Patel 2021:16) that gave rise to first immigration policies, for example, the 1905 Aliens Act limiting the number of Eastern European, especially Jewish migrants in Britain, or earlier laws introduced in White-settler colonies that aimed to regulate the movement of 'Asiatics'.

The transition from Empire to the state entailed complex adaptation to and negotiation with the newly created terms of equality worldwide. However, despite eventual decades of state multiculturalism in Britain, many have discussed continuities and 'reluctance at the level of the British state to fully come to terms with imperial pasts and their relationship to British national identity' (Patel 2021: 19). It was argued that this also resulted in limited coverage of the history of colonialism in schools (Dorling and Tomlinson 2019), including 'the history of violence that colonialism entailed, but also the history of opposition to that violence in Britain' (Gopal 2019) and anticolonial resistance in the former colonies that prompted the changes. The legacy of the past was also seen in contemporary decisions regarding migration, for example, the Windrush scandal in 2018. It was therefore impossible for me to think about contemporary Polish and Eastern European migrations without recognizing that migration and race were central to understanding population movements in Britain.

I quickly saw that it was also impossible to understand Brexit and UK Polish migrations without reference to whiteness as an organizing principle of managing mobilities in the twentieth century. Since Britain entered the European Economic Community in 1973, millions of those formerly classified as 'European aliens' were granted the unrestricted right of entry, employment and residence. At the same time, non-White British citizens living outside the UK remained subjected to immigration control. In principle, the European Convention on Human Rights gave rights to colonial citizens living overseas, but many were also prevented from entering the UK for a long time (Patel 2021). Using their rights to submit individual petitions, some complained to the European Commission of Human Rights. Patel noted that this resulted in the case *East African Asians vs. United Kingdom* and an anti-racist ruling of the European Commission, which drew attention to the 'special importance' 'attached to discrimination based on race' in Britain. In subsequent decades, an active anti-European sentiment was also observed in sectors of British public life and political campaigns against the EU continued from the 1970s onwards (Dorling and Tomlinson 2019).

Importantly, the discussion so far suggests that Polish citizens and Eastern Europeans have existed in the British social imaginary for a long time as certified by legal acts such as the Aliens Act or the Polish Resettlement Act. However, the largest groups classified as 'Eastern European' living in the UK did not feature in British public discourse till the 2000s, that is, when the 2004 EU enlargement enabled Eastern European migrants to settle and work in the UK. Today, in British census measures, Eastern Europeans are still usually lumped together with all 'other White' people, which is contrasted with separate entries for White British, and Irish. Importantly, the 'other White' category is also not included in the Black, Asian and Minority Ethnic (BAME) category, which is widely used in statistical and anti-discrimination tools across the UK. At the same time, scholars have been drawing attention to the fact that they do not capture specificities of Eastern European experiences in the UK that include their xenophobic treatment since 2004, rising hate crimes after the 2016 Brexit referendum or poor working and housing conditions (e.g. https://www.birmingham.ac.uk/news/2021/who-are-you-to-tell-the-story-exploring-the-experience-of-central-and-eastern-european-migrant-artists). It thus becomes crucial to think about the very form of whiteness of Eastern Europeans. Before doing that, however, it must be stressed that Polish and Eastern European migrants enjoy 'a certain level of invisibility and palatability in Britain that people of colour can never access' (Cowan 2021).

When comparing their participants with other migrant communities, researchers working with Eastern European migrants in Britain have drawn attention to them benefitting from their pre-Brexit legal status and whiteness. It has been argued that Eastern Europeans 'pass' as White and hence can access resources and jobs more easily than other migrating groups. Some media have acknowledged the hard work ethic of Eastern European migrants, and defined them as looking 'like us' and 'sharing a European cultural background, possessing a "White" phenotype and thus not standing out visually in the public space, sharing similar socialization patterns and Christian religion' (Halej 2014: 246). However, at the same time, many have talked about degraded, 'non-quite white' form of their whiteness (Parutis 2011). Polish migration has, for example, been compared to invasion and natural disaster (Spigelman 2013) in line with othering discourses aimed at non-White immigrant communities (e.g. Hall 1995; Baker 2013), and some talked about Polish and Eastern Europeans' unusual habits and their pushing up crime rates' (Fomina and Frelak 2008). While, as shown above, the whiteness of Eastern European and other EU migrants is crucial to understand the migration policies in the past century, many have long argued that EU citizens have been 'othered' in the UK precisely because of their migrant status (e.g. Gilroy 2004) and that putative whiteness does not prevent them from discrimination and xenoracism. For example, Ryan (2007) describes how the Irish were described as 'uncivilized others and primitive'.

To me, this paradox was best explained through non-essentialist and critical definitions of race. Carby (2019) argues that race has to do with the ways in which people are classified through practices that link differences to individuals and groups and ways in which these differences become institutionalized. 'It is a verb not a noun' (Carby 2019: 65), which is embedded in particular timespace configurations. It is hence not 'essentially about skin colour' or being contained in semantic terms that delimit such categories (Lemon 2002), but it has also to do with 'who points to whom, where and when, how and in relation to what' (Lemon 2002). It is best understood as a result of a process of racialization through which stories of 'authentic and singular' racial categories emerge.

Historically, in the British Empire, 'British race' or 'British whiteness' was seen as a superior racial category which organized the ways 'to manage other races' (Hicks 2020). Tabili (1994) notes that 'racial categories and racial subordination were reconstituted on British soil' before the post-war Caribbean migrations and as early as the 1920s and 1930s. Subsequent decades resulted in the introduction of racialized policies that aimed 'to manage black civilian and military personnel' (Carby 2019: 65). As shown earlier, the encounter with racialized others also prompted re-evaluation of what being a national subject meant and how it related to new racialized divisions. When discussing race politics in Britain, Paul Gilroy (2004) also talks about 'the gradual synonymity of "race" and nation which betrays the genesis of ethnic absolutism and its new racism' (147). Whiteness has been construed in contrast to blackness, but also against other shades of whiteness. This new type of xenoracism is thus directed at all migrant and displaced communities.

As, traditionally, many migrants have described their initial encounter with Britain 'through the prism of the British class system' (Patel 2021: 67), I was gradually becoming aware of the fact that the new xenoracism was also tightly linked to economic disadvantage and penalty. Since the 'Eastern Bloc' constitutes a lower-income area in Europe and as many Polish and Eastern European migrants are in fact economic migrants (House of Commons 2016), these groups are most often portrayed as homogeneous and working-class in British media. Some studies report that regardless of class background, members of the British public have been observed to assess the positioning of Eastern Europeans through racializing discourses and talk about their inability to perform 'whitely scripts' (Halej 2014). At the time of writing, the non-quite white form of Eastern European whiteness was also exemplified by the coverage of Russia's invasion of Ukraine in 2022, where some parts of the British media were building solidarity with Ukrainian refugees by only now discovering their whiteness (https://www.theguardian.com/commentisfree/2022/mar/02/civilised-european-look-like-us-racist-coverage-ukraine). The Eastern European category is, however, dynamically (re)produced together with its internal hierarchies, with 'whitening of Hungarians, and darkening of Romanians' (Fox et al. 2012), and the dominant role played by the Polish.

I established that Eastern European migrants have been observed to orient themselves to the dominant British discourses of whiteness in contradictory and complex ways. On the one hand, they have been shown to differentiate themselves from other 'visible' migrants and to reproduce notions of normality 'inherently coded white' (Halej 2014). In Bristol, a study based on fifty interviews and ten focus groups with participants with ties to Hungary and Romania, combined with a project on daily routines of ten participants classified as 'Poles', revealed that this may result in reproduction of racializing practices and racism towards others. In this project, the participants also recognized the difference from the main White British public, but it was not essentialized/racialized (Fox and Mogilnicka 2017). On the other hand, constraints of Eastern European whiteness have also been reported and contested by participants in research projects. While recognizing their own 'white phenotype', some of Halej's respondents in Manchester, Norwich and Winchester, for instance, raised concerns about experienced xenoracism and awareness of negative attitudes and stereotypes circulating in England. In Manchester, Rzepnikowska (2018) examined twenty-one narrative interviews with variously positioned post-accession Polish women before the Brexit vote, six of whom were re-interviewed in 2017. The study showed that the participants experienced xenoracist abuse during both periods, with an increase after the vote.

While the othering of Eastern Europeans in the UK operates along the colonialism-immigration continuum in the context of the history of the British Empire, with Eastern European being a 'boundary term' (Halej 2014), the ways in which Polish and Eastern Europeans have been observed to orient themselves and articulate this boundary must also be understood in relation to the concepts of race circulating in Eastern Europe and Poland in particular. To do so, one must also note that these migrations and mass dislocations cannot be grasped without reference to the history of exploitation, starvation, slave labour, warfare, changing borders and xenoracism in Eastern Europe, including Poland, over the last few centuries. When the history of European great land, often multi-ethnic empires such as the Habsburg monarchy, the Kingdom of Prussia and the Russian Empire in the late eighteenth and nineteenth centuries is considered in conjunction with subsequent subjugation of Eastern European territories to the Nazi and

Soviet totalitarian regimes in the twentieth century, after decolonial thinkers, this part of the world is best described as 'a zone of multiple colonialisms' (https://keywordsechoes.com/multiple-colonialism). Despite West-centric tendencies of postcolonial perspectives, I knew that scholars working with the notion of Mittel Europa and history of Nazi occupation in Eastern Europe, identified parallels between European colonialism and Nazism in that both relied on assumptions of biological racism, sustained through the development and propagation of eugenics programmes. This logic was most painfully enacted in the Holocaust that the Nazis organized in today's Polish and Eastern European territories.

Slavic-speaking populations have also traditionally been seen as inferior to 'Germanic Westerners'. In the past, Slavs were often compared to 'slaves'. Their perceived degraded whiteness has historically also shaped their possibilities and trajectories of movement in multiple corners of the Western world, for example, in the twentieth century they were not welcome in the United States with their race being seen by some as pointing to inferiority and being 'immune to certain kinds of dirt. They can stand what would kill a white man (Ross 1914). Most visibly, the inferiority and racial difference between Germanic and Slavic-speaking populations were however enacted through the rhetoric and policies of Adolf Hitler, whose aim was to keep the Germanic and Slav worlds apart due to racial inferiority of the latter. Moreover, during and after the Cold War, in the Western imaginary, the Soviet Union and its dependent Eastern European states have often been portrayed as 'only partially European' or 'even Asian' (https://keywordsechoes.com/multiple-colonialism).

At the same time, the concept of whiteness further participated in 'nesting orientalism' in Eastern Europe as many have tried to prove their Western or European credentials for centuries. Historically, ideals of whiteness also guided colonial efforts in the region, both of the Russian Empire and formations with colonial ambitions, for example, the Polish-Lithuanian Commonwealth. Slavery of Roma was also present for a few centuries. When referring to the Soviet era, due to discourses of internationalization that often idealized its anti-racist stance, some postcolonial thinkers have historically found it difficult to talk about colonization and racism in the context of the USSR. It must be acknowledged that during the Cold War, the Soviet Union publicly 'declared itself against racism' (Lemon 2002). However, the concepts of race and superiority of whiteness were not erased from its public life and state policies. Importantly, racial slurs were also not eradicated both outside and inside Soviet state institutions (Lemon 2002). Leder (2014) also argues that the USSR's policies were quickly built on Russia's imperialist past, and it must be noted that ideas about ethnicity and race were incorporated into its 'internally imperialist, but externally anti-imperialist' state-centric structure (Condee 2006). By now, policies of 'russification, exploitation of non-Russian republics, domination over other Central and Eastern European states' together with deportations, forced labour, history of ethnic cleansing and crimes against indigenous populations have been widely acknowledged (https://keywordsechoes.com/multiple-colonialism).

When rethinking whiteness in the context of Polish migrations, one must also note that the concept has been sustained 'through self-identification and identification of the Other people' (Balogun 2020) throughout the history of the Polish territories as well. Historically, groups defined as non-White such as Jews or Roma have been othered and discriminated against by some parts of Polish society. Although the main eugenics programmes have usually been discussed in the context of the Western tradition, it has been argued that such programmes also shaped understanding of whiteness in Eastern Europe. Bolagun (2020) traces the beginnings of such practices in Poland to the first half of the twentieth century. These were also propagated by Polish nationalists in the interwar period and later also assumed in both Nazism and Communism's reliance on blood ties as a defining feature of a nation. The nationalistic state policies of the Soviet era codified the 'purity of the nation' with an assumed whiteness of its 'national character', and race has been habitually defined in terms of being 'normal'.

The importance of ethno-racial imagination must also be acknowledged after the transformation to neoliberal capitalism. It has been argued (Bolagun 2020) that despite the presence of anti-racist activists, 'a sense of purification' remains embedded in the public images of 'real Poles' and non-White citizens and residents 'are [still] assumed not to be biologically integral to the Polish nation' today. Institutionalized practices such as census measures also make people of colour invisible. Bolagun's interviews with mixed-race citizens and residents reveal that 'Polish centrism' and racism have an impact on their self-identification and well-being. While the 2020 worldwide Black Lives Matter protests prompted some discussions on the use of racial terms in sections of Polish society (https://notesfrompoland.com/2020/06/12/czy-murzyn-obraza-zapytalismy-czarnoskorych-polakow-jezykoznawcow-historyka-i-aktywistke/) and there is a social movement which has been actively helping migrants and refugees from the Middle East and Africa at the Poland-Belarus border in 2021–2 (https://grupagranica.pl/#co-robimy), in the 2010s and 2020s, some nationalistic groups have also mobilized discourses of White power and supremacy. Exclusionary racial discourse also motivates recent decisions regarding migrations at the aforementioned Poland-Belarus border. When discussing the rising Islamophobia in Poland from 2015 onwards, Bobako (2018) also noted that it may be observed both in the liberal and nationalist public discourse. Such a paradox, Bobako argued, lies in the specificity of the semi-peripherality of the Polish state, which entails its economic marginalization and instability as well as commitments to European modernity and the West which rely on 'affirmation of individualism, human rights, sexual freedom and secularism'.

Exclusionary practices and moral panics surrounding discussions on migration in Poland have also been reported (Garapich 2016). Such discourses portray migration as pathological and at the same time, actively erase the history of the global Polish diaspora and its role in shaping connections and possibilities of the Polish-speaking world. The estimates of the diaspora range between 4–5 million (Brubaker 2005) and 20 million people (gov.pl). Large Polish settlements have as a result been found in multiple corners of the world: not only the United Kingdom but also Germany, the United States, Canada and Australia as well as Argentina, Brazil, and Kazakhstan, Ukraine, Lithuania and Belarus. These movements of Polish populations also have a long history. For example, in the nineteenth century, after joining the Haitian Revolution, some Polish groups settled in Haiti. At the turn of the twentieth century, a quarter of all new migrants in the United States were classified as Polish (Thomas and Znaniecki 1918), with Chicago even becoming the third largest Polish city in the world. Importantly, movement between America and Poland was also reported (Okólski 1999), with 20–30 per cent eventually going back to the Polish territories. As mentioned in the previous section, the largest population movements in Polish history were, however, triggered by the Second World War (Okólski 1999), for example, deportations to forced labour or 'Germanization' in German territories, prisoners of war and deportations to the East (Luczak 1984). It is estimated that after the Second World War, one in seven inhabitants of Poland from 1938 was living abroad (Walczak 2012).

Despite this variety of Polish experiences worldwide, the 'presentation of Polish homogeneity [has been observed to serve] as a way of maintaining stability in the state' (Balogun 2020) and tightly links Polish national imagination to sedentariness. Traditionally, in the Polish language, *naród* (nation) and *narodowość* (nationality) are used to refer to belonging to a nation, defined as a group of people living in the same territory, speaking one language, sharing a common history, culture and political and economic interests (sjp.pwn.pl). Importantly, such discourses of sedentariness often portray migrations as 'abnormal' or pathological and have been observed to contribute to stigmatization and othering of migrating individuals and groups in Poland where some are continuously framed as undeserving or disposable in public discourse. For example, Urbańska (2018) argued that those who 'leave their children behind' (www.greeneuropeanjournal.eu/on-the-move-experiences-of-migation-from-poland), especially migrant mothers, are often construed as 'a new social deviant'. Urbańska also noted that stigmatization usually affects working classes migrating from smaller cities and rural areas rather than 'privileged managers or Eurocrats'. Various forms of stigmatization of those migrating and returning migrants have also been reported in non-academic literature. For example, in his reportage *Białystok*, an account of life in a once multicultural city in eastern Poland, where before the Second World War the Jewish population made at times 75 per cent of the whole population (Kącki 2015: 56), Marcin Kącki discusses the city's lack of memory and rising nationalism, anti-Semitism and racism in the 2010s that led to, for example, a violent fire attack on a multiracial couple who met in Britain.

These emerging 'themes that do not sit comfortably with one another' (Akomfrah) reminded me of contradictions and complexities in the processes of unsettling of contemporary systems of domination, where ethno-racial thinking remained implicitly operationalized to reproduce and justify local and global flows of socio-economic inequalities. Navigating between these conflicting and multiple observations, I had to acknowledge that global capitalism 'has transformed the material conditions of life' for many and created huge benefits for some. However, to imagine and recognize another, more equal world, we must also admit that 'it is not an illusion that capitalism [also] generates great harms and perpetuates eliminable forms of human suffering' (https://www.versobooks.com/blogs/4419-why-be-anticapitalist). This recognition in turn urges us to engage with dominant ethno-racialized, classed, gendered, and other ideologies of European modernity by reframing histories around movement rather than statis, undoing superiority of whiteness, and going along with emerging non-linear forms of social transformation. As this chapter shows, we can only start doing it if we pay close attention to the ways in which systems of domination mutually reinforce one another to form unstable, but recognizable meanings and knowledge projects. Seeing intersectionality as a 'critical social theory in the making' (Collins 2019) that aims to enhance ethical social justice frameworks, I propose to turn to discourses of normality among those on the move and by bringing contradictory logics and rhythms in relation to one another, explore how new 'modes of being, thinking, knowing, sensing and living, that is an otherwise in plural' (Mignolo and Welsh 2018) are formed. Only then will we be able to start carving a new way through our difficult genealogies shaped by 'the hands of others' (Leder 2014), and at the same time, take responsibility for our own personal and collective actions. Looking for new possibilities and relinking with new meanings, we must first, however, pay close attention to language and (socio)linguistic imagination in erasing and highlighting intersectional struggles and granting legitimacy to particular models of conduct and ideals of normality. In the next chapter, I argue that only by looking closely at the enactment of material sociolinguistic performances can we fully harness our capacity to challenge ongoing coloniality (Quijano 2000) and demand politics of togetherness (Stroud 2001) glued by difference, transience and imperfection.

2

Politics of Sounding Out and Being Heard

Looking at the colonial paradigm and its consequences: 'languages' and locations

To understand the ways in which systems of domination mutually reinforce one another to form unstable, but recognizable meanings and knowledge projects and relations between them, I had to recognize that signs, communicative routines and sensory inclinations guide us towards expressing particular orientations and subject positions, and create propensity for the future. These signs and their intelligibility never operate in a vacuum, but rather emerge as a result of 'extended interactions between individuals, institutions, ideologies and ideas' (Brown 2003: 21). The chaining of signs in communicative encounters is thereby always embedded in particular chronotopic (Bakthin 1981) frames, that is, timespace configurations. It is also 'cycled through the experience of particular perceivers' (Faudree 2012), which I saw very clearly when my participants let their stories momentarily freeze in my academic project. I quickly noticed different subject positions expressed through semantic content. Changing acoustic rhythms and my interlocutors' metacommentary linking sounded differences to people, however, continually reminded me that 'information and communication pass through rhythms: repetitions and differences' (Lefebvre 2013: 52). To study mechanisms through which signs, objects, contexts and selves are linked to assemble particular images of normality in these situated accounts, from the beginning, I had to therefore recognize that poetic devices were actively used in the construal of meaning and logic of emerging transnational projects.

These sounded repetitions and differences are, however, not always taken seriously by studies of migrant discourse. In fact, many sociological and anthropological works centre on texts as core units of analysis and present quotes in English or only mention the name of the language in which the utterances were spoken. The latter, a conventional way of linking discrete and quantifiable language labels to people, helps us to not forget about linguistic diversity in a world dominated by powerful hegemonic codes of wider communication such as English. However, these labelling practices are tightly linked to politics of sounding and listening, where particular representations of collective memory (Bauman and Briggs 2003) have historically separated discourse from the sensorium and simplified the relationship between human and institutional bodies, erasing their continuous entanglement in sociocultural timespace of multiple dimensions (Munn 1992: 116).

To avoid dangers of simplified linguistic representations, I therefore needed to devise a way of using the existing body of knowledge about the signs I was encountering without blindly perpetuating colonial understandings of linguistic divisions. Given my exposure to linguistic discussions, I was aware that linguists also talk about quantifiable and bounded languages. They often quote statistics of world languages to make the wider public aware of the increasing number of dying languages and uneven realities of language relations. Following an established linguistic tradition where the focus is most often put on linguistic structure, such scholars identify relevant syntactic, phonological, and morphological patterns typical of particular named languages. The patterns are often established through linguistic fieldwork conducted by a trained linguist, and with reference to the body of literature and other available recorded language sources, if such exist. Linguistic fieldwork usually entails writing down stretches of elicited discourse, translation and deduction of grammatical rules (Deumert et al. 2020). The definitions of named languages are not, however, limited to linguistic structure, and institutionalized linguistic knowledge must often admit a number of other criteria to name a code 'a language'. For example, next to linguistic structure, linguists consider issues of mutual intelligibility, geographical area, ethnolinguistic identity, existence of a writing system and political realities. The linguistic form is then frozen in time, assigned to a group of people and institutionally labelled as typical and representative of a particular linguistic code that falls under a particular label such as English, Polish, Swahili or Mandarin. Linguistic stats based on such definitions are then widely used as authoritative sources of linguistic knowledge.

Reading critical sociolinguistic and linguistic anthropological works, I was acquainted with the historical conditions in which this linguistic knowledge had been forming. I had to take into account the fact that the field of linguistics, which was usually traced back to the beginning of the nineteenth century, operated within its own changing assumptions about the relationship between linguistic data, the researcher, their technologies and the object of study. Such knowledge like all academic knowledge was thereby 'tentative and done with its own temporality' (Deumert et al. 2020) and involved participation in authorization and authentification of legitimacy of collective linguistic representation. Scholars in this field had themselves been actively engaged in the construction of languages (Bauman and Briggs 2003).

From the beginning of the twentieth century, building on ideas developed in Europe, the primary focus in language sciences started gradually being put on analysis of linguistic structures. It is often argued that the interest in the systematic and rule-governed nature of language change and structure began to flourish after the introduction of Ferdinand de Saussure's programme of structural linguistics with its dyadic understanding of the linguistic sign. Since the 1920s, structural linguists preoccupied themselves mainly with the production of grammars of various linguistic systems. Despite later developments and redefinitions of the object of analysis, with most significant improvements coming from, for example, Chomsky's push away from structures independent of human will towards the workings of the creative potential of the human brain, most linguists have remained predominantly interested in grammar, and traditionally the field has equated grammar with language (Deumert et al. 2020). The historical perspective hence demanded acknowledging that descriptions of linguistic structures themselves had been highly influenced by Western definitions of 'language, notions of languageness and metalanguages' (Makoni and Pennycook 2007).

Chomskyan distinction between 'competence' and 'performance' also further pushed the field towards the study of workings of abstract bounded systems based on biological predispositions. Rather than acknowledging the multifunctionality of language (Jakobson 1960), in line with Western imagination, the preference for particular functions of language has tended to dominate the field. As a result, linguistic knowledge has historically prioritized the referential function of language. Many have also presented denotational codes as static through their insistence on invariance in grammatical models. With an interest in linguistic universals and parameters, today many in this tradition may still rely on their own intuitions when developing their theories without reference to naturally occurring data. They often test their intuitions about particular grammatical constructions against 'those deemed to have similarly intimate knowledge of the target language' (Li Wei 2013), usually 'native speakers' of 'a language'. I knew that such data collection methods were, however, later criticized by some who worked with some collected data. For example, today those working in what are often defined as 'core' subfields of linguistics such as phonology, syntax or morphology may examine linguistic patterning against large corpora in corpus linguistics. Additionally, with technological advancements, many projects have also employed experimental methods which often rely on designed tasks to elicit particular language forms and situated stretches of discourse.

Despite ongoing methodological improvements, I quickly noticed that major projects in the core areas have traditionally presented very limited information about the context of interaction, participants' backgrounds and trajectories. For example, projects foundational for our understanding of sounds of world languages have relied on very small numbers of often student participants or groups defined as native speakers. When studies focusing on such sounds as stops, which I closely examine in this book, are considered, I couldn't ignore the fact that the groundbreaking project conducted by Lisker and Abramson in 1964 examined initial English stops in isolation produced by four speakers of American English. Today the field moved on to include larger samples and occasionally less controlled discursive performances, but Yao's (2007) study, which was one of the first to rely on casual interview data, still focused on stops in initial positions produced by nineteen residents of Ohio, United States. Importantly, the findings from such projects are usually labelled as representative of, for example, British English, American English. Admittedly, many insights from such projects also serve as a basis for dictionaries, grammars, language tests, speech recognition software and teaching materials. These practices and ideas have also travelled from the global West and North around the world and actively shaped how linguistic systems are imagined and recognized today.

I consequently knew that quantifiable languages were 'an artefact of classificatory procedures rather than reflection of communicative practices' (Romaine 1994: 12). These in turn were tightly linked to particular assumptions about the body, society, history, place and objectivity, often erasing the fact that elicited discourse is always situated and fragmentary. Relying predominantly on utterances of the self, they may make us also momentarily forget about the role of the researcher and the dialogic nature of discourse (Bakhtin 1981). With my project, I saw very clearly that the audience in discourse production cannot be ignored in any discursive encounter. I had to therefore first recognize linguists' overwhelming reliance on particular, not universal, understandings of the relationship between language, nation and geographical location.

Gal reminds us that European philosophies of the Enlightenment and German Romanticism together with consequent political practice resulted in 'making a connection between the categories of "language" and "nation" appear a necessary, natural, and self-evident one, used as much in everyday political discourse as in scholarly arguments' (1998: 324). The science of language, established in the late eighteenth century, propagated an idea of language as natural and 'independent of individual voluntary acts and therefore not the creation of any self-conscious human will or intervention' (324). Such a conceptualization of language actively participated in the emergence of modern nation-states. Linguistic objectivity eradicated 'the "personal" and the "willed" from the project of scientific observation and analysis' (Gal 1998: 324), which in turn enabled people to seek justification for allowed political actions such as the formation of nation-states in the objective characteristics of language. Apart from scientific epistemology, aesthetics also played an important role in the process as a uniform language was seen as a tool for communication among rational and mobile citizens allowing them to become modern and aware of their political rights (Hobsbawm 1990).

I knew that scholars had offered various explanations for the embodiment of the collective spirit in the social category of a nation with Ernest Gellner's (1983) and Benedict Anderson's (2006) theories triggering the debate and arguing for nationalism and nation-states as being products of modernity. While for Gellner nationalism was understood as a political principle brought about by industrialization, for Anderson it emerged with the popularity of capitalism and the development of print as a commodity allowing for the creation of imagined communities. In both theories, language played a crucial role: for Gellner, through standardized, shared languages people became loyal to 'high' culture, and through schooling mediated in the languages, nationalism was created; for Anderson, by propagating selected vernaculars by means of print, print-languages created nationalism. Both theories and those that followed successfully questioned the narrative of the self-evident relationship between language, nation and place.

Linguistic anthropologists and sociolinguists, especially in postcolonial contexts, have further challenged ethnolinguistic modularity and the predetermined character of nationalism assumed in many of these theories, and stressed the role of language ideologies in the creation of national identities and shaping the indeterminacy of ethnolinguistic identity. It has been thus noted that 'the national vision' is not limited to the imagination of the nation, but it includes the imagination of language and linguistic communities (Eisenlohr 2007: 25), often perpetuating ideologies of elites (Eisenlohr 2007, Ramaswamy 1997). A contemporary example comes from Jacqueline Urla's (1993) study of Basque nationalism, where it has been argued that despite the fact that many nationals do not speak the Basque language, the imagination of Basque as a national language is a factor at play in conceiving of the nation.

Reflecting on the consequences of linguistic assumptions, I therefore often thought of Fanon's assertion that '[t]o speak means being able to use a certain syntax and possessing the morphology of such and such a language, but it means above all assuming a culture and bearing the weight of civilization' (1952: 2). Linguists' assumptions have thereby historically framed participants and actively shaped the history of global politics of sounding out and being heard. In Irvine's (2008) discussion of the history of African linguistics, we see that European models equating language with identity and place travelled with linguists and missionaries who codified and observed colonized populations from the nineteenth century onwards. Working mostly with brief wordlists usually in refugee communities and among freed slaves, often away from larger communities of language users, emerging linguistic representations of African 'languages' linked linguistic forms to geographical locations visually freezing them on maps. The descriptions presented reduced versions of studied communicative practices, rarely looking at 'social deixis other than pronouns and kinship terms' (Irvine 2008: 331) and leading to simplified static grammars independent of local social life. Similar practices were reported in other colonial contexts and it has also been argued that the pursuit for objectivity in literacy materials made many equate language with the written code. This was also accompanied by modelling representations on the Roman alphabet in line with European orthographies.

The relationship between the colonizer and the colonized was not considered in such projects, and ethnic labels were often invented (Makoni and Pennycook 2007) in line with colonizers' imagination. 'Suitably objectified languages' were hence 'powerful naturalizing instruments for colonial power' (Errington 2001: 34), reminding us that linguistic research 'is never far from military activity' (Irvine 2008: 329). The linguist also came to be seen as an expert who could turn noise into meaning (Deumert et al. 2020) for other, usually European audiences and who frequently participated in designing languages for political purposes. Pointing to differences between colonial policies and regulations, Errington (2008) demonstrated for example that in the Dutch colonized Indonesia, the Dutch government decided not to use Dutch, but employed linguists to design the standard form of Malay as the language of governance. The code was then renamed to Indonesian and picked up and promoted by Indonesian nationalists. It has thus actively shaped today's linguistic imagination where it has become a code of the majority and has been given the status of a national language.

I was aware that these linguistic representations often disregarded the fact that speakers whose languages were studied were very often displaced due to, for example, war or genocide, illness, population mixing, assigned work on plantations (Mufwene 2010). Differences between exploitation and settler colonies were also not reflected in such models, and multilingual dynamics, with people's differential access to sites of power and varying intensity of contact, eradicated and portrayed as of secondary importance. Finally, in many cases, assumptions about the 'native speaker' led to inadequate understandings of the role of language transmission. Today, various projects show that in colonial contexts, the question of power mediated access to linguistic resources and frequency of contact, and linguists working in colonial contexts often did not acknowledge that transmission is more dependent on home practices than schooling in standardized, written codes (Mufwene 2010). They also often forgot to take into account the fact that these practices remained entangled in colonial policies that promoted education modelled on Western cosmology and linguistic imagination. For example, Mufwene reminds us that in India, the 'Macaulay doctrine' from 1835 reserved the right to education in English to the privileged classes, and limited education of Indian 'masses' to selected 'indigenous' languages.

The ignorance of colonial linguists resulted in epistemic violence (Deumert et al. 2020), which, to me, was perhaps most visible in discussions surrounding creoles (DeGraff 2001). DeGraff (2001, 2020) argued that due to the institutional structuring of creole knowledge production, with its colonial funders and founders, traditionally creoles were contrasted with 'regular' languages based on their 'abnormal' patterns of emergence and transmission. The myth of 'creole exceptionalism' was largely based on studies focusing on linguistic structure and carried out in the context of limited availability of historical data. DeGraff warned, however, that creoles cannot be defined based on linguistic structures, but only in sociohistorical terms. When entering the debates, one thus cannot forget the circumstances of creole emergence, that is, their development mostly among non-European slaves employed for sugar cane and rice cultivation; or among Aboriginal populations in Australia (Mufwene 2010). In such contexts, the enslaved population constituted the majority of speakers of creoles as the colonizers usually obliged enslaved individuals to use their European languages, limiting exposure to that code and putting people together without any consideration for codes that were brought along.

I noticed that historically, linguists paid little attention to such social dynamics. Instead in their studies of creoles, they were highly influenced by Schleicher's *Stammbaum* model that grouped languages into families, and remained widely used in historical linguistics. Comparing orders and levels of linguistic forms, the model sought to account for Darwin-influenced evolutionary theories of language. The 'image of branching descent' (Errington 2001: 32) actively legitimized particular conceptions of linguistic difference among the academic community and simultaneously naturalized '"grades of man" from primitive to advanced' (DeGraff 2020: e.296). With changing data sources, later projects successfully debunked many myths surrounding creole genesis and formation. For example, today, it is widely accepted that discourse plays a major role in creole formation, and despite the fact that no one questions the impact of language transmission, L1 acquisition is no longer treated as catalyst for grammatical elaboration. Rather, most scholars recognize multiple factors in the development of creoles, with language contact being considered together with, for example, population growth or social history of language use.

I also knew that it had been argued that partial evidence from colonial linguistic projects sometimes provides the only remaining evidence and 'cannot always and everywhere be dissolved into the reproduction of colonial interest' (Errington 2001: 34). We may, however, assert that when read critically, such sources shed light on the metalanguage framing discussions on dynamics of human talk, complexity of linguistic forms and the process of institutionalizing particular linguistic practices. This in turn made me approach labelled codes used in these descriptions as metadiscursive regimes (Bauman and Briggs 2003), which through their insistence on linguistic purification, standardize and link particular linguistic systems of domination to particular visions of social and political cohesion imagined to be embodied in one voice.

Moving beyond epistemologies of ignorance (Deumert et al. 2020), grounded in 'not knowing' as well as 'not wanting to know' (Khan 2020), I eventually came to see that these standardized codes were tightly linked to governmentality and had an impact on embodied experiences of many until the present day. Descriptions of simple and reduced grammars of creoles have, for instance, travelled outside academic debates, and the colonialist ideology of 'bad, broken or abnormal languages' surrounding creoles has been mobilized in various media outlets till today. DeGraff also notes that the hegemonic whiteness (Hudley et al. 2020) and erasure of history of racial capitalism to which this ideology is tightly linked still contribute to the politics of exclusion and inclusion worldwide. For example, education systems in many postcolonial contexts still rely on colonial European languages rather than providing tuition in local varieties and creoles; for example, French is widely used in schools in Haiti, English in Jamaica, Latin America and Africa.

In multiple corners of the world, ideals of standard language are still used as benchmarks against which other ways of communicating are evaluated and around which models of reality have been construed. They also regiment moves and actions of some more than others, remaining tightly linked to gendered processes of racialization and socio-economic disadvantage. Studies of the material effects of linguistic profiling, 'an auditory equivalent of racial profiling' (Baugh 2003), have shown for example that in telephone conversations studied in California, speakers of African American English faced discrimination due to stereotypes about their non-standard speech which in turn limited their housing opportunities. In the UK, the latest projects report that accent bias leads to downgrading of 'working-class and ethnic minority accents' and upgrading of those historically associated with upper-class speech (https://accentbiasbritain.org/wp-content/uploads/2020/02/Accent-Bias-Report-2020.pdf). Although weaker in professional settings, such bias may still impact the perception of job applicants and employment. Less standardized varieties are often linked to lack of competence or illegitimacy of individuals and groups (Rosa 2016), and assumed static conceptualizations of the relationship between language, place and identity propagated in state policies lead to images of 'languagelessness', where some are continually portrayed and evaluated as lacking a language.

To me, the material effects of language standardization were perhaps most visible in institutionalized contexts such as court trials where testimonies and accounts of those using non-dominant resources were repeatedly dismissed and portrayed as not credible. For example, examining the speech of Rachel Jeantel, the leading witness in Zimmerman's trial for the killing of Trayvon Martin in the United States in 2012, Rickford and King (2016) demonstrated how the jurors' unfamiliarity with the witness's way of speaking led to acquittal of Mr Zimmerman. Based on the witness's use of African American English with Caribbean influences, her credibility was questioned, testimony misunderstood and eventually dismissed. Similarly, in Blommaert's work on asylum hearings in the UK (2010), the Home Office's lack of up-to-date understanding of language relations in Rwanda made a case for asylum unsuccessful. Blommaert showed that Joseph, a man who grew up in the context of genocide in Rwanda and whose linguistic repertoire was organized in small, functionally specialized English, Runyankole, Swahili and Kinyarwanda chunks, was declined asylum mainly due to his linguistic profile not being evaluated as legitimate. Rather than considering severe constraints on the asylum seeker's language choice, the authorities ignored the importance of time for language and place relations, questioned his authenticity and ordered to send him to Uganda. Linguistic policing and surveillance were also evident in Khan's discussion of encounters between various UK government-run organizations and racialized and securitized (Khan 2020) predominantly male Muslim and brown bodies. Khan described, for example, how pronunciation patterns or use of linguistic codes unknown to the state authorities may lead to accusations of radicalization or detainment, pointing to the ways in which particular ways of sounding and looking come to be continuously associated with images of a 'dangerous Other' under constant suspicion and assessment.

These observations made me aware of the fact that listening subjects' own unfamiliarity with linguistic differences had been repeatedly reported to limit freedoms and movements. As shown earlier, lack of a thorough consideration for linguistic difference has resulted in 'the burden of adjustment on groups who are outside positions of influence and power' (Baugh 2003), only highlighting that definitions of languages are continually used to control and persuade others to a particular way of seeing the world. Observations from such projects convinced me that active living was not always set up along the oppressor–oppressed axis in linear ways and, thus, required a theory that came from people's lives rather than one based on purely abstract categorizations. I therefore had to turn to sociolinguistic and linguistic anthropological projects that had resisted dominant invariant portrayals of language and could enable me to better understand how sociolinguistic tools may be reused in an effort to carve a more material and affective way of thinking about language.

Seeing what we know: Situated orientations towards the standard

To move away from linguistically standardized 'regimes of purification' (Bauman and Briggs 2003), but not to erase the role of materiality of the code, I turned to research that had historically challenged ideas of uniformist and universalist understandings of language. I knew that many scholars had questioned a possibility of ignoring the role of the context for language production and development. I was also aware of the fact that early dialectological work provided perhaps the earliest evidence of differences in pronunciation, grammar or lexicon within various European and Western nation-states. Largely interested in historical questions surrounding language structures distributed in geographical space, the traditional dialectological method allowed scholars to draw attention to the ways in which linguistic differences were reorganized across dialects or 'non-standard' ways of communicating in different locations, and reflect on the role of the linguistic context.

I couldn't, however, stop thinking about dialectology's flawed assumptions favouring ways of communicating of non-mobile, older, rural, male speakers who historically featured in these studies and who at the same time were imagined to be sources of authenticity and genuine linguistic forms. I knew that with increased availability of portable recorders and a growing interest in the local social order, from the mid-twentieth century onwards, such assumptions were later challenged and ideals of authentic speakers were eventually extended to other people. Having read about Labov's alternation to the method and question of inquiry of dialectology, I also knew that early sociolinguists of variation[1] later tested various linguistic theories against recorded spoken data, repeatedly demonstrating that linguistic structures correlate with social structures (e.g. Labov 1966; Macaulay 1977; Trudgill 1974; Wolfram 1969).

Considering the context in which these projects were carried out, I was aware that these scholars designed studies of 'precise patterning' of various linguistic variables such as the presence or absence of (r) in American English or use of (ing) in British English, and sought to explain their occurrence in relation to such categories as social class, ethnicity, race or gender. They captured the heterogeneity of linguistic expressions and, at the same time, repeatedly reported the role of linguistic pressures on variation. I knew that these studies helped debunk many myths surrounding 'language deficit' debates. I was aware, however, that their primary interest was in historical questions about sound change, giving priority to quantitative analysis of variants associated with such social categories in speech communities defined 'by participation in a set of shared norms: [. . .] observed in overt types of evaluative behavior, and by the uniformity of abstract patterns of variation which are invariant in respect to particular levels of usage' (Labov 1972: 120–1). The interest in linguistic variation in these early studies had to do with their focus on the vernacular as the most natural, most automatic and maximally systematic speech, grounded in an assumption that an adult's linguistic system reflects a critical point in acquisition. As Bucholtz and Hall (2016) noted, the preoccupation of these studies with linguistic patterning did not allow for reflection about 'the place of language in a broad communicative field encompassing the full range of embodied practices' (177). It also led these scholars to imagine the vernacular as reflecting the speaker's assigned place in a socio-economically stratified community as well as a natural object of scientific inquiry that would objectively capture the 'orderly differentiation in a language serving a community' (Weinreich et al. 1968: 101).

Despite the projects' important recognition of class for linguistic production, I didn't see class only as rank in a socio-economically stratified community. While engaging with these studies, I acknowledged the importance of looking at socio-economic indices consisting of the speaker's income, education and occupation. I was, however, troubled by the argument that differences in language could be explained mostly in relation to self-correction, ideals of prestige and assumed desired upward mobility of the speech community. In the end, I was hesitant to follow these projects' heavy reliance of the logic of the nation-state as I couldn't disregard the fact that historically they erased mobile speakers and recently arrived migrating populations.

I also found these projects' objective different from my own. I was indeed interested in the sonic experience, but I wasn't only preoccupied with the study of ongoing sound changes without raising participant self-consciousness. While engaging with this literature, I noticed that in these projects, scientific objectivity was also often imagined to be maintained by rapid and anonymous interviewing techniques and random sampling, which differed from my approach to both knowledge production and interviews. Finding Labov's definition of style as attention paid to speech far too limiting, I also didn't follow the variationist methodology: the sociolinguistic interview during which various speaking styles are elicited through reading minimal pairs, reading word lists and passages, and conversation with the interviewer. This had to do with the fact that from the beginning, my understanding of style was influenced more by a Welsh cultural theorist, Raymond Williams, who wrote:

> No generation speaks quite the same language as its predecessors. The difference can be defined in terms of additions, deletions, and modifications, but these do not exhaust it. What really changes is something quite general, over a wide range, and the description that often fits the change best is the literary term 'style'. . . . For what we are defining is a particular quality of social experience and relationship, historically distinct from other particular qualities, which gives the sense of a generation or of a period. (1977: 131)

I found the critique of assumptions made in these early variationist projects a helpful guide for finding a way to deal with my data. Arguments against static, predetermined and bounded understandings of social categories, preference of citizen bodies and an assumed consensus model of society (Bucholtz 2009) were crucial for my thinking about the sociolinguistic dynamics I was studying. I couldn't ignore the tensions I was observing. Not to erase them, I found inspiration in Silverstein's reflections based on the work of Labov's contemporaries, also interested in the role of language in society, but often working in the contexts of less standardized communities, Hymes and Gumperz. In his writing, Silverstein drew my attention to the contextualized use of language and the ways in which members of communities control contrasting forms. I decided to begin with his assertion that all linguistic behaviour is equal to 'unstable mutual interaction of meaningful sign forms, contextualized to situations of interested human use and mediated by the fact of cultural ideology' (Silverstein 1985: 220).

Rather than discovering patterns of language change in static communities where the standard was always seen as a desired code embodying upward mobility, to me, the early observations showed situated orientations towards the standard register and helped me understand the sociohistorical processes of standardization and enregisterment (Agha 2007) in such American cities as New York City or Philadelphia. Here, after Agha (2007), 'enregisterment' is equivalent to 'processes and practices whereby performable signs become recognized (and regrouped) as belonging to distinct, differentially valorized semiotic registers by a population' (81). This body of research helped me see that rather than monitoring one's speech towards the standard only, speakers do things with language (Austin 1962) and navigate between the demands of the push and pull of 'identity-indexing' and 'context-creating/effectuating' (Silverstein 2016) features deployed for particular communicative purposes. It also made me aware of the fact that particular task formats, for example, reading aloud, may create standard register anxieties, which as Labov demonstrated, are linked to the dynamics of sociocultural space.

To me, it was most useful to see standardized norms as part of registers, i.e. particular 'cultural models of action that link diverse behavioural signs to enactable effects, including images or persona, interpersonal relationship and type of conduct' (Agha 2007: 145). I assumed that like other registers, standard registers were composed of 'the emergent patterning of linguistic and non-linguistic tokens within observable events of semiotic activity and interaction' (Agha 2007: 186). They were reflexively shaped and changed both in form and in value, spreading through historical processes of socialization based on valorizations and countervalorizations among members of groups that made use of them, where 'widespread schemes of speech valorization associate particular forms of speech with commonplace value distinctions' or where social effects emerge from the organization of co-occurring signs in interaction (Agha 2007: 15–16). As shown earlier, I was aware that standard registers become norms against which other ways of communicating are evaluated as they get to be promoted by institutional action of various sorts.

I noticed, however, that speakers' evaluations of standard norms always depend on their proficiency and awareness, which are 'mediated by large scale communicative processes' (Agha 2007: 169) and remain 'tightly linked to asymmetries of power, socio-economic class, position within hierarchies, and the like' (Agha 2007: 146).

Johnstone's work on Pittsburghese in south-western Pennsylvania (Johnstone 2016a, 2016b) helped me think about the idea of the processual nature of emergence of registers, be they standard or not. In her work, Johnstone traced the emergence of English in Pittsburgh to eighteenth-century colonial migration from the British Isles. As the city life was initially relatively geographically isolated, she argued that the local Scottish-Irish-influenced way of speaking gradually became dissimilar to other ways of speaking American English. This was particularly pronounced in terms of vowels that only diverged further due to later 'in-migrations' triggered by nineteenth- and twentieth-century industrialization. This also attracted immigrant industrial workers, such as those from Polish territories, who usually brought and used other linguistic resources with them. Not until after the Second World War, however, did the local working-class population become aware of their distinct way of speaking. Johnstone argued that the local dense and multiplex social networks reinforced local norms. Living in 'insular neighbourhoods within a walking distance of their steel mills and other factories where the adults worked and children went to school' (Johnstone 2016b: 360), speakers of what got to be known as Pittsburghese did not have many opportunities to notice the difference and relatively few had a chance to position themselves towards other ways of speaking. Changes in the 1960s and 1970s, which made the local population more mobile, and used to speech stereotypes mass-mediated via TV, and which coincided with grandchildren of immigrants no longer speaking home languages and often moving away from immigrant religion, resulted in increased consciousness of linguistic differences. Tightly linked to class and regional affiliation, the reflexive negotiation of norms led to the emergence of the term Pittsburghese, explicitly linking the 'dialect' to the place only in the 1960s. Later economic changes, which also involved relocation of many Pittsburghers from the city, made the link between this enregistered style and social identity only more pronounced. Johnstone (2016a) noted that this led to the creation of a dictionary of the local dialect as well as its commodification as features of Pittsburghese got to be frozen in time in the written form on sellable objects of different sorts. Today, the features associated with Pittsburghese continue to be imbued with different values in the ongoing process of its resemioticization as those for whom the signs are meaningful position themselves towards social images associated with the local speech.

Such a processual emergence and commodification of a register made me aware that practices through which links between forms and their meanings are forged are also key to understanding standard register formations and people's orientations to these norms. Agha's discussion of RP, received pronunciation, often equated with Queen's (now King's) English in Britain, but estimated to be used by 1–3 per cent of the UK population today, reminded me that reflexive activities through which human beings shape links between styles and social images differ, for example, in terms of explicitness and ways in which linguistic phenomena are typified to be indexical of certain attributes of speakers. Remembering that everybody speaks with an accent and that in the UK accents continue to be reflexively shaped both through institutionalized and everyday practices, I knew that RP had historically been also tightly linked to images of upper class and education. Agha's discussion of the formation of this register fleshed out the unequal access to social space and these images. He demonstrated that, perceived as a supralocal accent, associated with Standard/Southern British English, which in turn is widely used in the written form and valued in public life, RP has historically been associated with positive social images lifting its speakers up in relation to others relying on less valued ways of speaking. Being recognized by wider society and propagated through historical processes, it was gradually enregistered as an object of value. 'Giving a system of register values a measure of stability in time' (Agha 2003: 264), with its relation to particular social identities erased, it also found its way to phonemic representations of British English that travel around the world in print and online dictionaries to this day. In Britain, with time, the perception and production of valued speech also started changing, potentially impacting the images of exemplary speakers and hence, certainly for some, moving away from RP's images of historical tradition and authenticity and impacting public imagination. Similar processes have been observed in other countries.

Building on such processual understandings of standardized speech, I wanted to develop a way to study how people on the move, who operated with communication technologies that enabled multipresence in various sites and extended possibilities of action, were participating in processes of enregisterment in transnational timespace and how this impacted upon situated emerging images of normality and authenticity. To do so, I needed to consider what happens when speaking and listening subjects interact in situated events.

Against fixed knowledges: Weaving images of the self and other

To grasp how signs, standard or not, were assembled 'within contexts of constraints and facilitation' (Kroskrity 2021), I decided to work with the Peircean (1931–58) triadic sign. Such an understanding of the semiotic sign assumes that its meaning cannot be understood without its pragmatic framework, but rather is always 'the product and producer of relations' (Faudree 2012). It has been argued that Peircean signs mediate and fuse material and ideational modes into a triad: sign, object and interpretant, and enable us to better understand how signs, objects, contexts and selves are linked. I wanted to see how such an understanding of signs may flesh out the relationship between the political dimensions of globalization and language.

To do so, following Peirce and later Silverstein (2003), I also relied on the division of signs into icons, indexes and symbols. For Peirce, an icon resembles the object that is being referred to, an index points to something other than the referent and symbols are arbitrary signs established by social conventions. Building on this division, Silverstein proposed that sociolinguistic differences index other phenomena in interaction, that is to say, a linguistic sign describes and stands for phenomena lying outside itself, where micro social frames of analysis are linked to the macro social ones by means of the indexical order, which comes in ordinal, integral degrees (Silverstein 2003: 193) in a non-linear manner. He argued further that 'any n-th order indexical presupposes that the context in which it is normatively used has a schematization of some particular sort relative to which we can model the appropriateness of its usage in context' (Silverstein 2003: 193). Such an order leads to a contextual entailment produced through ideological engagement with the meaningfulness of the n-th order, which is created by culturally ritualized usage of the n-th order, its so-called ethnometapragmatics. The n-th order can then be conceptualized as $n+1^{st}$ order, hence a different relationship guided by different values can be formed. For example, after indexing place, Pittsburghese could for some become indexical of particular ethnic, Polish, images of masculinity. Such orders and their understandings always compete and are in a dialectical relationship with one another. The indexical meaning of any linguistic sign rather depends on its appropriateness to the context as well as its effectiveness in context, that is, its presupposition and entailment, which are mediated by a metapragmatic function (Silverstein 2003). In this model, the metapragmatic function is most often implicit as it has to do with the organization of talk itself, which makes it inherently dialectical and, as Silverstein argues, ideological, and thus anchored in cultural conceptualizations of the world connected to people's values.

Subject-creating dimensions of listening are hence active processes that rely on the literacy of listening and geopolitical positioning of all parties involved. Research actions and communication are also tightly embedded in the politics of voice, which often promotes modern and neoliberal understandings of subjectivity. Faudree (2012) further argues that in situated events, the political and social aspects of voice must be considered in relation to its sonic dimension precisely in order to understand how sonic recontextualization constitutes stratified forms of modernity and participates in processes of authentication and purification. To avoid dichotomy between language and other sonic phenomena such as music, she proposes a basic unit of analysis as an always 'socially situated, relationally understood sign' whether spoken or written, performed or embodied. Speaking subjects must therefore always be perceived as acting in the present ritual moment, temporarily inhabiting it and always conveying their historicity (French 2012).

Such a relational aspect of the linguistic sign production and its embedding in stratified communities were well known to me from ethnographic, locally oriented projects that often employed a Marxist understanding of class relations, where class was seen as a formation and an 'ultimately economically driven process that splits populations into subgroups' (Milroy and Milroy 1992). Having read about, for example, the Milroys' project in Belfast, I knew that social networks had been observed to impact sociolinguistic production. Working in three working-class neighbourhoods in the time of Protestant–Catholic tensions in Northern Ireland in the 1970s, these scholars observed that speakers with weak inter-group ties, that is, in this case younger women from the Catholic area, were using, for example, more backed /a/ than both older women and men in their area, and women in the two other neighbourhoods. Discussing the women's working conditions and family arrangements, they pointed out that orientation to sociolinguistic differences depended not only on class relations, but also on 'differences in the circumstances in which women and men typically find themselves' (Eckert 1989: 255).

As the gendered context of discourse production was important to understand my observations, I found Nichols's work (1983) on Black women's use of standard forms in the south of the United States helpful in identifying processes in which gendered differences in language use emerge. Nichols argued that those with jobs that required more use of the standard were more likely to use it. She further claimed that women and men do not participate in the economy in the same ways and their sociolinguistic performances must be understood in terms of access to jobs. As with many other projects, I couldn't forget that these studies fleshed out that the configuration of contact and interaction under particular economic conditions had an influence on standard register orientation.

Rereading these projects in the 2010s, I noted that they did not reject the supremacy of the standard linguistic market (Bourdieu and Boltanski 1975), but pointed to the workings of hegemonic heteronormative masculinity and highlighted the creative potential of those in relatively powerless positions. Although they were moving away from male, educated, and rational scientific authority, when I was reading them, I couldn't help but see that they still relied on static categories equating a speaker's identity largely with category affiliation and didn't necessarily extensively reflect on the researcher's perception of these signs. Nevertheless, reading them from a historical perspective made me see that they must have brought into focus the fact that men's work is not evaluated in relation to their use of the standard and that linguistic practices constitute symbolic capital on particular linguistic markets (Bourdieu 1977).

However, the relationality between social categories and linguistic signs fleshed out in these projects wasn't enough for me as I was already discussing insights from the so-called third wave of sociolinguistics of variation with my supervisors and other graduate students at Oxford. I knew that the idea of the linguistic market was further explored by Eckert in her two-year-long ethnographic project in Detroit, Michigan, in the late 1980s. Invested in debates on language change, Eckert argued that the study of adolescents' participation in the Great Vowel Shift, a series of changes in pronunciation observed in northern American cities, may help further understand how speakers locate themselves in the gender order when entering the heterosexual market. To explain the changes, she relied on the concept of communities of practice (Lave and Wagner 1991), defined by engagement, shared repertoire and joint enterprise. Working in a high school in a predominantly White suburban area, where ethnicity was downplayed, she noticed that newer changes in the Northern Cities Shift such as backing of (e) and (ʌ) were best understood along a continuum of local categories of jocks and burnouts, who differed in their orientation to the city life, college education and class background. Having examined the use of vowel changes that entered her participants' linguistic repertoires at different intervals in time, she showed that the oldest changes were led by girls, while later changes were best explained in relation to the burnout/jock distinction. This enabled her to posit that gender 'does not have a uniform effect on linguistic behaviour for the community as a whole, across variables, or for that matter for any individual'

(Eckert 1989: 253). Her observations drew my attention to the differentiation within the gender category and foregrounded dynamics of the heterosexual market in the United States, where women competed with women, and men competed with men.

The findings from this project made me aware that the use of sociolinguistic differences was tightly linked to the value that comes from enacting a particular kind of woman/man image. At the same time, women's and men's orientation was best understood in relation to differences of power as 'women . . . are constrained to exhibit constantly who they are rather than what they do' (Eckert 1989: 259). Reading Eckert's further work with the California Style Collective, I knew that she proposed that 'resources from a broad social landscape will be identifiable not only by which resources it [the style] uses, but how it uses each resource and how it combines all its resources', with choices being neither neutral nor random, but having 'some kind of meaning for the speaker who takes them up' (California Style Collective). All these observations made third-wave sociolinguists argue that individual linguistic variables do not have specified meanings, but rather 'the construal of any verbal gesture is embedded in a construal of its context at every level' (Eckert), and it is through participation in discourse that we continue to reinterpret forms in contexts and imbue them with meanings.

I also linked these arguments to observations coming from other projects on the relationship between language and gender, where it had been repeatedly shown that researchers cannot assume uniformity of gendered linguistic performances, but must rather always consider their embedding in particular timespace configurations as category norms are not identical across the globe or history. Here, I remembered Cameron's (2014) point about the changing ideals of femininity that enabled changes in women's and men's speech in England. I also thought about various studies of gendered pronouns and pronominal change in the English language (e.g. Silverstein 1985). Additionally, Keenan's (1974) work on divergent gender stereotypes across cultural contexts resonated with my own observations that Polish and Eastern European performances of femininity and masculinity that I was familiar with might also be enacted in other ways than those associated with dominant Western images of woman/man reported in sociolinguistic studies so far. I knew, for example, that in her study of Malagasy-speaking women and men, Keenan noted that contrary to American stereotypes, in Madagascar at the time of her project, women were more direct than men, which was manifested in their reliance on the ordinary, direct speech register, *resaka*, rather than the more ceremonial and indirect *kabary*.

Such observations together with later projects that also challenged the assumed heteronormative masculinity, for example, in the United States by showing that men's language use is itself not linguistically uniform (Kiesling 2019), made me convinced that in any partitioned sociocultural space, people rather negotiate, propagate, and legitimize their ideas and multiple sociopolitical, economic, and other interests in and through communicative practices. Thanks to ideologies' primarily communicative character, bodies hence only become, for example, female/male by operating within discursive systems in which they are recognized (Butler 1990). At the same time, language ideologies are not true or false (Gal and Irvine 2019), and remain 'mutually constitutive' (Woolard 1998: 10) with social relations.

Noticing that in any time and place, they are multiple, ever-changing, 'partial, interest-laden, contestable and contested' (Woolard 1998: 10), and having engaged with Gramsci's (1971) writings on hegemony, I knew that the multiplicity did not mean, however, that all ideologies were equivalent or similarly accessible. Reading about dominant, residual and emergent (Williams 1977) aspects of sociocultural practices and images, I was perfectly aware of the fact that some ideologies have wider impact. While at Oxford, I found myself going back again and again to Stuart Hall's writings on ideology, which continued to stress the fact that particular groups may have total social authority by imposing ruling ideas on subordinate groups and 'winning and shaping consent so that [their] power . . . appears both legitimate and natural' (Hall 1977). As a result, others operate within an ideological space which 'appears to lie outside history, to be beyond particular interests' (Hall 1975).

To understand how such dominant images of normality were perpetuated and spread, I also went back to the literature in which it had been argued that it is through semiotic processes and repeated practices in which particular combinations of signs are used that they may become tropic and lead to the partitioning of social space (Silverstein 2003). Rereading Irvine and Gal (2000), I knew that this may be achieved through such semiotic processes as iconization, fractal recursivity and erasure. Irvine and Gal argued that iconization is 'a transformation of the sign relationship between linguistic features (or varieties) and the social images with which they are linked' (37). In this process, linguistic forms operate as images of social groups displaying their nature/essence as speakers make connections on the basis of shared qualities of linguistic signs and social images. For example, in Irvine's analysis of the Wolof greeting in Senegal, we see that different caste members are linguistically differentiated through the process of iconization, where the contrast between laconic and austere with impulsive and elaborated speaking styles associated with opposing social groups is seen as derivative of speakers' temperament. Through fractal recursivity, these oppositions, 'salient at some level of the relationship', are projected 'onto some other level. For example, intragroup oppositions might be projected outward onto intergroup relations, or vice versa' (Irvine and Gal 2000: 38). Fractal recursivity enables a link between 'subtle forms of distinctiveness with broader contrasts and oppositions' (Irvine 2001: 33) and reproduces meaningful distinctions within partitions creating subcategories. In Irvine's discussion of Wolof griot and noble speaking styles, these are not only the two extreme castes that use the speaking styles, but everybody in society draws upon them reproducing subtler distinctions in rank. Finally, as Irvine and Gal noted, through erasure, some speakers and their linguistic practices are made invisible as speakers pay attention to certain aspects of distinction, and ignore others.

To understand how to think with my situated audio-recorded data, like everyday life, full of imperfections and complexities, I came to a conclusion that the standard register must be seen as the strongest demarcation of a uniform public culture and domination (Silverstein 2016). While coming to this conclusion, I was also discussing sociolinguistic studies incorporating insights from Queer Theory (Butler 1990, 1993) with my cohort at Oxford, which made me aware of their research focus on the ways in which particular actions link linguistic forms to groups through ideologies of gender. As a result, I was convinced that I needed to move away from discourse and materiality dichotomy, and additive models of structural location. By looking at the ways in which my participants were making use of available semiotic resources in situated encounters, I decided to examine what a focus on material enactments might add to discussions on the ways in which categories are assembled in transnational timespace and how different forms of categorization compound to produce qualitative differences in experiences of discrimination and privilege.

To grasp how my interlocutors were situationally positioning themselves towards particular images and to understand the role of sonic recontexualization for emerging social relations, I quickly realized that I needed to further consider processes by which such signs are produced and imbued with emergent meaning. Here I found inspiration in Judith Irvine's work on speaking styles among Wolof speakers in Senegal. In line with other projects mentioned above, Irvine argued that ways of speaking were always positioned and not universal, but culturally specific. While doing so, she also recognized the importance of stylistic aesthetics, defined as both distinctiveness and consistency of linguistic forms, proposing that it centred upon 'locally relevant principles of value', which 'motivate the consistency of stylistic forms' (Irvine 2001: 23). I also followed her assertion that ways of speaking were characterized by the Bourdieu-influenced concept of distinctiveness. I remembered that for Bourdieu, 'social space' constituted space of relationships 'constructed on the basis of principles of differentiation' (Bourdieu 1985: 196). In his analysis of French lifestyles and tastes, the pursuit of distinction, expressed in different styles, resulted in separations that were perceived and recognized by other members as legitimate differences. I therefore had to study the ways of speaking that I was encountering as part of a sociocultural framework and in relation to other 'contrasts, boundaries and commonalities' between them (Irvine 2001: 22).

To do so, like Irvine, I found myself going back to early British cultural studies. I was drawn to Hebdige (1979), which describes how different semiotic codes such as dress, posture or music choices were forming different working-class youth subcultures: Mods, Teddy Boys, punks, Rastas and so on in the UK in the 1970s. Hebdige's assertion that style often constitutes 'the area in which the opposing definitions clash with most dramatic force' (1979: 3) resonated with me and my observations. I could also see this clearly in his comparison of the semiotic practices of teds and punks. To remind the reader unfamiliar with British youth subcultures, for teds, the style is 'static, expressive, and concentrates attention on the objects-in-themselves' (Hebdige 1979: 124), leading to their combination of aristocratic Edwardian style with Black rhythm and blues. In contrast, for punks, it is 'kinetic, transitive and concentrates attention on the act of transformation performed upon the object' (Hebdige 1979: 124), which results in their 'confrontation dressing' and music choices and dances undermining established conventions. In his analysis of the ways in which selected objects, codes and practices became meaningful and organized to express resistance to existing social norms based on particular social experience and position, Hebdige argued that the objects were homologous (Gramsci 1971) with the group's main concerns, practices, relations, experience and collective image, all of which were linked to its values. Building on his arguments, Irvine further argued that speaking styles cannot be 'assumed a priori to be an utterly different matter from style in other realms of life' (21). To be meaningful, they must rather be interpreted by a group of people 'whose actions are informed by it' (Irvine 2001: 22).

In order to fully understand the type of data that I was examining and its mode of participation in a relational, material and sensual world, as mentioned at the beginning of the book, I couldn't help but see that I was dealing with fragments, which were giving me access only to situated performances. I was mindful of the studies that were continually reminding me of the role of the social situation, showing that single features of pronunciation may be used in different combinations to achieve distinct effects. Together with my cohort, we were, for example, discussing Podesva's (2007) work on aspirated intervocalic /t/, a feature associated with various enregistered styles used among groups ranging from 'geek girls' (Bucholtz 1996) to 'gay men' in the United States. In his study, Podesva traced the use of this feature in the speech of a self-identified gay speaker, Heath, and conducted a fine-grained analysis of his linguistic performances in multiple situations in the San Francisco Bay area. He showed that the participant used the variable more frequently when he was enacting 'a competent and educated persona' in the clinic where he was working as a doctor. However, he also showed that in another situation, at the barbecue with friends, Heath's bursts of aspiration were longer, which invoked 'fussy hyperarticulateness/prissiness'. This in turn, in this context, enabled him to enact the gay diva persona.

I knew that the situatedness of talk was also tightly linked to the researcher's choice of data collection methods, a point that was very clear in Sharma's work on a register that is often referred to as 'British Asian English' in the UK. In her analysis of young and old individuals' use of features associated with the register such as retroflexion of /t/, the FACE vowel, the GOAT vowel and coda /l/, Sharma's (2011) work first drew my attention because she reported gendered differences between younger British Asians in Southall, London. When she compared the speech from the sociolinguistic interview of younger women with younger men, she noted that women made more use of Standard British English pronunciation patterns, with a dramatic decline in their use of retroflexion. Sharma argued that this had to do with their membership in multiple communities and network-linked practices as in contrast to younger men, younger women tended to shift away from traditional Punjabi roles to more Western ideals of femininity. When investigating their use of the variables further through self-recordings, she established, however, that rather than avoiding Punjabi features altogether, younger women compartmentalized their speech and made use of retroflexion at home.

Her further work with Rampton provided more fine-grained detail about the linguistic practices observed in Southall, clearly showing the situatedness of talk not only in relation to space but also time. Using the lectal focusing index, a 'proportional measure of fluctuation in style over the course of a segment of interaction' (Sharma and Rampton 2015: 12), Sharma and Rampton analysed thirteen phonological variables typical of such enregistered styles as Standard British English, 'Vernacular British English', and 'Indian English' in relation to generational differences among Punjabi men. They observed that older men regularly deployed 'Asian' variants, which was indexical of their ethnopolitical valuation and served as acts of identity, whereas younger men seemed to 'exploit such orientations less, possibly operating at a lower level of awareness, as part of a 'fused lect' (Sharma and Rampton 2015: 25). According to Sharma and Rampton, the discrepancy in the strategic use of the variants could be explained in the context of the changing sociopolitical experience of the Punjabi community over the last sixty years: from being a minority Asian community, where now older men were exposed to 'Indian Asianness' through close ties with India facing hostile attitudes in Britain, to being a majority Asian community within Southall, where the young men had been brought up with weaker ties to India and a more positive ethnic experience enabled by state multiculturalism in the UK. The authors concluded that the differences in the way phonological variables were employed by the two groups could be seen as a shift to a more 'fused new' ethnicity.

Thanks to studies focusing on the moment-to-moment unfolding of discourse, I also knew that subject positions are inhabited, contested and transformed by those who have access to the shared sign forms in the very communicative encounter through stance-taking (DuBois 2007). Following projects examining both linguistic structure and Foucault-influenced discursive systems of knowledge (Bucholtz and Hall 2016), I was aware of the different ways in which bodies get to be labelled, assessed and regulated by others through discursive practices. Here I kept thinking about the very first class I took in linguistic anthropology, when Jane Hill talked about her work on Mock Spanish and language and race in the United States and Mexico. I remembered her pointing to the ways in which a single moment in interaction can index multiple meanings, where White American English speakers created images of cosmopolitan selves, relying on images of lazy Latinx others (Hill 2008).

I found Bucholtz and Hall (2005) and others' proposals to pay attention to the ways in which speakers orient themselves to the talk itself convincing. To do so, I drew on Dubois's (2007) concept of stance-acts as dialogically accomplished public tri-acts (163) 'of simultaneously evaluating objects, positioning subjects (self and other) and aligning with other subjects with respect to any salient dimension of the sociocultural field'. After Rosa and Flores (2017), I also noticed that such a focus on the mechanics of interaction helps reveal how 'authentic signs of racialized models of personhood' get to be linked to 'objectively distinctive or non-distinctive' (Rosa and Flores 2017) registers, and how research production is embedded in the dynamics of racialized linguistic perception. Thanks to these projects, I knew that in situated communicative events, processes of authentication are not always perfectly delimitated, but rather depend on particular historicities of interpretation and scale of space–time relations in which some events are understood as meaningful. The weaving of combinations of chronotopes may thereby lead to discursive connections that although presumed to be located in different timespace frames, are locally valid and legitimate. For example, in her work on Asian Americans in the United States, Chun (2001) demonstrated that despite being often imagined as a 'model minority approximating whiteness' (Rosa and Flores 2017) through raciolinguistic ideology of lacking a racialized English register, her participants situationally positioned themselves against ideals of the privileged American whiteness by drawing on selected lexical and syntactic features of African American English.

This enabled me to see that it is through a series of stances that sociocultural value is (re)produced or reconfigured, and clusters of semiotic resources operating at multiple levels are deployed. Kroskrity (2021) further argues that 'subjective milieus of individual people are the locus of potentially destabilising desires that have the potential to maintain and disrupt the norms' (132). To me, this was visible in Kiesling's (1998) study of men in an American fraternity, where their speech was examined in three different situations: when socializing, engaged in interviews with the researcher and during weekly meetings. His quantitative analysis of individual rates of (ing) showed that the men used [ɪn] the most in socializing encounters, and the least in weekly meetings, despite the fact that they were talking to the same people during both. Kiesling explains these differences together with other individual differences in relation to stances that the men were taking in these encounters. Being aligned with particular images of masculinity, the high rates of [ɪn] enabled the men to use them to take 'hard-working' stances, stances of solidarity with those around as well as those of resistance to the fraternity's hierarchies (Kiesling 2019). In contrast, when giving opinions 'based on their seniority' or rank, those who used the variable the least expressed authority in line with official fraternity structure. Kiesling's project didn't allow me to ignore the fact that semiotic configurations are continually created, de-constructed and reclaimed (Kroskrity 2021) through people's actions and desires that have communal effects.

I was fully aware that these actions and desires can lead to the maintenance of established norms, but they may also disrupt these norms and structures that uphold them if more durable effects are sustained. I knew that this observation had been shown to have important effects for the conduit of social meaning in the context of globalization and migrations. Over the years, I have engaged in various discussions about the creation of multicultural forms of solidarity and identification with my students in London and became perfectly aware of the register that is often labelled as Multicultural London English. The structural tradition, which historically focused on non-dominant 'immigrant' ways of speaking 'host languages' of Western societies (e.g. Cheshire et al. 2011), brought into the spotlight the fact that the studied multi-ethnic registers often rely on linguistic configurations that cannot be directly traced to one 'source language'. Rather, due to contact between migrating groups speaking various codes, new registers that people of various backgrounds may draw on have been emerging in parts of various cities with a history of migration. In London, MLE is usually traced back to the 1980s and argued to be based on East London Cockney, but highly influenced by postcolonial migrations which brought among others Jamaican Creole, Punjabi, Bengali, Tamil, Yoruba, Akan, Turkish and Arabic to the inner city. In their work with recorded semi-spontaneous conversations of adolescent speakers of MLE (in total over 120 hours) in interactions with one another in the presence of the researcher in two boroughs with different ethnic composition, Hackney and Havering, between 2004 and 2007, Cheshire et al. (2011) argued that those who repeatedly used features associated with MLE identified predominantly as Londoners. Cheshire further claimed that MLE, which most users referred to as 'slang', was usually associated with a '"cool" tough figure from a multi-ethnic urban neighbourhood' (2020: 322), self-differentiating from traditional White Cockneys or RP-speaking upper and middle classes as well as non-Londoners. With time, MLE found its way to mass media, for example, through films set in inner-city boroughs, social media or grime music. It was later picked up by others in multi-ethnic parts of various British cities (e.g. Drummond 2018) and today, as Sharifi (2021) shows may be creatively used to go beyond traditional colonial discourses of racial difference thanks to its speakers' positive orientation towards the shared experience, neighbourhood, practices, music and multicultural bonds.

Rather than being 'transmitted without passing through language' (Bourdieu 1994), as such projects suggest, I had to recognize that the linguistic habitus is formed through discursive interactions (Agha 2007) as individuals and groups often continue to contest over-deterministic models of dominant language varieties through their everyday communicative practices. Such 'an agentive process of habituation' (Mahmood 2005), as Agha (2003) notes, 'is mediated largely by metalinguistic processes' and implicit activities, which often involve racially hegemonic modes of perception of others. For example, the social images of MLE among non-MLE speakers (Kircher and Fox 2019) have been observed to include references to 'sounding black', lack of education or aggression, potentially bringing a threat to the purity of the standard. Such strong language ideologies of others, with limited exposure and experience, drew my attention to the constant gaze of listening subjects and their continual attempts to '(de)authenticate' the organically emerging processes of subject formation.

With this knowledge, I felt that I was gradually finding a way to avoid 'the danger of a single story' (Adiche 2009). In my view, most of the projects described in this section, similarly to various studies on world Englishes, enabled scholars to successfully reclaim what such dominant language labels as English may mean. Far from being uniform, they rather stressed that English-sounding performances are always situated, embodied, embedded, enactive and extended as well as emotional and open-ended. I noticed that it is only through institutionalized historical processes that hierarchies of ethno-racial and linguistic authenticity and legitimacy emerge (Rosa and Flores 2017) and shift our focus away from the processes through which categories are intersectionally assembled and communicatively enacted.

However, while the studies above made me aware of the multiplicity of soundings and codings, operating within limitations of research projects and practices, in the context of migration, they did not often provide me with the full picture. First, as mentioned before, I couldn't ignore the fact that recently migrating individuals had been traditionally excluded from most variationist projects in the structural tradition. Second, focusing on dominant performances of migrating groups in Western societies, I couldn't help but see that some projects described in this section may make us also momentarily forget about non-dominant resources that may be accessed at any moment in the everyday life of multilingual participants (Garcia et al. 2021).

Here I kept thinking about Harris's (2006) close examination of self-representations of linguistic practices among thirty South Asian teenagers in Blackhill, London. Harris observed that the Blackhill youth creatively combined local London features with their Asian linguistic resources to present themselves as Brasians. By analysing selected phonetic and grammatical features of their speech – for example *T-glottaling, I done it, innit*, and the speakers' use of family languages and ways they were woven into distinct configurations – he demonstrated that local London features dominated in the teenagers' speech, simultaneously making their new ethnicities 'unambiguously dominated by Britishness' (Harris 2006: 92). However, diasporic ties to traditions from the Indian subcontinent enabled the speakers to inflect this Britishness in a new way and pointed to 'a particular encounter with the world being experienced in a contingent social context' (Harris 2006: 77), where the present coexisted with the historical and the global inflected the local on a daily basis.

As a result, in the context of migration, as I realized early in my fieldwork, the erasure of multilingual dynamics ran a potential risk of producing the 'subaltern who was only able to engage linguistically in the present through the words of the metropolitan language' (Stroud 2018: 17). To better connect language struggles to wider dynamics of power and turn towards transforming existing structures (Rosa and Flores 2017), I had to therefore move towards research that put those using multiple linguistic resources at the centre and rather than partially, although most often not intentionally, silencing those on the move, engages with borderland thinking to further challenge the monolingual mindset of modernity.

Recognizing multiplicities of times and spaces: Multilingual discourse and scale-making

As personally, I have always been drawn to less obvious stories and debates on radical difference in literature, film or art, and as my own family history spanned transnational space, I knew that migrating populations often operated on the margins of dominant structures of the modern nation-state. This positioning required a consideration for complex practices of navigating between multiple liminal spaces 'created by multiple kinds of borders' (Collins 2019). As has been often shown, the actual social relations in such contexts only highlight hybridity and unpredictable fusion as never-ending and always present. While engaging in intersectional and decolonial debates, I became aware of Gloria Anzaldua's writing (2012 [1987]) about the borderlands between Mexico and the United States, in which she stressed the contingency of social arrangements and constant mixing of languages, cultural norms and writing genres. Closely reflecting on her own experiences of life as a daughter of farmworkers in a deprived area of south Texas, she drew my attention to the contradictions of her experiences, where both Mexico and the United States were seen as home, neither of which allowed for full acceptance. The constant encounter with the two systems of oppression only stressed the fluidity of categories and simultaneity of multiple social perspectives with the importance of maintaining a centre that called for social justice and fight against material forms of oppression. Her work reminded me that sociolinguistic enactments at such intersections are only partially structured and remain in dynamic movement. It made me fully aware of the fact that rather than only enacting static 'non-dominant' binary positions, individuals living at intersections of systems of exclusion may use the contradictions to their own advantage, developing a complex concept of social self with new consciousness. This new mestiza continued to be enacted through *multiple* linguistic resources: English, Castilian Spanish, North Mexican varieties, Tex-Mex, Nahuatl and their constant *mixing*. I noticed that it was in the very mixing that the mestiza was formed and synergy of cultures and values achieved, where the new becoming was possible.

Anzaldua's observations were echoed in works produced by multilingual activists and decolonial researchers from around the world that I was reading. For example, when discussing the 'new emergence' of one of the indigenous peoples of Canada, Nishnaabeg, Leanne Betasamosoke Simpson (2011) talked about the constant contestation of colonialism and neocolonialism in the individual and collective process of 'learning through language' among the Nishnaabeg people. To explore the resurgence of the indigenous thought with its 'non-hierarchical, non-authoritarian and non-coercive values', and to recreate 'the cultural and political flourishing of the past' (51) in the present rather than simply returning to pre-colonial norms, Betasamosoke Simpson called for acknowledgement of fluidity and 'diversity of political and cultural viewpoints within the Nishnaabeg worldview' (53) in conjunction with a deep understanding of the culture, language, philosophies and so on. Similarly, Stroud (2018) and Williams and Stroud (2015), working in the context of post-apartheid South Africa, foregrounded the importance of the diversity of voice, where a new sense of self and citizenship together with a transformed sense of the past self emerged as 'new actors' engaged in 'unsettling encounters'. They showed how through transformation of meanings and repurposing Afrikaans discourse genres, stand-up comedy performers creatively engaged in Afrikaans performances and sought recognition in the public space 'to determine a new course of events' (Stroud 2018: 21).

I thus knew that my participants would be constantly moving and transforming the relevant social images as they would draw on multiple voices and forms in every utterance (Bakhtin 1981). At the same time, I noticed that models built on monolingual assumptions did not enable me to understand the polycentricity of multilingual practices. In order to locate the production of social memory and knowledges in performance (Connerton 1989), I needed to better understand how multilingual speakers reconfigure what language means through their continuing engagement with various configurations of dominant and non-dominant resources and how this may impact the complex processes of their subject formation that become enregistered under particular historical, political and economic circumstances.

Having gathered a lot of observations from around the world, I knew that not surprisingly, entangled in specific webs of connections and multiplicity of historical relations, reported actual practices differed across multilingual populations. For example, imagined as distinct and shaping different identities (Kroskrity 1998), three varieties used in Arizona's Tewa community, Tewa, Hopi and 'American', were observed to be kept separate. In contrast, in New York City, multilingual practices among members of the Puerto Rican community (Zentella 1997) were valued and celebrated as an expression of hybrid positioning. Looking at Zhu Hua's (2008) work on family conflict talk, I further noted generational differences among members of the same community – the UK Chinese community – and lack of one-to-one associations between linguistic forms and cultural values.

Drawing on Tsing's (2015) ecological theory and based on his own long-term ethnographic research with multilingual Mono and Tewa communities in the United States, Kroskrity (2018) proposed that actual multilingual practices may only be understood in relation to 'larger complex[es] of relevant beliefs and feelings, both Indigenous and externally imposed that may complement, contest or otherwise dynamically interact with each other to modify language ideologies and linguistic practices' (134). Rather than only limiting himself to observation of semiotic configurations, he foregrounded the need to talk about language ideological assemblages as processes through which potential histories are made (Tsing 2015), political economic forces work and wider connections between practices and structures are forged. Drawing on assemblage as used in art, I would add that it is formed through acts of creating meaning through devices *found* and *scavenged* by the artist/speaker, and mediated 'through implicate order [. . .] and [. . .] complex chain of reactions [that] is necessarily non-linear' (Betasamosake Simpson 2011: 91). It is through the *way* in which various semiotic–material resources are assembled that the relationship with the forces is developed and rebalance achieved.

To understand 'subjective milieus of individual people' in multilingual contexts I had to carefully consider the dynamics of situated multilingual speech and how socially meaningful ways of communicating are created. Agha (2009) noted that in the everyday life multilingual speakers negotiate 'register models for type-hybridized practices with the persons with whom they engage through such practices' (10). In situated speech, they draw on multiple cultural frameworks, where a specific linguistic behaviour may be perceived as appropriate according to one categorial dimension within 'several dimensions of categorial structure' as linguistic expressions form category clusters (Agha 2009: 6). Multilinguals' linguistic practices are therefore tightly connected to interactional frameworks that map their social roles and relations. During interactional events, such speakers transpose linguistic items across contexts of use, which often results in reanalysis and transformation into new models of conduct (Agha 2009). Garcia et al. (2021) further propose that multilingual speakers engage in translanguaging practices that do not rely on separate systems that correspond neatly to language labels, but rather possess a unitary system built 'through social interactions of different types' (Garcia et al. 2021). They do so even when they are 'in the monolingual mode' (Zhu Hua and Li Wei 2021) as they negotiate between opportunity and necessity (Zhu Hua and Li Wei 2019) in everyday life.

I hence assumed that the formation of the multilingual subject is tightly linked to the relation of the self to others, time and space. At the same time, as in studies focusing on dominant monolingual performances, the politics of accessibility and availability still enable and restrict multilingual capabilities and make particular ways of seeing, acting, feeling and sounding in the world more acceptable than others. To understand multiplicities of multilingual repertoires (Kroskrity 2018) and their situated enactments, I noticed that scholars have found relief in the Bakhtinian (1981) concept of *chronotope*, timespace, which enables us to study interactant's orientations to relevant depictions of time-space–personhood through a close examination of dialogically configured and diagrammed text patterns. Working with literary genres, as suggested before, Bakhtin argued that time and space are always interconnected, and a close examination of different chronotopic representations enables us to analyse plot and character development in which particular actions are meaningful and recognizable (Agha 2007a, Woolard 2013). Such an inseparability of time and space from human action also draws attention to the lack of uniformity of timespace configurations in relation to human agency and consciousness. This in turn also helps us understand processes through which particular temporal and spatial realities become hegemonic in particular multilingual contexts.

While getting to know my data, I noticed that chronotopic analysis could be productively used to study both the performances of embodied memory and their connections to power-laden processes of expert knowledge production. Many have argued that dominant narratives of modernity rely on chronotopes built around a linear conceptualization of social progress and 'an irreducible break between the past and present' (Das 2016) excluding other timespace configurations often found in migrant and diasporic narratives (e.g. Eisenlohr 2007; Lempert and Perrino 2007; Woolard 2013). For example, Eisenlohr (2007) noted that in contrast to linear depictions of 'historical time' typical of narratives of modernity, in Mauritius, diasporic reality centred upon 'messianic time' that enabled a link between dominant Mauritian society and an immanent quality of 'heroic and virtuous ancestors' (242).

By focusing on the ways in which migrants decode their sociolinguistic worlds and invoke particular, often contested historicities of origin and change (Woolard 2013), I noticed that projects relying on chronotopic analysis also highlight what chunks of history become relevant to whom in the new locale (Blommaert 2007b, 2015) and how this is linked to the logic of capitalism, patriarchy and the nation-state. I established that recent studies focused on semiotic processes through which migrants locate themselves in relation to circulating images of personhood, time and space (Agha 2007b), how they selectively engage with conventionalized norms and typifications (Gal and Irvine 2019), and how their choices change the 'value of communicative resources in accordance with users' shifts in social and geographical mobility' (Das 2016). For example, Gal and Irvine (2019) described how a migrant woman from Dakar, Senegal, living in Michigan, United States, moved away from the traditional noble/griot register contrasts when evaluating Wolof practices. Looking for a place in the new 'world of social ranking and history' (Gal and Irvine 2019: 230), the woman turned to 'old-time rurality and purity contrasts with urban "tainted" French-infused modernity' (229). With the change in location, similarly to other migrating individuals, the participant's point of view also changed and as Gal and Irvine argue, her units of comparison were no longer the same. Rather the change in locale prompted the change in salience of contrasting qualities and reanalysis that led to a new reassemblage of relevant contrasts, where the salience of gradient variation in Wolof was evaluated not only in contrast to the Wolof-speaking population, but also in relation to noticeable differences between the speaker and other ethnic groups in the United States.

Additionally, in her work with Catalan-Castilian bilinguals in Barcelona, Woolard (2013) noted that social contexts in which people with similar social location or experiences operate may be construed via different chronotopic frames that enable different visions for the self's development and action. Comparing interviews conducted among the same working-class Castilian-speaking participants in the Barcelona area at two intervals in time, 1987 and 2007, she reported that those who spoke little Catalan at school made use of

Catalan at later stages of life with most positively orienting themselves to the variety. Woolard argued that to describe their sociolinguistic transformation, the participants relied on three distinct chronotopic frames: biographical chronotope, sociohistorical chronotope and 'adventure time in everyday life' chronotope. She noted that the different chronotopes enabled the construal of 'sociological and politicized versus psychological and apolitical readings of personal experience'. For example, when the only speaker who expressed an anti-Catalan stance discussed his sociolinguistic practices, he explained them in the context of sociopolitical changes in the Catalan nation and the Spanish state, portraying himself as unchanging. In contrast, another participant mobilized a rhetoric of personal transformation where the evaluation of Catalan and Castilian was not linked to linguistic authenticity and the unchanging self, but rather to anonymity and a personalistic stance taken also in the context of salience of global English, which erased the relevance of Castilian-Catalan contrasts due to the superiority of Northern European modernity over 'Southern archaism'.

To me, these projects successfully challenged circulating modernist assumptions that 'people will always self-identify with the languages they know best or in which they have acquired dominance over their life trajectories' (Das 2016). They rather showed that discourse always operates in relation to identifiable available contextual normative universes and cannot be understood without their thorough understanding. Rather than just moving between geographical spaces, transnational bodies operate within multilayered ordered indexicalities which systematically give preference to some forms of semiosis and exclude others and these are chronotopes that 'invoke orders of indexicality valid in a specific timespace frame' (Blommaert and de Fina 2016). Studies of multilingual migrant and diasporic discourse hence help us further understand 'the new mobilities paradigm's' insistence on examining how the world is constantly moving, but remains entangled in politics of exclusion and contributes to 'experiences of immobility' (e.g. Sheller 2018). For example, in her work with various migrating groups, ranging from refugees from Syria to resettlers from Eastern Europe living and working in Berlin, Schulte (2021) shows that spatiotemporal similarities and differences between migrating groups and those assumed by the modern nation-state may have significant effects on newcomers' life opportunities and contribute to their delay in socio-economic mobility. She argues that differences in timespace relationships may impede the migrants' and refugees' access to employment and higher education opportunities within the German state.

I concluded that the chronotopic analysis enabled 'a more nuanced understanding of how social actors perceive, construct, organize, and evaluate normative behaviour' (Karimzad 2020) in multilingual contexts. These projects also repeatedly emphasized that emerging semiotic representations that linked time and space to social types in transnational timespace were shaped in indeterminate and dynamic ways. For example, in his work with Iranian-Azerbaijani migrants in the United States, employing discourse analytic and ethnographic methods, Karimzad showed that his participants became more conscious of 'the mismatch between the immediate chronotopic contexts and migrants' brought-along images of them' (Karimzad 2020), especially in earlier stages of migration. This led to complex linguistic practices as in the case of a participant who asserted that she could neither use English when talking to fellow members of the Iranian diaspora, nor found it 'right' to address others in English in the presence of Iranians. Karmizad argues that with increased frequency of encounters with the new social contexts, and through moments in which contrasts became recognized, metapragmatic re-evaluation may lead to the relative resolution of 'semiotic uncertainty' and reconstruction of normative images.

I noticed that to fully understand the dynamic ways in which timespace frames are linked to social types, I had to consider various scalar distinctions that define their scopes of communicability and creativity (Agha 2007a; Blommaert 2019). I noticed that it had been argued that scales link scopes of understandability to the value of discourse showing that different semiotic resources are always simultaneously deployed, but they are not equivalent and form different orders subject to the politics of inclusion and exclusion. In his study, Karimzad (2020) further showed that as discourse unfolded, his participants shifted their scales, and construed images via alternative chronotopic frames. Norms are hence themselves scaled phenomena which develop intersubjectively in interaction and are discursively organized through orientations to perceived appropriateness criteria and complexes of evaluating authority (Blommaert 2007a). Scales are made as relevant chunks of history, chronotopes, are taken up by a particular range of audiences for whom they are meaningful (Gal and Irvine 2019), which enable connections between discursive spaces. I realized that the scope of communicability hence depends on those who take particular communicative behaviour up, the ways in which they engage with it and whether the practice is institutionalized.

Carr and Lempert (2016) argued that it was precisely a close examination of the pragmatics of scale that enabled us to critically distance ourselves from scalar distinctions whether in monolingual or multilingual contexts, 'whether our own or others and focus instead on the social circumstances, dynamics and consequences of scale-making as social practice and project' (9). By closely examining how people imagine and order things, events or encounters, we may better understand the tensions between what is assumed or expected and what happens on the ground. A critical examination of the ways in which scales are made through particular sign behaviour and what scales reach across and connect domains of users further illuminates the ways in which social contexts are discursively construed, recognized and maintained. At the same time, a juxtaposition of models with differing claims also highlights that the view from nowhere in fact does not exist and that these are 'communicative, and specifically linguistic, practices [that] are the means by which models are put to work organizationally, institutionally, and interactionally in [multidimensional] projects of scale-making' (Gal 2016: 254). The ways in which scaling reaches and shapes relations between people, however, also involve bodies, technologies and other non-human entities that afford the semiosis and 'impose limits on those who try to scale them' (Carr and Lempert 2016). To fully grasp how perspectives orient speakers when they employ various '*senses* of scale' [emphasis added], I therefore need to focus on their materialization and embodiment.

Focusing on sensorial modes and their materiality: Opening the debate to transformations of concepts and realities

To analyse the production of perspectives on norms and practices in my situated encounters, I chose to focus on my participants' scaling made through the chaining of relevant semiotic signs. I wanted to understand what points of fixing were being formed and what were their relationships to other points. I wanted to study how my participants were assembling self and collective images through their very interactional moves and bodily engagements during their encounters with me. While doing so, I found inspiration in my own everyday life in transnational space, replete with encounters with various types of illness among my loved ones and frequent visits to hospitals. As I realized with time, in my case, these experiences put the spotlight onto the body and physicality of discourse production. Over the years, my interest in embodied aspects of discourse production was only reinforced through work with multimodal analysis, where I examined how different semiotic potentialities were connected to the body and the senses.

Given the discussion in previous sections, I was aware that the refocusing of sociolinguistic and linguistic anthropological discussions onto social units defined by engagement, such as communities of practice (Eckert 2012), enabled scholars to shift attention to the ways in which indexical signs were linked to the bodily hexis. These projects fleshed out how through engagement in various joint endeavours such as making a family, being a member of a film club or working in a particular profession, individuals developed shared communicative repertoires and formed dynamic social formations. I also knew that studies focusing on participation framework (e.g. Duranti 1997; Hanks 1996) highlighted participants' alignments and their characterization as a way to better understand how participants' interactional moves and sequential organization of communicative encounters enable category formation. I was aware that these projects expanded the focus of analysis beyond speech and fleshed out how individual metalinguistic consciousness is best understood as a result of sociohistorically formed orientations rather than psychological states (Hanks 1996).

At the same time, I found myself going back to Jacquemet's work in which he argued that the overemphasis of these projects on elective networks, shared knowledge and goal-oriented engagement, and their heavy reliance on prioritizing face-to-face interactions, did not allow us to fully understand power dynamics of the globalized, digitally mediated world. Jacquemet (2019) talked about the digital revolution, which had a profound impact on the possibilities of action of my participants and which since only the late twentieth century, enabled the mobility of the linguistic sign at an unprecedented scale. I found relief in his work as he did not ignore the fact that the development of global diasporic networks with multiple linguistic ties and the 'offline-online nexus' had revolutionized access to linguistic resources and made 'deterritorialization of both communicative practices and social formations' (Jacquemet 2019) an integral part of everyday life. Jacquemet proposed that this has led to the 'emergence of media idioms that presuppose translocal modes of production and reception' and give access to relevant procedural knowledge and 'historically and culturally distant communicative environments' (48). He also claimed that the new communicative environment remained heavily indexically structured, but interactions were 'performable across multiple media' without clear-cut boundaries. They were also recognized by particular populations. Noticing that the new communicative environment relied on 'emerging networks' and 'heteroglossia of juggling voices and partial identities', he posited that it was crucial to understand how people 'move in and out' of the emerging social formations and what a 'recombinant potential' in such an environment may be.

I knew that those studying specific ways of binding discourse or texts available for circulation in mediatized society had shown that these were highly dependent on the medium used (Bauman 2004). They also demonstrated that the processes of recontextualization of original discourse and the ways in which it moved across time and space were affected by the practices in which producers engage to recontextualize it, as well as by its very materiality. The materiality of the medium, that is its physical 'stuff', had also been shown to impact the dynamics of multimodal communication (Kress 2010) with the different modes of communication, such as gesture, sound, still and moving images, writing and colour, organizing representation and communication in line with their specific resources and affordances. These modes were thus 'shaped by both the intrinsic characteristics and potentialities of the medium and by the requirements, histories and values of societies and their cultures' (Kress and van Leeuwen 1996: 34). I was aware that any type of discourse analysis entailed a thorough knowledge of dominant modes in particular cultures and contexts. This was visible for example in Irvine's (2016) fieldwork in Senegal, where for some, oral tradition and memory contributed more to the long-term maintenance of local discourse than writing practices. Sharing the experience of living in transnational space with my participants, I quickly noticed that spoken discourse and informal digitally mediated written communication constituted dominant modes among Polish speakers living and working in white-collar jobs in the UK.

At the time of writing, I have already engaged in advanced discussions on the explorations in affordances of various modes in diasporic contexts thanks to my postdoctoral work in London. This made me perfectly aware of the fact that these affordances impact the formation of relations and knowledges in migrant contexts. For example, Sahra Abdhullahi and Li Wei (2021) demonstrated that in situations of intergenerational language and cultural shift, embodied communication and language brokering enabled mutual understanding despite language barriers. Examining audiovisually recorded instances of everyday home interactions observed among different generations within families with ties to Somalia, but living and working in the UK, they showed how the families created meaning when completing tasks and when involved in storytelling activities. This project stressed that such changes, often 'important for self-actualisation of those younger generations' (Abdhullahi and Li Wei 2021: 162), are negotiated and enacted through various modalities that offer particular possibilities for action. I had to therefore recognize that the study of meaning potentialities of each of the modes, their functions in communities as well as relational multimodal assemblages, enables a better understanding of 'the life in the making' and its multisensory (Li Wei 2018) character.

The attention to the materiality and sociality of the senses in academic debates in recent decades (e.g. Howes 1991; Pink 2006; Porcello et al. 2010) has made me also aware of the profound changes in the multisensory dimension of social life in the late twentieth and twenty-first centuries and their impact on the culturally constituted nature of the sensorium. I knew that various projects examining people's engagements with objects and technologies such as digital video communication, websites that allow sharing of the moving image, mobile communication, surveillance technology or online games have revealed that actions and reactions in such environments are enabled by the coming together of human and non-human entities. For example, Keating (2005) showed how members of the deaf community in the United States used sign language in computer-mediated spaces, successfully integrating it into their common routines and practices next to developing new ways of engagement. This in turn offered extended possibilities of action and changed their capabilities. I noticed that such changes often pose challenges to the ontological status of agents involved in actions and events (Gershon and Manning 2014), which makes a priori distinctions between human and non-human entities increasingly difficult (Bauman 2004). Following Bucholtz and Hall (2016), I saw the move beyond the materiality-discourse dichotomy as a way to investigate how the changing communicative environment impacts the relationship between the self, others, time and space in the context of multipresence in various sites.

Unlike many in anthropology of the senses (e.g. Howes 1991), I did not find arguments to reject 'language, discourse and semiotics as modes for encountering and understanding the sensuous cultural world' (Porcello et al. 2010: 59) convincing. I did not want to divide sensorial knowledge from linguistic knowledge. On the contrary, I rather followed Porcello et al. (2010) and others who claimed that discourse is part of processes of embodiment and sense-making. Rather than relying on Cartesian duality, treating '[k]nowledge and communicative action [as] moments in a single process' (Gal and Irvine 2019: 89), I saw such an approach as a way to rethink modernities' insistence on dichotomies between the mind and body, and contribute to discussions on sensing as a means of knowing. I finally realized that the focus on the material form in relation to the recursivity of revelation (McDonald and Tidius 2020) could be used to flesh out the practices of domination and reproduction of colonialisms and solidarities. It could thereby generate new knowledge about authentic category reproduction and stratified forms of modernity.

Given my interest in contemporary diasporic contexts as well as consideration for the global impact of the recent Covid-19 pandemic, I thought that with this book, I could start carving a way to reformulate the primacy of face-to-face interactions for sociolinguistic production and at the same time, flesh out its significance for counterbalancing visuality and textuality. I knew that the focus on the surface representations of signs of migration and connections between particular scalar metaphors and rhythms may build on other projects and show how the participation framework may be understood and how sonic connections between speakers are forged in this new communicative environment. I also noticed that the analysis of the material form of discourse could enable me to start thinking about differences in face-to-face situations and 'technosocial situations' (Gershon and Manning 2014), where it could be argued that it is the very sensory experience that is different. Unlike in mediated encounters, be they written or spoken, I noted that the co-presence of face-to-face interactions relies on different materiality, which, as Gershon and Manning (2014), argue may be 'associated with richness and evidential possibilities for mutual monitoring'.

To me, face-to-face communication always involved the 'space of appearance' (Arendt 1998), where meaning was produced and shared, was always there even if my further analysis relied on audio recordings and did not allow the study of interactions between modes to the same degree. I couldn't help but notice, however, that the sensory experience in verbal communicative acts also relied on particular, material events, sounds, only recorded for research purposes, which were later studied through relevant technologies. I knew that the affordances of this particular mode were different from gesture or colour, and operated within a particular culture of reception. They were thus specific kinds of 'expressive form[s]' that 'lend[ed] themselves] to participation' (Rancière 2013: 7) and presented themselves to the sensory experience in particular ways.

These collected transient flows of energies unfolded in time and space and were highly malleable. They were also characterized by physical properties and the ways in which they were interpreted by the human brain. Obviously, they were 'events heard', rather than 'objects seen'. It could be argued that the soundscapes that I recorded were at the same time 'physical environments' and 'ways of perceiving that environment'. They also operated within a changing culture of listening (Thompson 2002), which for many, through the reformulation of the sound-space relationship and technological manipulations from the 1930s onwards, made soundscapes modern too, often 'indistinguishable from the circuits that produced them'. I noticed that in the case of sounds of language, lack of careful attention to the sounded experience may, however, erase its bodily production and response, which are its integral parts.

I knew that many who ignored the sonic experience relied on the assertion that speech is perceived as a fairly unified activity. Given my training, I knew that as it is well known in phonetics, it is at the same time a series of transformations enabled by the human body and physics of speech. Crucially, for spoken discourse in face-to-face encounters, the body remains the centre of sensory experience and perception. I knew that sounds of language rely on the action of the brain as well as that of muscle systems that enable skilled articulatory movements: those used for breathing, in the larynx and head and neck. These in turn generate sound waves of speech and bring acoustic energy onto the eardrum of the listener, which 'the auditory system translates [. . .] into neural impulses which we experience as sound' (Johnson 2003: 3). As it unfolds in time and space, the sound sets the body in motion. At the same time, as suggested before, I knew that voice phenomena such as fluctuations of pitch, phonation type or articulation of phonemes are used and understood in relation to particular sociocultural contexts. They thereby do particular interactional and sociocultural work, which is then linked to broader categories (Bucholtz and Hall 2016).

I decided to use this existing body of knowledge together with institutionalized knowledge about the sounded signs that I was investigating as proxies to get closer to the workings of the bodily engagements with the world and emerging matter-energies. Rather than allowing the understanding of meaning-making to resort to the written word, which often relies on the most invariant forms and which has for many outside language studies been in fact the case (e.g. a reminder in Barad 2003), I wanted to propose that a well-known practice of phoneticians, the close listening to what is and what is not there, may be used to help us better understand the formation of scale-making projects and 'possibilities of occupying the limits of normative structures', guiding us towards 'acoustic social becoming' (LaBelle 2018). I therefore chose to focus on the materiality of discourse, its physical properties together with embedding in sociopolitical economic dynamics, as a way to 'theorize the sound as a way of knowing' (Shankar 2016) and investigate power dynamics as a property of materiality. Carefully examining transient situated sociolinguistic performances in the context of migration, their rhythms, vibrations, resonances and tonalities, together with silences and intensities, and 'their conditions of ambiguity and fluctuation', I ended up following LaBelle's call and proposed to see also sounds of speech as 'support structures for emancipatory practices' that themselves may unsettle and go beyond the logics of visibility. In the next chapters, I explore how extended from the depths of the human body and entangled in the energetics of particular social formations, the materiality of sounded signs of migration used to scale things, events and actions in situated encounters may contribute to advances in politics of 'radical compassion', care and sharing. I want to see what happens if we do not allow for erasure, carefully examine what explorations in soundings and resoundings do in the world and what people's own observations tell us about this particular sensory experience and dynamic perception (Levon and Fox 2014). This in turn may help us bring the body with its physicality back to the studies of meaning-making in the globalized world and demonstrate how people on the move 'adapt their bodies and brains to the languaging activity that surrounds them' (Thibault 2017: 76). It is also hoped that by doing so, we may come closer to finding a way out of 'the cognitive box of imperialism' allowing us to 'bring the old into the new' (Betasamosake Simpson 2011) and acknowledging that 'to become one is always to become with many' (Haraway 2006).

3

Weaving Webs of Material–Semiotic Practices in a Community of Movement

Listening to the echoes of the globalized Polish sociolinguistic landscape

To approach my collected soundings and resoundings as part of emerging transnational expressive cultures and projects with particular dominant sensorial modes, I had to understand 'the surface of "depicted" signs, the split reality of' (Rancière 2013) the community, and the rhythms of its constitutive parts. I saw that the existing body of knowledge about the globalized Polish linguistic landscape could help me map who had historically had a share in its dominant linguistic representation and how it was related to delimitations of time and space. I hoped that by doing so, I could make sense of the politics of sounding and listening in contemporary transnational space, and show that surface representations of signs of migration were not simply linear representations plotted in geographical space. Given my knowledge of other contexts, I knew that they were rather particular delimitations of what was imagined to be common to the community and its organization, which at the same time revealed the logics of repetition, renewal and recognition, and their relation with otherness and the self.

To begin my investigation into formations of specific images in situated Polish-sounding performances of collective memory in transnational space, I had to trace processes through which multiplicities of different realities were woven by my participants (Law 2019). To do so, I knew that I had to start with tracing where the threads came from, what they historically excluded and what automatisms and functions of speech produced particular habits and consequences of their patternings. I wanted to understand why the heterogeneous elements of the social–material world that I was encountering didn't quite fit with the common myth portraying Poland as 'a country with only one distinct culture and one language – Polish' (Bidzińska 2016: 53).[1]

First of all, thanks to works in historical studies of the Polish language, I noticed that this 'one language' had not been uniform across time. According to Bajerowa (2012), the earliest evidence for Polish 'language norms' could be found on monuments in today's Polish territories dating back to the thirteenth century. Since the development of print in the sixteenth century, the norms, both orthographic and grammatical, were being standardized and historical changes were tightly linked to gradual 'social stratification' and population movements (Bajerowa 2012: 24) as well as scientific and technological developments. These historically also included changing communication channels through which the norms spread. Bajerowa distinguished three main stages in language development: *staropolska doba* ('Old Polish stage': the thirteenth to fifteenth century), *średniopolska doba* ('Middle Polish stage': sixteenth to the second half of the eighteenth century) and *nowopolska doba* ('New Polish stage': from the second half of the eighteenth century onwards). She further proposed that historical criteria were key for Polish standardization processes as today's linguistic landscape in Poland could be best explained as a result of 'the history of the nation existing without a state', eighteenth-century partitions of Poland, unsuccessful uprisings, deportations, world wars, the Cold War and communist policies.

I was aware of the historical differences in geographical demarcations of today's Poland and their consequences for linguistic practices. I established that between 1795 and 1918, the Habsburg monarchy, the Kingdom of Prussia and the Russian Empire enforced different conditions for the use of Polish. For example, the Prussian authorities actively fought against the use of Polish in today's western and northern Poland. Polish was also banned in schools by the Russian Empire, but under Austrian rule it was used in schools and institutions except for the postal service and military (Bajerowa 2012). In the pre-twentieth-century period, Polish was characterized by intense language-mixing practices with French, Italian, Czech, Ukrainian and Latin (Bajerowa 2012). Due to political dynamics, the Polish nobility cultivated Polish as a unifying force for the Polish nation, while the need for and later, the emergence of the Polish nation-state were presented as self-evident and natural (Garapich 2016). As a result of continuous efforts to maintain Polish during the partitions, in 1918, when the independent Polish state was established, the so-called *język ogólny* ('standard Polish') was largely associated with the Polish nobility who made up 1 per cent of the population (Bajerowa 2012), and, in the early twentieth century, remained in intense contact with Jewish, German, Lithuanian, Czech, Belarusian, Ukrainian and Russian communities. Due to urbanization and population growth and the emergence of the working class, the wider population gradually started coming into contact with *język ogólny* (Bajerowa 2012). Language norms were mainly propagated through literature and printed texts, mediated by communication technology. Polish was maintained in schools and the church, with a more traditionalist, purist approach to the language in Kraków, and a more progressive one in Warsaw.

In 1918, when the independent Polish state was established, Polish was a fairly stable variety (Bajerowa 2012) in terms of grammar. In the interwar period, efforts were made to systematize its lexicon and orthography. Due to deportations, the Holocaust and war damages including the almost total destruction of Warsaw during the Warsaw Rising, in 1945 the Polish state emerged as a one-nation state where the intense contact with Yiddish, Ukrainian or Belarusian radically stopped. However, as discussed before, internal population movements and resettlements from territories beyond the Polish borders continued to contribute to further population mixing. I noticed that subsequent further urbanization and changing class realities also accelerated the change of the profile of the Polish language user. Polish was no longer a literary, elite language. It became accessible to a wider audience thanks to technological advancements such as radio and TV and the near-eradication of illiteracy (Bajerowa 2012).

I also observed that the mass-mediated form of society, characterized by polycentricity of language norms, made the spoken rather than written language more available to all. At the same time, the centralized government of the People's Republic of Poland and the state-centric character of social life contributed to further homogenization and standardization of the language, with the government propagating cultural norms disassociated from the intellectual elite (Bajerowa 2012). The forced linguistic homogeneity was modelled on the Warsaw variety, while regional variation was actively erased and portrayed as an aberration. I was aware that today, some still imagine *język ogólnopolski/ ogólny* to be used by 'all Poles' in 'all public situations, and institutions', 'taught in primary, secondary and tertiary education' and 'its proper command [to be] a condition to participate in the national culture' (Bajerowa 2012: 23). At the same time, it was often perceived as a variety spoken by most educated individuals and sustained through strong monolingual ideologies that also influenced how linguistic diversity was perceived.

I saw that the forms of domination associated with standardized language have been challenged, however, by the recent changes in Polish society. Kontra et al. (in press) argue that the linguistic landscape in the last fifteen years has been rapidly changing as Polish society has been participating in global and translingual processes. They note that 'speaker attitudes and researchers' orientations have become increasingly open to linguistic diversity and interest in variation' (in press: 15). I became aware of the fact that some discussions about Polish language norms have been taking place in recent years. I was reminded that today dictionaries may include not only norms of 'correct Polish', but also 'permissable' ones, differentiating between *norma wzorcowa* ('ideal norm') and *norma użytkowa* ('everyday norm'). These changing dynamics were, however, most visible in debates surrounding representations of gender and sexuality (e.g. Pakuła 2021), which have entered popular discourse, everyday interactions and media coverage, created space for language activists' efforts and increased awareness of the role of language in shaping social relations (Kiełkiewicz-Janowiak 2019).

To fully grasp how different realities may 'interact, conflict or ignore one another' (Law 2019), I needed to better understand the material stuff that made *gwary* ('local varieties') and various sociolects in Polish territories, which have historically been contrasted with standard Polish by those working within the dialectological tradition. I noted that many linguists distinguished five dialects of Polish and 'new mixed' dialects (Urbańczyk and Kucała 1999), and today the standard remained most invariant in the written form. Minority language varieties remained variously labelled and recognized depending on their size and status. For example, Kashubian was officially recognized, while Silesian was still waiting to be so. At the same time, increasing stylistic variation (Bajerowa 2012) and resistance against 'former speaking habits and [their] official constraints' (Duszak 2002: 217) were reported. Crucially, Bajerowa (2012) argued that these 'non-standard' ways of speaking and communicating could be seen as operating at the peripheries of the standard as 'their grammatical aspects' resembled standard Polish, but the lexicon differed significantly making them comprehensible only to those who use them.

As a speaker of Polish, I was also aware that it remained replete with 'foreign elements' (Walczak 2012: 527), with multiple historical lexical and grammatical influences from Latin, German, Italian, Hungarian, Turkish, French and English. Language-mixing practices have been reported in multiple academic and non-academic outlets that I had been reading; for example, in the aforementioned reportage *Białystok*, Kącki showed that historically, mixing practices in rural areas in eastern Poland had been a norm rather than an exception. After the Second World War, due to the political influence of the USSR as well as ongoing globalization and technological advancements, Russian and English influences and the so-called internationalisms increased. Kontra et al. (in press) also note that in the last decades, 'mixing practices' and other language varieties have become more widespread in Poland, with perhaps the most rapid recent changes being triggered by the arrival of large groups speaking East Slavic varieties, such as Ukrainian, Russian, Surzhyk, for example, before and due to the Russian military aggression on Ukraine in 2022.

I noted that contact with English received increased attention, with some (Sztencel 2009) arguing that after 2000, it became 'more intense' than in previous decades. This was also noticed by my participants, which is visible in an interview with a 25-year-old 'Polish Pole' man who had spent six years in the UK. In the excerpt, Bartosz commented on mixing practices in the corporate sector that he observed during his internship in Warsaw in the 2010s, which he evaluated negatively as 'ugly'.

jako język urzędowy był angielski i wszystkie jakby materiały były po angielsku, było też dużo pracowników którzy przyjeżdżali z zagranicznych biur, więc z natury rzeczy rozmawialiśmy sporo po angielsku, ale jeżeli byli tylko Polacy to rozmawialiśmy tylko po polsku, to znaczy jakby zamiarem było to żebyśmy rozmawiali tylko po polsku, ale do czego dochodziło to że rozmawialiśmy w okropnej okropnej mieszance polskiego i angielskiego [. . .] nigdy się jeszcze nie spotkałem z taką mieszanką polskiego i angielskiego jak właśnie w biurze w Warszawie mając do czynienia z ludźmi którzy nigdy- naczy ludzie którzy używali tej mieszanki to byli ludzie którzy nigdy nie mieszkali za granicą, tylko jakby być może ta kultura korporacyjna tam coś takiego proponowała

(the official language was English and all like materials were in English, there were also many workers who came from non-Polish branches, so naturally we spoke English a lot, but if there were only Poles, we spoke only Polish, I mean our intention was to speak Polish, but it turned out that we spoke an ugly mixture of Polish and English which [. . .] I'd never encountered such a mixture of Polish and English as in the office in Warsaw talking to people who'd never, I mean people who used the mixture had never lived abroad, but like, maybe this corporate culture offered something like this.)

As my project was taking place in the context where standardized English was the dominant language variety of British society and where multiple forms of English were accessible in the everyday offline realities of my participants, I was interested in tracing circulating meanings and forms associated with 'English' in Polish society. I suspected that being exposed to different English-influenced forms and styles before coming to the UK, my participants would be weaving their evaluative and aesthetic judgements and enactments of permissible verbalized practices also in dialogue with previous models of indexicality and figures of speech. To get a wider picture of what webs of meanings they might have been operating with and situating themselves towards, I reviewed literature focusing on the presence of English features and loanwords in Polish in the past few decades (Chłopicki 2002; Grybosiowa 2003; Otwinowska-Kasztelanic 2000). I knew that English features in Polish were widely recognized in the public domain and that members of Polish society often agreed that 'English features' were 'foreign elements', but the stereotypical values associated with them varied for different social groups, with differential evaluations of the forms diverging by ideological stances regarding social changes happening in Polish society.

The increasing spread of English had been attributed to foreign capital investments entering the Polish market, and ongoing globalization and specialized literature favouring English loanwords, especially in economics and computer science (Korcz and Matulewski 2006). Some differences in the evaluation of features at different levels of linguistic structure also existed. Most scholars differentiated between English grammatical and lexical phenomena. For example, Otwinowska-Kasztelanic (2000) argued that among 250 respondents to her questionnaire, English grammatical borrowings were more acceptable if they were frequently used in the media. Acceptability was also greater among younger respondents, with 15- to 20-year-olds being least likely to comment on recent grammatical changes in Polish. Otwinowska-Kasztelanic suggested that the younger generations' grammatical system was already different due to the influence of English. She also reported overall disapproval of English loanwords. However, Sztencel (2009) observed 'a tacit social consent to English infiltration' (13).

To get a picture of emerging delimitations of speech from noise and its impact on conditions of intelligibility and processes of authentication in transnational space, I had to recognize simultaneous multiplicities of associations. I was perfectly aware of the fact that for many, these associations could be positive and serve as emblems of globalization and being modern Poles who, thanks to them, can easily function in the EU (Kołodziejek 2008). However, I was also aware that others may perceive them as snobbish, which was most often contrasted with being down-to-earth. Studies reported English features to index social prestige (Sztencel 2009) 'and in extreme cases [. . .] professional snobbism' (Korcz and Matulewski 2006: 160), especially of management boards of big companies (Maternik 2003). Lubaś mentioned most extreme negative associations linking them even to 'stupidity and cultural primitivism' and new social phenomena promoting utilitarian over patriotic/national values, propagated by the middle classes (Lubaś 1996). I was also aware that the use of English features may also be linked to the 'East' vs. 'West' debate, with sentiments towards the West fluctuating between superiority and inferiority with material standards to measure the progress imposed by the West (Peteri 2010). Here I also noted that Western elements, including English, became desirable commodities for some in Poland and may be understood within the tradition vs. modernity/conservatism vs. innovation dichotomies.

At the same time, as there were large Polish-speaking communities in the English-speaking world, I also knew that the English-like phenomena may be indexical of being from abroad, with some mixing practices, for example, *Ponglish* historically being often linked to working-class migrations, especially to America. As today these groups come into regular contact with Poles in Poland, both in person and via communication technologies, translanguaging practices and English-influenced ways of speaking Polish may also index being 'not really Polish'/'foreign' in terms of one's Polishness defined on the basis of the place one comes from and sedentariness. These were also mediated by large-scale communicative processes such as instances of parody in Polish media ridiculing English-accented Polish.

When existing literature operating within the standard language ideological Polish-English dichotomy was considered, Standard British English and American English were typically seen as norm providers and evaluated as more valuable than other ways of speaking English. Kontra et al. (in press) note that in recent years, 'substantial migration to the UK and Ireland put many Polish people in direct contact with the English language or, rather, with many different Englishes that they had never heard of'. This in turn was shown to affect how the 'markedness continuum of world Englishes' (Diskin and Regan 2017) was actively evaluated and exploited in migrant contexts. In Ireland, Diskin and Regan (2017) noticed that Polish migrants views of world Englishes were situated along both a cline of markedness, and the degree to which the variety appeared different as compared to an abstract benchmark of "English", and desirability' (204).

When reviewing studies of members of the Polish diaspora globally, I quickly saw that most projects focused on establishing language maintenance by means of statistical demographic data, the problem of identity understood as a psychological construct, and proficiency levels and the domains in which the Polish language was used by such speakers across the globe (Clyne 1991; Dębski 2009; Janik 1996; Miodunka 2003; Nowicka McLees 2010). In comparison to other contexts, at the time of the project, data concerning the knowledge and use of the English language among Polish-speaking migrants in the UK were limited. According to Błasiak's (2011) study, almost 50 per cent of the newcomers claimed to know English very well, an additional 23 per cent reported a good knowledge of English and 15 per cent claimed to know English at a satisfactory level with 13 per cent indicating poor knowledge of English and less than 1 per cent no knowledge at all (Błasiak 2011). Błasiak claimed that almost 30 per cent of the Polish-speaking participants that she studied spoke what she also calls 'Ponglish', a combination of Polish and English replete with insertions, calques, interferences, code-switches, alternations and so on from both language varieties.

In her study of Polish migrants in Bath, Bristol, Frome and Trowbridge, all in England's West Country, White (2011) also observed various levels of language knowledge of Polish-speaking migrants working in the UK. According to White, her participants expressed the need to acquire the language as they perceived it as a necessary tool to function in British society. With different outcomes, many migrants succeeded in learning some English. Many husbands seemed to speak the language better than their wives when surrounded by English colleagues. Some men, however, did not speak the language even after living in the UK for several years due to the fact that they usually worked with other speakers of Polish and thus did not need English at all. Many of the people interviewed by White expressed frustration because of what they perceived as 'inadequate progress in learning English' (White 2011: 164), which was raised by some participants in my later work in London as well and linked to limited or inadequate English language provision provided by the state.

While these projects enable me to see that both contact with and access to resources potentially had an impact on the ways in which sounded linguistic objects may be imbued with emergent meanings, other projects coming from the UK and Ireland which were looking at variation turned out to be more useful for understanding the productivity of the semiotic–material sign forms in which I was interested. When reading about the studies of English phonetic variation used by post-EU-accession Polish migrants in the UK and Ireland, I noticed that it was often observed that their engagement with English norms was translated in dynamic and complex sociolinguistically meaningful ways. For example, Meyerhoff and Schleef (2012) demonstrated that although teenagers that they identified as Polish and interviewed in London and Edinburgh did not have access to the same 'richness of information', as they call it, about the social meaning of (ing) as 'native speakers', some systematization of the feature was observed and linked to social networks and gender differences. Drummond

(2012) also showed that Polish-speaking migrants in Manchester used the local STRUT vowel more if they had an English-speaking partner, a positive attitude towards the city and an increased length of residence. In Dublin, social identity and class inconsistency were also shown to be crucial for the use of the local phonological variation (Kobiałka, 2016). Finally, Schleef (2017) demonstrated that based on interviews with him, after two years in England, continuous systematization in the use of T-glottaling in English, a feature associated with Londoners, can be observed with (t) becoming a stylistic resource allowing the teenagers to project identities, and signal alignment with Poland/disalignment with England in complex ways.

These projects provided some sketches of what could potentially influence how heterogeneous elements pattern in transnational space, but didn't necessarily take relevant politics of recognition fully into account. I was in the end interested in how dominant images erased the ways around which the ability to speak and sound out was related not only to properties of spaces but also to possibilities of *time*. Based on my later ethnographic fieldwork in community organizations in London, in 2021, together with Prof Zhu Hua, we noted that there were emerging differences in the conceptualization of the language and timespace relationship even among post-war and post-EU-accession organizers, although most of those participating in the politics of ethnic representation in the UK relied on the historical narrative of the Polish nation and standard language ideology. We also argued that the bounded understandings of languages and preference for linguistic purity were echoed in the very conceptualization of ethnic identity among interviewed community organizers, where Polish and English cultural resources were seen as belonging to separate and bounded cultural systems authenticated by particular linguistic practices. We argued that among UK Polish community organizers, observed appropriate performance in English was also usually evaluated within a UK culture of standardization, where multi-ethnic, class or regional ways of speaking were evaluated against the benchmark of Standard British English (e.g. Milroy and Milroy 2012). They also remained underpinned by UK racial discourses, with whiteness of the British population assumed as an invisible norm. In our project, despite noticeable regional, class and historical differences, Polish and English were also most often conceptualized as discrete and separate entities. The presence of language mixing was acknowledged, but the interviewees usually expressed less positive attitudes towards mixing. We argued that such preferences and practices hid the ways in which the denotational code was susceptible to the politics of access and workings of symbolic dominance, where a historically shaped class-based ideal of the standard language associated with sedentary settlement served to erase asymmetrical power relations and less representative ways of speaking. Our ethnographic work revealed that next to standard monolingual institutionalized and colloquial practices in self-labelled Polish organizations, mixing practices were organically emerging in both oral and written communication, reminding the reader that in everyday life the community-making is dynamic with speakers rarely occupying one homogeneous space.

Already in 2012, I was convinced that situated aesthetic judgements may help flesh out the complexity of presenting multilayered messages to the senses, which could bring me a step closer to the potential distribution of the sensible. By not erasing aesthetics, 'a system of a priori forms determining what presents itself to sense experience' (Rancière 2013), but rather examining my participants' own situated aesthetic judgements, I hoped I could start the discussion about the ways in which semiotic–material conditions of discourse production enabled and restricted the construal of emerging transnational images in this particular context.

Going through my collected accounts and fieldnotes, I quickly noticed that most indexical meanings associated with English-like features operating in Poland had already been recursively projected onto the UK Polish community by 2012–14. However, new models of indexicality, specific to the British context, were also emerging. For all participants and other Polish migrants approached by me within the last decade, in the UK, English and English features in Polish may often be linked to 'success and integration' into British society, which is demonstrated in an interview with Ewa, a 25-year-old Polish Pole woman working in the corporate sector in London. The excerpt also shows a projection of the down-to-earth vs. snobbish opposition onto the migrant community as Ewa links the new ways to 'showing off'.

> *być może te osoby w ogóle nie zauważają że przeskakują, że cały czas się przełączają, między polskim a angielskim [.] i być może być może właśnie te osoby są najlepiej zintegrowane [.] chociaż czasami w weekendy [.] chcę pójść na piwo i rozmawiać po polsku z kimś, no więc są takie osoby które- którym właśnie chcą rozmawiać po polsku i potem przychodzi ktoś i cały czas nie wiem szpanuje swoim angielskim*

(maybe it's easier, that there are people who find English easy maybe that these people don't even notice that they switch [. . .] and maybe these people are more integrated [.] although sometimes on weekends [.] I don't want to think in English, I want to go for a beer and speak Polish with someone, so there are people who want to speak Polish and then someone comes and shows off)

English features, including phonetic detail, were also often linked to one's networks and participation in the Polish community. In another interview, Daria, a 23-year-old in-between woman from London, comments on the use of English features in Polish among her friends, including a cosmopolitan speaker whose speech is analysed later in this book, and links them to the diasporic orientation and 'being cool'.

> *niektórym się zmienił [. . .] to raczej są ludzie którzy są otoczeni Anglikami bo jednak wielu Polaków trzyma się w tym polskim środowisku i jest taka tendencja że jak już się znajdzie tych Polaków to oni są taką grupką i wszystko robią razem i potem są te osoby które się odłączają i raczej mają [. . .] Anglików w swoim otoczeniu [. . .] ten polski [. . .] im upada tak? więc jak mam koleżanki które mają na przykład chłopaków Anglików albo mnóstwo koleżanek Angielek no to częściej wtrącają angielskie słowa albo nawet trochę akcent im się zmienia, tak więc rzeczywiście to zauważyłam [. . .] może to jest związane z jakąś modą byciem fajnym [. . .] no myślę, że to nie jest najlepiej odbierane jednak jest takie, jest taki sentyment do Polski i do polskiego, szczególnie w takich grupach dosyć zamkniętych, że jednak powinno się kultywować i dlatego oni wszyscy razem się przyjaźnią, bo oni jednak chcą być tymi Polakami i chcą być razem, więc jak ktoś odchodzi od tego takiego modelu, prawda? no to wtedy trochę to im się mniej podoba, myślę, że to jest bardziej krytykowane, że a, albo udaje albo – tak udaje, że jest kimś innym, albo chce się odciąć od nas, myślę, że różne teorie mogą być tworzone*

(for some, it's changed [. . .] these are rather people who are surrounded by the English because many Poles stick to the Polish environment and there is this tendency that if you find the Poles, then they are a group and do everything together, and then there are the people who go apart and rather have [. . .] the English around them, then [.] this Polish [. . .] is deteriorating, so when I have friends who for example have English boyfriends or many English friends, then they insert more English words and even the accent is changing a bit [. . .] maybe it's connected with fashion, being cool [. . .] no, I think it isn't well perceived, there's this sentiment towards Poland and Polish especially in those quite closed groups, that one should cultivate and thus they're all friends, because they want to be Poles and want to be together, so when someone leaves this model, right? so then I think, they like it less, I think it's criticized more and or pretend or yes, pretend that one's someone else, I think there might be various theories being created)

The tensions in the judgements made me aware that they may also affect processes of authentication. For example, while some projected the East vs. West opposition onto the migrant community arguing for English features to be indexical of elitism, they also associated them with 'weird people' pretending to be someone whom they were not. The next extract comes from an interview with Marek, a 26-year-old Polish Pole man working in the corporate sector in London, who, like some other nationally oriented interviewees, explicitly asserted that he did not want to be in contact with such people.

ale koleżanka była z Polski i pamiętam, że było to takie- takie- bardzo niekomfortowe, to byli sami Polacy w pokoju, a ona po angielsku rozmawiała z nami, nawet jak ktoś do niej mówił żeby mówiła po polsku to zaczynała mówić po polsku i zaczynała używać angielskich słów i w ogóle mówiła z dziwnym akcentem więc nikomu się nie spodobała wszyscy mówili ze jakaś była dziwna strasznie [. . .] ludzie na pewno się zdarzają, tak no ja nie mam może dlatego nie mam wśród bliższych znajomych, bo to właśnie tacy dziwni są ludzie

(but the friend was from Poland and I remember that it was so uncomfortable, there were only Poles in the room and she spoke English to us, even when someone told her to speak Polish, she would start speaking Polish and use English words and in general, she spoke with a weird accent, so no one liked her, everybody said she was very weird [. . .] there are people like that for sure, but I don't have, maybe that's why I don't have closer friends like this because these are such weird people)

Although infrequent, explicit comments about 'social ostracism' occurred, where those speaking in new ways were excluded. Again, this mechanism was employed through fractal recursivity of the real vs. unreal dichotomy operating in Poland, where Poles living in Poland are imagined to speak 'standard' Polish and hence, those speaking in an English-influenced manner may be perceived as not 'really' Polish and not from Poland. From the interview with Adam, a 27-year-old Polish Pole living in London, the tension between the two opposing groupings is visible. Similarly to Marek, Adam does not want to be friends with 'weird' speakers and situates the tension within the West vs. East debate, describing those trying to speak in new ways as those that strive for social elitism in Britain by neglecting their Polish heritage.

znam ludzi, którzy próbowali, żeby za wszelką cenę im się zmienił akcent i zostali bardzo szybko spotkali się z ostracyzmem społecznym, więc raczej jak spotykamy się w grupie Polaków to, to - komentujemy polskie - nie, nie znam nikogo, kto by nie będę już za bardzo filozofował, tak, zostały ukamieniowane, nie żartuję oczywiście, bo niektórzy chcieli być bardziej angielscy niż Anglicy no to, to –to nie jest tak, że się taki antagonizm wytworzył wśród Polaków, tylko ogólnie to jest śmieszne zjawisko, i to zarówno Polacy, jak i Anglicy tak samo to oceniają no, no więc no niektórym to się zmieniło, a niektórzy po prostu z nami nie utrzymują kontaktu, naczy nie ogólnie w naszym gronie przyjaciół nikt nie nie ma takiej sytuacji, niektórzy to robią, ci, którzy to robili tak jak powiedziałem nie utrzymujemy za bardzo kontaktu z takimi osobami, ale myślę, że dla niektórych to też jest próba polepszenia swojej pozycji społecznej, tak? mimo wszystko angielski, Anglia i Zachód w świadomości wąskiej grupy osób wiąże się z jakąś elitarnością, i próbują to podkreślić, co, co jak powiedziałem jest dosyć śmie, śmiesznym zabiegiem . . . miałem koleżankę, która chciała być – osiadła w Anglii, ma już teraz rodzinę tutaj i, i jej mężem jest Anglik, i tak, i stara się za wszelką cenę, że tak powiem – odseparować od, od kultury polskiej, a to wynikało z negatywnych doświadczeń w Polsce

(I know people who tried to change their accent at all costs and became, quickly faced social ostracism, so when we meet, then, then we comment on Polish, no, I don't know anybody who, I won't theorize too much, yes (in a joking manner) they (FEM) were stoned, no, I'm joking, of course, because some wanted to be more English than the English so then, then . . . it isn't that this antagonism's emerged among Poles, but generally it's such a funny phenomenon and both Poles and Brits see it, so, so some've changed that and some are no longer friends with us, I mean no, among our friends no one has such a situation, some do it, those who did that, as I said, we aren't in touch with such people, but I also think that for some, it's also an attempt to advance their social position, yes? nevertheless, English, England and the West for a small group of people are associated with elitism and they're trying to stress this which, which as I said is a bit fu, funny [. . .] I had a friend who wants to be . . . who settled in England, has a family here now and, and her husband is English and yes, and she tries at all costs, so to say, to separate herself from Polish culture and this is related to her negative experiences in Poland)

I was interested in understanding how such aesthetic judgements of expressive culture were woven with sensorial modes of knowing and how they delimitated speech and noise, and space and time. I had to therefore make further decisions to critically examine the collected chronotopic representations of migration experiences and their embedding not only in individual subjectivities, but also contextualized attitudes and interests.

Finding a way to study performances of collective memory in a moving world

I wanted to investigate how particular moments in knowledge production processes were embedded in individual and collective histories and how sensory inclinations guided my participants in their aesthetic judgements and recognition of particular ways of apprehending acceptable norms and practices in transnational space. To do so, I had to consider both their enactments of embodied memory and expert knowledge. Given my continuing reflections on the relationship between the researcher, the body, society and knowledge production, I came to see experts as structurally positioned individuals who were actively involved in production, authorization and legitimization of collective memory (French 2012). Following Carr (2010), I also saw expertise as 'something that people do rather than something people have or hold' (18), which is tightly linked to positions of power.

The collected accounts were therefore particular events in the wider project on which I performed discourse and phonetic analysis. They were based on events in which particular people voluntarily decided to share their accounts with me, having been informed of the purpose of the encounter, their rights and later handling of the data. The announcement sought participants who were Polish-speaking with UK higher education degrees, willing to share their views and experiences of living and working in Britain and transnational space. It thereby framed the data collection process according to the demands of my PhD programme and discipline. The encounters also operated within a particular culture of research activities, which included silences as some people that I approached were not willing to share their views in a recorded encounter. This reminded me that research is a public activity in which 'publics are created when texts engage [participants] in particular sorts of ways . . . inducing them to feel part of a social group that shares a particular orientation towards specific publicly circulating cultural forms' (Briggs 2007: 555). This is evident in the production and perception of interviews. They were also selective and not representative of the whole Polish-speaking population that shares this positioning. Their number was rather determined during fieldwork as I achieved saturation (Small 2009) of the emerging ideological orientations.

The selection criteria also depended on my understanding of sociocultural space in the UK. During fieldwork, I made multiple trips to London, learnt about the neighbourhoods my participants lived in, their work, networks, motivations to migrate, views on language and culture, and plans for the future. Seeing class as a relational category, historically and dynamically shaped and economically driven, I established that most lived in private, often shared rented flats, with only three people suggesting ownership of their flats[2]. They worked in white-collar jobs with most working in the corporate sector in London (fourteen out of thirty recorded: eleven Polish Poles and three cosmopolitans). The jobs were not all the same, but the findings and other observations may suggest that similarly to Poland, the corporate sector was one of the main job providers for Polish-speaking middle classes at the time. Differences in jobs, of course, may influence one's orientation and explain the palette of ideological intensification of the reported chronotopic representations. Other jobs included social media and advertising, architecture, education (including higher) and public sector. These latter jobs were mostly performed by the so-called in-betweens and cosmopolitans. Given the educational background, white-collar jobs and living arrangements, I couldn't help but see that the participants' experiences in the UK were different from many other Polish-speaking people I met at the time and have worked with over the years. At the time, I reviewed statistics for South-east England, which enabled me to get a picture of wealth distribution in Oxford and Greater London and better understand class dynamics of which my participants and I were becoming a part. Given the UK's strong class structure, where such measures as income, inherited wealth, education and profession are most often used to define one's class background, rather than seeing my participants through the lens of the Polish state and defining them only as elites, in relation to the wider British public, they must be seen as having a middle-class background, perhaps most often closest to the profiles of the middle- or lower-middle classes (Dorling 2019). A handful of (multi)millionaires that Poland had at the time were not approached in this project.

As gendered differences emerged as a theme quite early into my project and as the project operated within intersectional frameworks, an effort was made to include equal numbers of women and men in discourse and linguistic analysis, but more people were approached in not recorded conversations. Crucially, gender is also seen here as a *relational* category, not a category operating in a vacuum. It is rather a formation always entangled in ethno-racialized and classed relations that, in this case, I am also a part of. It is not therefore seen here as a binary essence, but rather as a category that continues to emerge in discourse. In my situated encounters, it is confined to the ways in which speakers present themselves, which includes gendered linguistic practices and reported partners, and ways of echoing societal discourses on gender roles at the time next to engaging in discussions on gendered aspects of life in these particular encounters and, where possible, during other observations. As the project rested upon voluntary participation, aimed to engage with a particular demographic, operated within particular constraints and relied on unfolding of discourse in interaction, recruitment methods did not enable me to investigate non-binary representations, and the recorded sample included only one interview with a self-identified gay Polish Pole speaker. Hence, the relationship between the observed ways of speaking and sexuality must be explored in the future and there is no intention to treat gender as an analytically separable category.

As mentioned before, my analysis centred on the production of perspectives on norms and practices. The interviews consisted mainly of accounts within complex stretches of discourse compressing multiple historicities (Blommaert 2015) into one 48-minute to 1 hour 32 minute–long synchronized ideological enactment. Due to limitations of my project, as suggested before, at the time I was not able to follow everybody to the same degree and admittedly, some met with me only for the interview. The focus of the project aimed at enabling the participants to order experiences of migration and engage in scale-making in situated encounters. After Gal and Irvine (2019), I approached scaling as 'a relational practice that relies on situated juxtapositions and comparisons among events, persons, things and activities' (218). At the same time, I had to recognize that in such accounts 'speakers attempt to construct a favorable presentation of self' and mitigate for less favourable representations, which uncovers 'everyday cultural frames through which agency and responsibility are understood' (Hill and Zepeda 1993). Each of the accounts was different, shaped by unique experiences, memories and emotions. There were nineteen key questions covered in all interviews and designed to enable me to collect information on a number of topics related to participants' experiences of living in the UK, language ideologies and views on ethnicity and nationality, Polish and British culture, and so on. The exact wording of the questions differed from interview to interview, with each beginning with an equivalent of, 'So, can you tell me your story in the UK?' intended to allow the participant's response to set out the direction of the interview. I determined the order of the key questions and the additional questions in our interaction and with reference to the information provided by the participant. Thus, after the first question, the interviewee's interest in talking about a particular topic dictated how much time was spent on each question.

Bringing the voices of individual people, building on arguments in Black feminist thought, I wanted to move away from top-down theories of communicative practices in transnational space towards recognition that individual consciousness constitutes 'a fundamental area where new knowledge can generate change' (Collins 1990). At the same time, I saw interviews as part of a powerful, shaping and contestable process of knowledge production in which complex subjects operating within multiple positionalities and motives mobilize particular actions and events to construe their perspectives and produce situated images for particular purposes. It must be remembered that this particular discourse genre through 'theory of communicability' (Briggs 2007) often makes participants' discourse 'transparent, magical containers of beliefs, experiences, knowledge, attitudes'. This is tightly linked to Locke's ideas of the liberal notion of the state, subjectivity and language, changing imagination of public/private relations that are crucial for structuring social participation as well as Romantic ideals linking words to authenticity (Briggs 2007). Briggs argues that this often makes us forget that interviews 'produce discourse that seems to transform inner voices into public discourse', although they are in fact always socially situated cultural and political artefacts that highlight communicable cartographies through which academic projects frequently produce subjects and knowledge. They are most often imagined to centre on an individual, but, importantly, through processes of recruitment and analysis, these individuals are inserted into systems of social organization, which, in the case of my project, centres upon categories salient in these accounts and the life of the diaspora.

It must be noted that it was my decision to use such category labels as 'Polish Pole', in-between and cosmopolitans. These came from fieldwork, but were also situated within larger societal discourses on nationalism, cosmopolitanism, multiculturalism and social organization relevant for this context. By doing so, I wanted to start thinking about ethnicity as a continuum rather than a binary category. In this project, this was confined to situated chronotopic representations, which enabled a construal of particular dominant images of time-space–personhood. Hence, as texts offer particular possibilities, the labels echoed dominant frames in these encounters. The label 'in-between' was admittedly my own invention as based on my analysis these accounts relied on distinctive chronotopic frames, but sat between the other two categories presenting contrasting orientations towards nationality, language and life in transnational space. The word 'cosmopolitans' came up in some interviews, and perhaps upon reflection could be supplanted by a more accurate label 'human beings', which was most often used in 'cosmopolitan' accounts. The dominant frames of representation presented in those accounts, however, echoed widely available discourses of cosmopolitanism circulating among various publics in the Polish-speaking world, where according to Słownik Języka Polskiego, a *kosmopolita* ('cosmopolitan') is understood as *człowiek nieczujący więzi z krajem, z którego pochodzi lub którego jest obywatelem, deklarujący swą więź z kulturą świata,* 'a person who does not feel a bond with the country they are from or of which they are a citizen, but who declares a bond with the culture of the world', and *kosmopolitanizm* is most often discussed as an attitude that seeks to go beyond territorial and political divides, and see the world as one.

These discourses were usually an integral part of the Polish curriculum covered in schools, where their origins are often traced back to Ancient Greece, whose history is usually thoroughly examined in primary and secondary schools, and together with other globally available theories, continue to circulate in public debates. This was especially evident with the rise of nationalism in Europe, including both Poland and Britain, in the 2010s.

In order to understand the complex pragmatics of the accounts I discuss in the next chapter, it must also be noted that I continually decontextualized and recontextualized these accounts and by doing so, subjected them to continuous transformations of scale, which does not allow for exact replication. In line with principles of critical sociolinguistics (Heller et al. 2018), one must note that the data and discourse are filtered through my sensibility. I am a cis-gender heterosexual woman researcher born and raised in Warsaw, with twenty-three years of experience of living and completing primary, secondary and tertiary education in the Polish state. I completed my first degree with a specialization in English and German linguistics, culture and literature at the University of Warsaw. I also had prior international experience as I studied and travelled across the globe, with longer stays in the United States, where I developed an interest and conducted my first graduate project on language ideologies among members of the Polish-speaking diaspora in Chicago, while completing my MA in social sciences at the University of Chicago. In the 2010s, I also had a transnational friendship network and a family history of many relatives living in transnational space with my own grandmother living in the UK after the war, but eventually settling in Warsaw. As noted before, my grandmother's family, however, settled as refugees in the north of England after fleeing Soviet gulags in Siberia and travelling through Iran, Palestine, Egypt and the former Rhodesia to Britain in the 1940s. I have visited them many times since I began my PhD programme. Apart from studies abroad, in 2012, I had also already had experience of working in the non-governmental sector in Poland and the Global South, as with new opportunities for cooperation emerging after Poland's EU accession, I was able to travel to work on a Polish government–financed educational project in deprived neighbourhoods of Phnom Penh, Cambodia, just before my PhD programme. Perhaps it is also important to note that I spent some time learning English in London in my teens, where I also attended a few summer schools in my early twenties.

During my DPhil studies at Oxford, I travelled to Poland every few months and have continued to do so for the last decade, most often spending my time in Warsaw, but also in Mazury, a low-income area in north-eastern Poland. I have also made use of communication technologies on a daily basis: talking to my Polish-speaking parents in Warsaw, and communicating in written and spoken form with contacts in various parts of the globe. At the time of the project, I was also engaged in discussions mostly with scholars in the United Kingdom, Europe and the United States through participation in various academic conferences and seminars, which also included online encounters with scholars in other parts of the world. All these encounters have had an impact on how I shaped my ideas about these observations, how I analysed the data and how I gradually made the findings available to the wider public. It does not therefore suffice to acknowledge my positioning, but it must be noted that like in any academic project, I was an *active* part of the project and power differences between me and my participants cannot be erased. As an individual, I shared many of the characteristics of the chosen population. Like them, I was among the first generation of Polish citizens who could make use of European citizenship and take up studies in the UK, but I had not lived in the UK permanently before my project. Crucially, however, unlike my participants, I had the power to control how discourse unfolded during our encounters as well as to gain control over the process of its recontextualization.

I have hence actively co-produced these situated accounts in collaborative processes of knowledge production. I also write this book after spending eleven years of living and working at various universities in South-east England, and settling in London in 2017. Importantly, the book comes after my two-year-long linguistic ethnographic work among differently positioned Polish-speaking families and organizations in Greater London post the Brexit vote, for which I worked with audiovisual methodologies with a team of scholars working with migrants with ties not only to Poland but also to China and Somalia, all living and working in the UK. These experiences together with, for example, the recent Covid-19 pandemic, rising collective consciousness of gender inequalities among those with ties to Poland, global anti-racist protests, the climate emergency and the ongoing war in Ukraine, have made me connect these observations to the current arguments in the humanities and social sciences in particular ways at the time of writing the book.

During fieldwork, the accounts were collected mostly in low-noise 'private' settings (participants' homes or places of their choice) over a period of one year from July 2013 to August 2014. They were recorded with a Marantz PMD 660 recorder and two lapel Audio-Technica AT8531 microphones, with the sample rate of 48 kHz with 16 bits per sample. The recordings were made with two audio channels and were digitized into Waveform audio files that were later analysed in Elan (Wittenburg et al. 2006) and Praat (Boersma and Weenink 2012). During the interview, I made use of the variety I would typically use when interacting with my peers back in Poland, inserting phrases and collocations typical for my peer group in informal settings, which put people at ease. This included some established English loanwords that I was familiar with, but my own way of speaking Polish would not resemble the new ways of speaking. As explicitly noted by my participants, the new ways of speaking also did not resemble images of stereotypically English-accented ways of speaking Polish that circulate in media and so on. Given the one-to-one nature of the interviews, the participants might have had a tendency to use more standard forms than in their everyday life, although based on my observations, where possible, it seems the clusters of features were used in other peer encounters. Other recorded data sets are necessary to confirm these trends.

In order to foreground the importance of a sounded perspective in the studies of emerging embodied transnational cultures and projects, during my analysis, I decided to conduct a holistic discourse analysis, that is, one in conjunction with an investigation whether and how phonetic detail was used in these accounts. To do so, I first transcribed the audio recordings in Elan, which is itself not a neutral activity. Following Bucholtz (2000), my transcription conventions must be seen as '[t]he choices' that 'link the transcript to the context in which it is intended to be read' (Bucholtz 2000: 1440). Although the participants did not expect typical [Qa][Ab][Qa][Ab] . . . interaction, each interaction is seen as a two-person interrogative chain (Goffman 1983) to some extent since as an interviewer, I provided feedback and interpretative frames in which the answers made sense. They were transcribed with standard Polish orthography, and closely examined in terms of sequential organization of the talk itself. In line with interactional prosody studies (Couper-Kuhlen and Selting 1996), I conducted a sequential analysis of 'local moves and countermoves' (Gumperz and Berentz 1993: 95), where an intonational phrase (IP) was defined as 'a stretch of speech that falls under a single intonational contour or envelope and ends in an intonational boundary marker' (Gumperz and Berenz 1993: 99). Such phrases were prototypically 'set off from surrounding phrasal units by pausing and constitute[d] semantically interpretable syntactic entities' (95). The boundaries between the phrases were established assuming that the units must 'make sense in terms of the rhythmic and thematic organization of the surrounding discourse' (Gumperz and Berenz 1993: 95). The division into intonational phrases followed the existing Polish Intonation PoInt project (Francuzik et al. 2002; Francuzik et al. 2005; Karpiński 2006) and was based primarily on perception of prosodic patterns established through close listening and visual inspection of the pitch tracking option in Praat (Boersma and Weenink 2012).

In line with critical approaches to discourse analysis, I first examined lexical choices, grammar, cotext and context, including ways in which tellership and tellability were construed in these encounters, how emerging discourse was embedded in relation to the interviewing activity and how the participants' orientations depended on temporal and causal order mobilized to create particular images and effects. After Cameron (2001), I observed that 'the text puts limits on what the reader can do with it' (92), and although utterances have a potential to be interpreted in multiple ways, 'what people actually say does not have an unlimited range of possible interpretations'. Rather, when considering likely possibilities, interlocutors rely on contextual information. In each interview, I therefore examined how displays of subjectivity were constituted through public stance-taking acts (DuBois 2007). Although such acts can be accomplished by multisensory and multimodal semiotic resources (Bucholtz 2009), which I saw very clearly in my later work with audiovisual recordings, my analysis of sounded experiences was confined to the examination of evaluation, positioning, and alignment in each interview, hence, to what was admissible to the world of verbalized ideas.

Stance-acts were not always complete within one intonational unit (DuBois 2007), but rather established in relation to particular objects, 'what the talk [was] about', in dialogic sequences and within the whole discursive event. I examined contradictory stances and the effects they created in these encounters to establish the dominant framework for each account. This included, but was not confined to, eight cultural foci that had been identified as central for the culture of the UK diaspora and often used by participants to distinguish between different Polish-speaking migrants in Britain. These included the degree to which one: self-identifies as Polish, says they care about the Polish language, maintains Polish traditions in Britain, is a member of one or more Polish organizations in the UK, intends to return to Poland, is religious, eats Polish food, has or would like to have a Polish-speaking partner.

After each interview, I also asked participants to list their networks: each participant provided information about each contact's place of origin, place of residence and relationship to the speaker, what language they speak with them and a ranking of the frequency of contact (on a scale from 1 to 5, where 1 is distant, rare and 5 is close, frequent). Afterwards, I established a network score for their social networks. The foci were then put together with network scores above 50 per cent to create an additional tool, which I called a Polishness Index

Table 3.1 Network scores for all speakers based on contacts other than kinship in descending order of the score[1]

Serial number	Interview	Gender	Network score
P4	Łukasz	M	83%
P8	Tomasz	M	74%
P15	Olaf	M	71%
P9	Maria	F	67%
P2	Ewa	F	65%
P10	Paweł	M	59%
P1	Adam	M	56%
P3	Kamil	M	54%
P5	Artur	M	50%
P6	Barbara	F	50%
P16	Ela	F	50%
P17	Stefan	M	50%
C4	Kaja	F	50%
P12	Emil	M	46%
P11	Bartosz	M	41%
I6	Adrian	M	40%
C1	Paulina	F	40%
C7	Natalia	F	38%
P7	Daniel	M	35%
I1	Agata	F	35%
C2	Rafał	M	33%
I5	Iwona	F	30%
P14	Monika	F	29%
I4	Daria	F	29%
C3	Iza	F	29%
C6	Maja	F	27%
I2	Sylwia	F	23%
P13	Marek	M	20%
C5	Jacek	M	14%
I3	Edyta	F	13%

[1] All names are pseudonyms. P- Polish Pole, I- in-between and C- cosmopolitans, ranked by Polishness Index scores.

(0–9) as it situated each speaker within the local understanding of the diasporic infrastructure in Britain (Table 3.1).

The focus on such situated performances of collective memory enabled me to flesh out processes through which these particular heterogeneous material–semiotic webs and images were woven and assembled for particular purposes. The final step was to decide how to examine the sonic dimension of discourse to highlight automatisms, bodily positions and functions of speech and their role in the parcelling of relations of domination.

Thinking with soundings as material events in a sensual world

As suggested before, in order to pay holistic attention to the accounts that I collected, I didn't confine myself only to 'their internal qualities and their embeddedness in social practice, but [I also examined] their materiality as physical [events] circulating in social worlds and phenomenally accessible to the senses' (Faudree 2012). During my fieldwork and analysis, I quickly understood that my participants made use of a wide range of symbolic resources, among which phonetic detail was just one. As the contrasting emerging rhythms were subjected to metacommentary and evaluation, I decided to focus my analysis on their sonic materiality and its role in scale-making through situated embodied momentary stance-acts. By doing so, I wanted to draw attention to the ways in which sounded signs overlapped, influenced one another and fitted together to assemble my participants' self and collective images. Such a focus was also motivated by my observation that also when studied as situated sociocultural artefacts, interview data cannot be seen as radically different from the mundane talk (e.g. Atkinson 2014). Sounds were still enacted, ordered indexicalities evoked, reproduced and reconfigured and affective and poetic devices actively used in the construal of meaning and logic of emerging transnational cultures and projects.

I wanted to see how discourse analytic and sociolinguistic tools could be reused to bring us closer to the processes through which time- and place-making processes were being linked to subject creation through sonic materiality and how particular rhythms were becoming dominant in this context through formations of points of fixing. I hoped that my focus on sonic recontextualization could contribute to our knowledge about ongoing processes of enregisterment in transnational space. To do so, I had to examine my recordings acoustically through the close listening technique and manual measurements of appropriate parameters. When doing so, I established a number of features that differed in the collected accounts: aspirated stops in onsets of nuclei of intonational phrases (measured as Voice Onset Time (VOT)), falling-rising intonation in declarative phrases as a floor control mechanism, as well as palatalized fricatives, vowel lengthening in nuclei of IPs, and occasional dark l. My preliminary analysis revealed that the two sounded signs to which I devoted most of my investigation were changing in particular contexts. Rather than ignoring standardized knowledge, I thought that in my context, it could be reused to elaborate sonic connections and 'possibilities of occupying the limits of normative structures' (LaBelle 2018).

As a result I started collecting knowledge about the two dominant varieties involved in this contact situation: reported measurements and observations for standard and non-standard Polish and English sound systems. I also noticed that standard varieties were often used as reference points by my participants, which had to do with the fact that together with Standard American English, Standard/Southern British English was usually taught to foreign language learners. I saw the institutionalized knowledge about these standardized varieties as a tool for understanding emerging matter-energies in surface representations of signs of migration, which at the same time could help unpack how such expressive forms were participating in sensorial-linguistic knowledge production. In other words, I focused on enactment and embodied material practice as a way to understand what webs and connections in epistemological claims were producing domination and how bodies and communities were socialized, lived, (re)produced and (re)configured in a never finished process of assembling self and collective images through 'felt' vibrations, resonances and modalities continuously materialized in sociocultural timespace.

To do so, I looked at the knowledge about the two standardized varieties as a sketch for understanding the possibilities and modes of transformation in my case. I knew that the two standardized varieties had been widely described and their sound systems offered particular possibilities. Standard descriptions of Polish showed that it had a rich consonantal system (31 consonants) with a tendency for heavy consonant clusters (Jassem 2003). The Polish vowel system consisted of six vowels and there were no meaningful distinctions in terms of vowel length. In contrast, the described consonantal system of British English was smaller consisting of twenty-four consonants with a more limited range of clusters (Ladefoged 2012). Standard/Southern British English, however, differentiated between 20 vowels (7 short, 5 long, 8 diphthongs). As my accounts were mostly Polish-sounding, I knew that other non-standard ways of speaking Polish were also often observed to resemble 'grammatical aspects' of the standardized variety (Bajerowa 2012); hence, their sounded dimension was likely to operate within acoustic parameters that have been established through an examination of other situated and ideological Polish-sounding performances.

I therefore used the institutionalized knowledge as approximations for understanding the surface representations of sounds that I was investigating, being mindful of the fact that I had to approach the existing findings in a particular way. Rather than seeing them as biological predispositions separable from abstract systems, I saw them as descriptions of particular material events in the sensual world that may highlight the embodied nature of situated discourse production.

To investigate these surface representations thoroughly and show how dominant norms were relied on and challenged in practice to construe images of time-space–personhood in this context, a number of specific decisions about particular sounded signs were made. Below I walk the reader through my decision-making in regard to one segmental, aspiration of stops, and one suprasegmental feature, falling-rising intonation.

Stops[3]

During my project, some participants explicitly identified stops as a feature undergoing change. This is visible in an excerpt which comes from an interview with Zuzanna, a woman working in the music industry in London. In the excerpt, she commented on the speech of one of the cosmopolitan women whose stops are analysed in the next chapter. Below, Zuzanna explicitly listed the changing *t* and presented an evaluative judgement towards innovative forms among other speakers of Polish, for example, '. . . my mom was terrified.'

moja współlokatorka to jest bardzo dobry przykład, ona jest tutaj dziesięć lat prawie y dziewięć i y mówi bardzo źle po polsku, nie mówi też jakoś świetnie po angielsku, o dziwo ma taki akcent trochę m- w sensie są takie pewne- na przykład takie litery jak l albo t, które brzmią inaczej w angielskim i ona mówiąc po polsku często wymawia te litery w jakby z angielskim akcentem, mówi słabo [. . .] moja mama nawet [.] była przerażona że [imię] tak źle po polsku mówi, no nie wiem jak to działa bo ona ma kontakt z rodziną w Polsce

(my flatmate is a very good example, she's been here for ten, almost, nine years and she speaks very bad Polish, she doesn't speak perfect English either, surprisingly, she has this accent a bit, I mean there are such, certain [. . .] letters like *l* or *t* that sound different in English and she, when speaking Polish, often pronounces the letters with [. . .] an English accent, she speaks poorly, for instance, she translates things literally from English into Polish, my mom [. . .] was terrified that ((name)) speaks such bad Polish [. . .] but I don't know how this works because she's in touch with her family in Poland)

I knew that many sociolinguistic projects had demonstrated that a difference in contrast between normatively recognized varieties can make the categorical presence of a feature in one variety and its absence in the second salient to speakers (Woolard 2008) and a candidate for accelerated language change as well as indexical iconization (e.g. Alim 2002). Non-age-related and 'non pathological [change in] a native language within an individual' (de Leeuw 2014: 25) at the phonetic level due to the acquisition of a new variety has also been frequently reported (de Leeuw 2014; Dmitrieva et al. 2010; Flege 2007), which has also been observed in the case of aspiration. As my participants learnt other varieties after their acquisition of Polish, usually beginning in classroom environments, and became immersed in multilingual practices mostly as young adults, I compared their use of aspiration to reported studies of the so-called 'taught bilinguals'.

When I considered aspiration, measured as Voice Onset Time (VOT), in such projects, there seemed to be a crosslinguistic tendency for VOTs to be affected. In Brazil, Major (1992) reported a correlation between proficiency in Portuguese and rate of attrition in English measured by VOT, in informal speech and with variability across speakers. Also, Flege (1987) reported that the VOT of L1 became similar to the VOT of L2 in the American English of Americans living in France and the French living in the United States for a decade, with interspeaker variability. Highly proficient Dutch speakers in English also produced their Dutch /t/ with a shorter VOT than less proficient speakers of English moving away from both the English and Dutch values (Flege and Eefting 1987). Finally, I noted that Nagy and Kochetov (2013) observed a drift towards English VOT values across three to five generations of immigrant communities in Toronto for Russian and Ukrainian, but not for Italian. There was a correlation between questionnaire-based ethnicity and VOT: the lower the score, the more English-like the VOT, with the first generation having higher ethnic scores and lower VOT values.

Based on existing descriptions, I knew that 'standard Polish' and Standard British/American English differed in their use of aspiration. In reported results for Polish, aspiration was not treated as a phonetic category (Jassem 2003; Waniek-Klimczak 2011): it was argued that it did not occur or if it did, it was 'extremely weak and generally escape[d] the speakers' attention' (Wierzchowska 1971). However, in contact situations with varieties in which aspiration occurred, it had been noticed. For example, as early as the 1950s, Doroszewski (1952) reported aspiration in some dialects of western Poland (Wielkopolska), relating it to the influence of German, where aspiration occurs. Additionally, in Polish, voiceless stops may be aspirated when they occurred in emphatically stressed syllables (Doroszewski 1952; Rubach 1974; Ruszkiewicz 1990). Polish distinguishes six stops: bilabial /p, b/, dental /t, d/, velar /k, g/ (Keating et al. 1981; Waniek-Klimczak 2011). The vocal cord vibration was the main cue for the voiced/voiceless opposition; there was no difference in the force of articulation and the opposition was neutralized in final positions. Polish was also reported to contrast negative and short-lag VOT (Keating et al. 1981; Kopczynski 1977; Waniek-Klimczak 2011). Finally, I established that stops were among the most frequent sounds in Polish as both studies measuring the frequency of Polish phonemes in 150,000-phoneme-long spoken discourse listed the three stops within the fifteen most frequent phonemes: Jassem and Łobacz (1971): 4=t(50.7), 11=p(31.7), 15=k(26.5); Rocławski (1981): 4=t(51.4), 11=p(31.7), 14=k(28.9).

In contrast, in Standard British English, similarly to Standard American English, aspiration was described as a phonetic category. Similarly to Polish, English had six stops: bilabial /p, b/, alveolar/t, d/, velar/k, g/. The voiced/voiceless opposition was preserved in all positions, but the primary differentiating factor between voiced and voiceless stops in syllable onsets was the force of articulation. In English, /p t k/ were aspirated when in the onset of stressed syllables (Lisker and Abramson 1964), reflected in the contrast of short VOTs of /b d g/ with long VOTs of /p t k/ (Rojczyk 2009). Most projects on English VOT were based on experimental data, but from the 1990s onwards some projects based on less controlled performances were also included (see Table 3.2). Keating et al. (1981), like all projects on the Polish VOT, reported a laboratory experiment. Most studies on the English VOT came from laboratory experiments on American English. Here, two experiments, including one based on British English, and

Table 3.2 Reported VOTs for Polish and English

	Mean VOT (ms)				
Stop	Polish Keating et al. (1981): Experiment on 42 initial, stressed stops in disyllabic words; 5 speakers of Polish from Łódź, Central Poland	American English Lisker and Abramson (1964): Experiment based on a list of initial English stops in isolation; 4 speakers of American English	British English Docherty (1992): Experiment on single initial stops in 207 words in isolation and as part of carrier phrases; 5 male speakers of British English, aged 18–21	American English Byrd (1993): Natural speech from the TIMIT corpus, 2342 sentences read by 630 speakers of American English	American English Yao (2007): Natural speech with stops in initial positions from the Buckeye Corpus, casual interviews with 19 residents of Ohio, USA
p	22	58	42	44	48
t	28	70	63	49	51
k	53	80	63	52	58
b	-88	1/-101	18	18	NO INFO
d	-90	5/-102	26	24	NO INFO
g	-66	21/-88	30	27	NO INFO

two natural speech projects are reported. I noticed that all but one English VOT values were higher than the Polish ones, with the smallest difference in velar stops.

Additionally, in English, I observed that the following linguistic factors could influence mean VOT: sentence position (e.g. Lisker and Abramson 1967), stress (Lisker and Abramson 1964), number of syllables in a word (Klatt 1975; Lisker and Abramson 1964), height of the following vowel (Klatt 1975; Maddieson 1997; Ohala 1981), speech rate (Allen et al. 2003; Kessinger and Blumstein 1997), place of articulation (Maddieson 1997), preceding segment (Repp and Lin, 1989,1990). Some studies also argue for the influence of gender (e.g. Awan and Stine 2011; Whiteside and Irving 1998)[4] and age (Ryalls et al. 1997). I found that systematic differences in VOT between speakers were also reported (Allen et al. 2003). Finally, my attention was drawn to the fact that in English, the VOT continuum was observed to do identity work. For example, Clothier and Loakes (2018) reported significantly longer short-lag VOT and more pre-voiced tokens of voiced stops among Lebanese Australian English speakers than among the 'mainstream' group. Moreover, when the interaction of ethnicity, gender and vowel height was considered, Lebanese women had longer VOT duration in line with more 'mainstream' Australian English norms and Lebanese men diverged further. Stuart-Smith et al. (2015) also observed that gradient shifts along the VOT continuum in stops from the Glaswegian speech corpus (e.g. oral histories, sociolinguistic interviews, conversational speech) indicated subtle sociolinguistic control among Scottish English speakers. While Docherty et al. (2011) reported longer VOT values for younger speakers in Scotland, controlling for local speech rate, Stuart-Smith et al. (2015) observed overall lengthening of VOT for both younger and older speakers in Scotland. The use of shorter VOT associated with Scots, as it was argued, participated in the construction of local, 'non-standard' personae.

At the same time, I was reading that in Poland, Konert-Panek (2009) also identified aspiration as one of the English features that 'occur[red] in the language of the young generation' and 'resemble[d] the phonetic system of English' (112). She further claimed that some social and professional groups may be more likely to implement such features 'due to their close contact with the English language' (2009: 114), cultural 'closeness' of languages in the globalized world and the 'international' character of English. Also, when Polish and English interact, voiceless stops were reported to be affected (Waniek-Klimczak 2011). Although Waniek-Klimczak confirmed that emphasis created favourable conditions for the occurrence of aspiration in Polish, she argued that its occurrence and duration depended on the speaker's experience of English and indicated proficiency in English, which suggested that if Polish was in a contact situation with English, aspiration was more likely to be observed. Conversely, lack of aspiration in stops in English was defined as a 'stigmatized dialect feature' with class, stylistic and ethnic characteristics (Labov 1966), for example, a feature of the immigrant English of Polish New Yorkers (Labov 1966; Newlin-Łukowicz 2014). Newlin-Łukowicz (2014) also observed that for second-generation Polish Americans, Polish-like VOTs in English were both linguistically and socially motivated and linked to participation in Polish community activities in New York and Poland.

In order to see whether stops were in fact affected in my sample, I started my investigation from preliminary analysis of stops in various positions. I noted that the variability across the participants occurred in non-cluster syllable onset positions in the nuclei of intonational phrases, and chose to identify, extract and analyse all audible tokens in up to an hour of each interview. Example (1) illustrates the context for the variable: an intonational phrase with a nuclear accent falling on the penultimate syllable of the last prosodic word of BryTAnię. The token is /t/ in the onset of the nuclear syllable TA, marked in bold capital letters.

(1) Maria
Wymarzyłam   sobie   własnie   Wielka   BryTAnię
dream-PAST-FEM-1SG   REF   precisely   Great   Britain
I dreamt precisely of Great Britain

To investigate the material–semiotic dimension of discourse production and ways in which voiceless stops were responding to change, all the participants' audible tokens of surface representations were first examined by mixed-modelling analysis in R (R Development Core Team 2009) using the Rpackage nlme (Pinheiro et al. 2015). All tokens' absolute VOTs were measured in Praat, with the second measurement conducted after a few months to secure consistency. VOT was measured from the onset of the stop burst to the first zero-crossing of the first periodic wave of the vowel following the stop. Figures 3.1 and 3.2 illustrate measurements for the same word (with different case endings) for a Polish Pole and a cosmopolitan, respectively. The examples show Polish Poles' dental stop as shorter than reported VOT for standard Polish (28 ms) in Keating et al. (1981) and cosmopolitans' dental stop's VOT exceeding the highest reported value of English VOT for /t/ in natural speech (49/51 ms), which results in an audible difference.

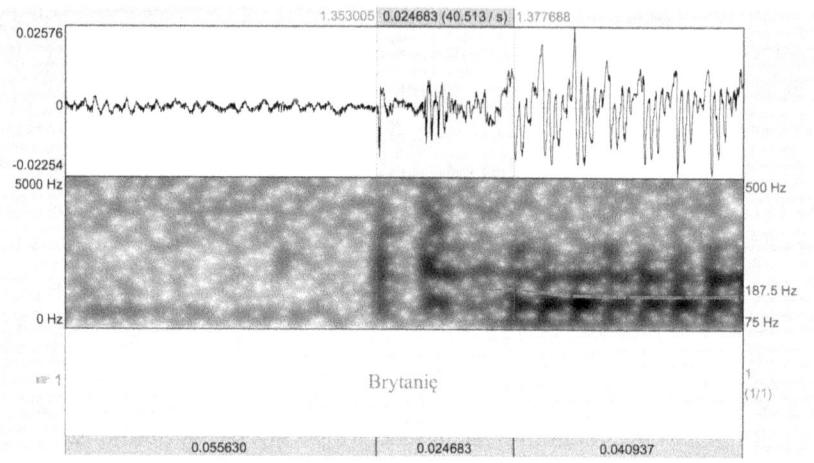

Figure 3.1 Measurement of VOT for a word-medial /t/ in *wymarzyłam sobie Wielką BryTAnię*, uttered by a Polish Pole (P9).

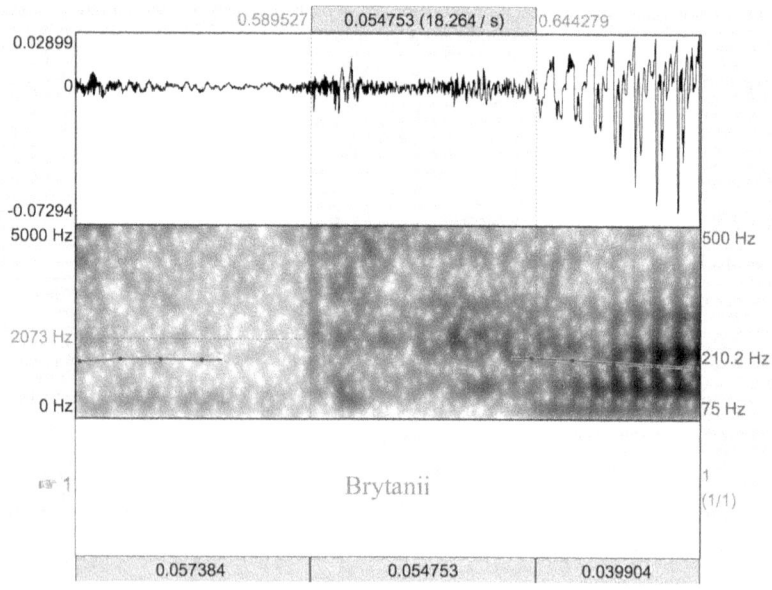

Figure 3.2 Measurement of VOT for a word-medtial /t/ in *dyskusji politycznej w Wielkiej Brytanii* uttered by a cosmopolitan (C1).

Fall-rises[5]

I now turn to my decisions regarding falling-rising intonation in declarative statements across the accounts. As the extract suggests, there was also awareness of differences in intonation among my participants. In the quote, Kaja, a 30-year-old cosmopolitan speaker living and working in East London, whose intonation was in fact changing as shown in the next chapter, pointed to the problems she had encountered when speaking English because of misinterpretations of her Polish-sounding intonation.

> naczy mam takie coś że niekiedy jak strasznie się spieszę w angielskim, to mój akcent naczy intonacja, ludziom się może wydawać że chcę im, że moja intonacja angielska, jakby mogą mnie nie zrozumieć poprawnie, jakby moje intencje tak po angielsku i to jest właśnie niekiedy jestem w tarapatach z tym właśnie, bo niektórzy ludzie w szkole jeżeli się na przykład coś spieszę i komuś coś powiem szybko, oni jakby myślą że jestem, że jakby rozkazuję im albo coś takiego, a mi się wydaje- naczy nie, boże nie w ogóle nie chciałam tego powiedzieć a mnie tak zrozumieli

> (that is, I have such a thing that sometimes when I'm in a hurry in English, my accent, that is my intonation– people might think that I want them, that my English intonation like they may not understand me correctly, like my intentions so in English and this is exactly sometimes why I'm, in trouble because of that actually because some people at school if I for example, I'm in a hurry and say something to someone quickly they like think that I'm, that like I'm ordering them or something like this and it seems to me that is no, God no not at all did I want to say that and they understood me that way)

To understand the productivity of this sign, I started my investigation with a premise that intonation was not referential, but indexical (Silverstein 2003) in nature. To me, it had a contextualizing function which consisted of cueing 'conversational interpretation by evoking interpretative schemata or frames' (Couper-Kuhlen and Selting 1996: 13) and was 'linked up to functions which derive from the situated use of language to accomplish interactional goals' (21). I observed that cosmopolitan women used an existing, but rare, Polish fall-rise pattern, more than others. To analyse its use and meaning, I employed conversation analysis and examined its general distribution. My analysis aimed at 'the reconstruction of patterns as cognitively and interactionally relevant categories which real-life interactants can be shown to orient to' (Couper-Kuhlen and Selting 1996: 48). By doing that, I followed interactional prosody studies that aimed to reconstruct the 'interactional text' which was 'laid down in real time discursive interaction' (Silverstein 1992: 58) and which was 'shaped by inferences from many contextual cues and therefore differed significantly from the effects of any particular one' (Agha 2007: 25).

In order to understand how the new intonational device helped establish positionalities, stances and alignments in interaction, I looked at how talk was locally managed and how interlocutors reacted to the interactional text. Following existing studies (Grabe and Karpinski 2002; Karpiński 2006), in my analysis, each intonational phrase had one prominent syllable (the nucleus/ the nuclear accent). The nuclear accent in Polish typically concerned terminal events in the phrase, as its unmarked position was the penultimate syllable in the phrase, with exceptions in emotional speech, when it could move towards the beginning of the phrase (Grabe and Karpinski 2002). The phrase also had a hierarchical structure at a surface phonological level. The hierarchical structure was in line with Wagner (2009), where the following elements were distinguished: utterance, major intonational phrase, minor intonational phrase, prosodic word, syllable, and in line with the Strict Layer Hypothesis that elements at one level can only dominate elements at a lower level (Selkirk 1986). The intonational phrase corresponds to the major intonational phrase (IP) in Wagner's hierarchy, where it is composed of at least one minor intonational phrase (ip) with one pitch accent. An example can be found in Figure 3.3 from an interview with Maria (P9). The nucleus falls on the penultimate syllable of the last word BryTAnię, marked in capital letters.

Based on existing observations, the fall-rise in the nuclei of declarative intonational phrases occurred in both standardized varieties, but reportedly, they differed in terms of pragmatic function and frequency of occurrence. In Polish, the nuclear intonation patterns reported for the tonic syllable in declaratives were: falling, rising, falling-rising. The most frequent pattern was the fall (Biedrzycki 1972; Francuzik et al. 2002; Grabe and Karpiński 2002; Karpiński 2006; Ropa 1981; Wodarz 1962). Rising intonation was also observed, but with much lower frequency (Karpiński 2006) and fall-rise occurred very rarely in limited contexts (Karpiński 2006). Karpiński (2006) stated that falling/

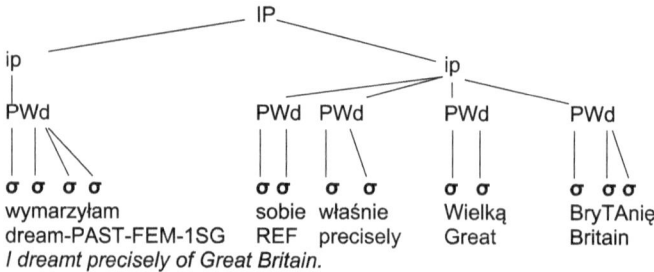

Figure 3.3 An intonational phrase, *wymarzyłam sobie właśnie Wielką Brytanię*, 'I dreamt precisely of Great Britain', produced by P9.

low tones were used for closed, complete, definitive utterances; and rising/high tones for open, incomplete utterances. He acknowledged rare occurrences of fall-rises in utterances expressing approval and admiration, and of rise-falls in utterances expressing surprise and disbelief. When observed, the fall-rise was said to occur in emotional contexts (Karpinski 2006) or if the speaker wanted to imply something (Mackiewicz-Krassowska 1973).

Similarly to Polish, 'English' declarative intonational phrases were reported to be realized with falling and rising intonation, but also with falling-rising and rising-falling intonation. The most frequent pattern for declaratives in Standard British English was falling (Grabe and Karpiński 2002; Grabe et al. 2005; Wells 2006). Rising intonation, especially high-rising terminals, was observed in multiple contexts (e.g. Cruttenden 1995; Levon 2014; Shobbrook and House 2003). Falling-rising intonation in declarative intonational phrases was claimed to occur in the London and Cambridge varieties of English (Grabe et al. 2005; Karpiński 2002), that is, where my study was conducted. In English, various meanings were also ascribed to the intonational tones. For example, Gussenhoven (1984) argued that falling intonation was used to introduce the background information and rising intonation was 'non-committal about whether a mentioned entity is part of the background', while falling-rising intonation was used to 'select an entity from the background' (Ladd 1996: 99). Falling-rising intonation was also observed to project continuation of talk (Local 1992).

In both standardized varieties, the falling intonation pattern was the default pattern for declaratives. Both also made selective use of rising intonation in declarative phrases. However, they differ in terms of the fall-rise in terms of both frequency of occurrence and context of use. My analysis indicated that the variability among speakers had to do with the ways they maintained the floor in conversation. In Polish, the floor was usually maintained by means of the unfolding of the propositional content, occasional lengthening of final sounds, fillers and other non-linguistic cues. Additionally, rising intonation was observed to be used to signal continuation of a sequence or as a way to control the floor (Karpinski 2006). Falling-rising intonation was not reported to have such a function in standard Polish.

However, in English, both rises and fall-rises were reportedly used for this purpose. Rising intonation, particularly high-rising terminal, was frequently reported. The feature was very often used by young speakers (e.g. McLemore 1991). It was also linked to the so-called New Yuppies (Cruttenden 1995) in Britain. Levon (2014) described high-rising terminal as a feature used to control the floor in interaction mostly by White women and to a lesser extent Black and

Asian men in context-independent situations. The use of high-rising terminal as a floor control mechanism was observed in other Anglo contexts, for example, Australia (Guy et al. 1986), New Zealand (Warren 2005) and the United States (Podesva 2006). Most importantly for this study, however, fall-rises were also found to be 'projective of more talk to come' in English (Local 1992: 275). Local (1992) argued that the use of fall-rises of pre-inserts was routinely associated with continuation of talk, which differed from 'standard' Polish.

The three intonation patterns used by the participants in declarative intonational phrases are presented in Figures 3.4, 3.5 and 3.6. Each intonational phrase is annotated on four tiers: syllable (r), prosodic word (PWd), minor intonational phrase (ip) and major intonational phrase (IP), with the nucleus indicated by an arrow above the pitch contour and marked in capital letters on each tier. The IPA transcription system is used in the syllable tier.

Figure 3.4 represents an intonational phrase, *jesteśmy Polakami*, 'we are Poles', ending in a fall produced by Adam (P1). The arrow points to the nucleus. The fall begins on the nuclear syllable [ka] and plateaus on the final syllable of the last prosodic word of the phrase [mi].

In Figure 3.5, rising intonation is demonstrated in an intonational phrase, *nie mam pojęcia skąd jesteś*, 'I have no idea where you're from', uttered by Daria (I4).

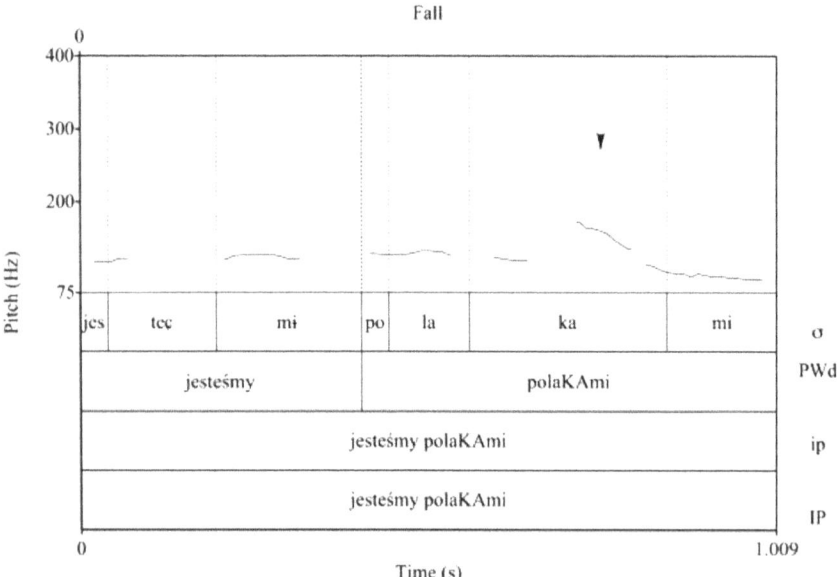

Figure 3.4 An intonational phrase, *jesteśmy Polakami*, 'we are Poles', ending with a fall produced by Adam (P1).

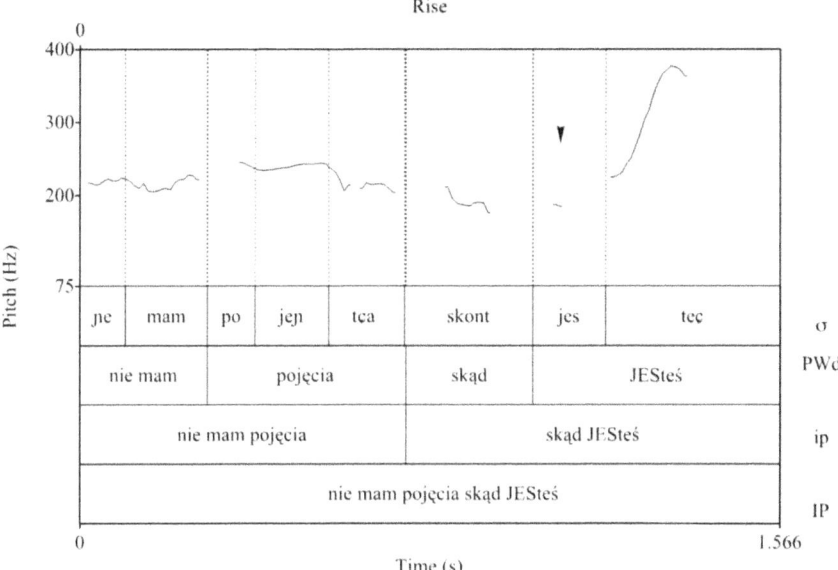

Figure 3.5 An intonational phrase, *nie mam pojęcia skąd jesteś*, 'I have no idea where you're from', ending with a rise produced by Daria (I4).

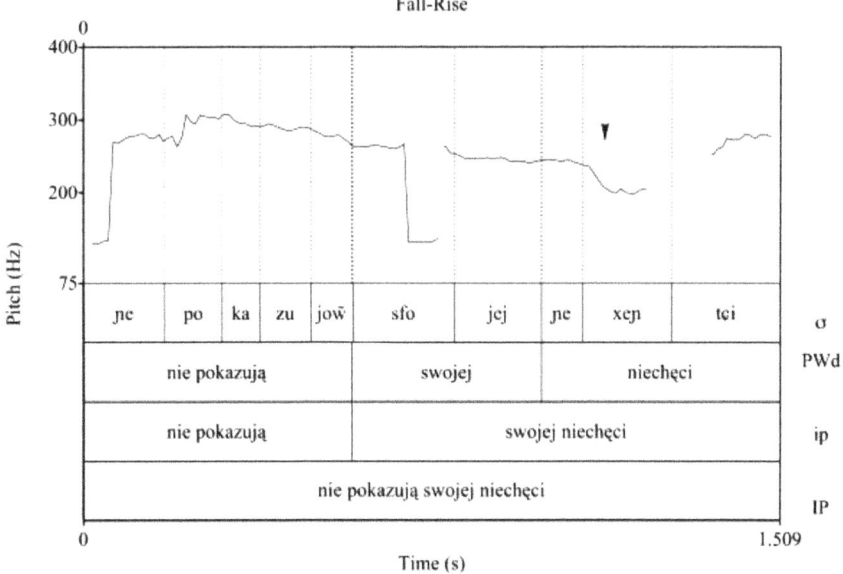

Figure 3.6 An intonational phrase, *nie pokazują swojej niechęci*, 'they don't show their aversion', produced by Natalia (C7).

The rise begins on the nucleus [jes], marked with an arrow, and is followed by a steep slope in the final syllable [teɕ] of the last prosodic word of the phrase.

Finally, Figure 3.6 is an example of a fall-rise produced by Natalia (C7). The nucleus of the phrase falls on the second syllable of the last prosodic word, *niechęci*, 'aversion', which is marked by an arrow above the contour. The intonation pattern begins with a fall on the nucleus [xɛɲ], which is followed by a rise that continues onto the final syllable of the prosodic word [tɕi].

These observations about the material forms of the signs that I was collecting made me see that the sensorial mode that I was investigating was highly malleable and its thorough investigation could guide me towards the possibilities of the discursive limits of my collected soundings. I wanted to use this knowledge to examine what the consequences of such weaves of heterogeneous semiotic–material forms and styles could be for our understanding of transnational space in this particular context. Finally, I ended up seeing that such close attention to the bodily dimension of discourse production could help me demonstrate that 'languages are not what human beings have, but what human beings are' (Mignolo and Welsh 2018), and operate within epistemic and ontological borders, rather than those of the nation-state.

4

Juxtaposing Dominant Images of Time-Space-Personhood

In order to flesh out the multiple ways in which my participants engaged in explorations of possibilities and movements of the spoken word in transnational space at the time, after I have made relevant analytical decisions, I moved on to bringing the distinct logics and rhythms in dialogue with one another. First, I wanted to establish whether my participants' observations about changes in speech could in fact be observed in my audio recordings. Hearing the differences, I first employed quantitative methods to trace the trends across the collected accounts. Due to time constraints and multiplicity of factors that I had to consider, I decided to confine my quantitative analysis to identification and close analysis of trends of two selected segmental and prosodic features constitutive of the emerging ways of speaking, both of which I named in the previous chapter. By doing so, I first wanted to draw the reader's attention to semiotic–material conditions of discourse production and their contribution to the domination of particular sociolinguistic norms and scalar metaphors.

My quantitative analysis is, however, not the only objective of this chapter, and the reader will quickly see that its larger part focuses on emerging stance-taking acts and their role in the construal of particular dominant time-space-personhood images. When doing so, they will also note that I bring contradictory logics and rhythms in relation to one another. My discourse analysis of selected interview extracts focusing on links between emerging conjunctures and observations will try to unpack the ways in which my participants were 'maintain[ing] multiple allegiances and locat[ing themselves] in multiple worlds' (Collins 2019: 32) producing situated embodied knowledges. By recognizing the sonic dimension of discourse, I will flesh out how the dynamics of this particular face-to-face sensory experience were shaping and were shaped by my participants' possibilities of action. At the same time, an acute observer will also recognize that by doing so I will not only put the spotlight onto the layering of oblique connections between these accounts, but also create a relation between them and elucidate what is at stake if we recognize that speakers always scale others, events and actions in transnational space.

Tracing trends across collective soundings[1]

In this section, I focus on a close examination of aspiration of voiceless stops, and the use of fall-rise as a floor control mechanism. Due to uneven numbers of women and men, herein I examine tendencies across emerging women's boundary projects.[2] To understand how these features patterned in weaves across my accounts, in line with established practices in sociolinguistics, I conducted quantitative analysis on all tokens coded for one dependent variable, ten independent variables (4 – sociocultural, 6 – linguistic) and one random effect, all presented in Table 4.1. As the data were not normally distributed, log-transformed VOT measurements are used. A random effect of speaker individuation was included for idiosyncratic variation, but word was not included as a random effect as word frequency was used as one of the independent variables.

To compare the three orientations among women, my mixed-modelling analysis was confined to 1408 tokens of stops produced by female speakers: 543 tokens of /p/, 546 tokens of /t/ and 319 tokens of /k/. Table 4.2 demonstrates the

Table 4.1 Variables used in statistical analysis

	Variable	Type
Dependent	Aspiration	continuous: VOT
Independent Linguistic	Following vowel	categorical, 2 levels: high, low
	Preceding phonetic segment	categorical, 2 levels: voiced, voiceless
	Speech rate[a]	continuous
	Number of syllables in a word	categorical, 3 levels: 1,2, more than 2
	Corpus word frequency[b]	continuous
	Place of articulation	categorical, 3 levels: bilabial, dental, velar
Independent Sociocultural	Ideological orientations	categorical, 3 levels: Polish Pole, in-Between, Cosmopolitan
	Number of years in the UK	continuous
Random effect	Speaker individuation	

[a] Established with Praat scripts: Lennes (2002), Ryan (2005) and de Jong and Wempe (2014)
[b] Established with Antconc (Anthony 2015)

distribution and mean VOTs for 15 women, showing that cosmopolitans have the longest mean VOTs: 35–47ms. For in-betweens, the range is: 31–36ms, while for Polish Poles: 29–38ms. All values are within a range of a Polish /k/ reported in a lab experiment (Keating et al. 1981) and English /t/ from natural speech studies (Byrd 1993).

Table 4.3 demonstrates that when significant, similarly to other projects (e.g. Mendoza-Denton 2008; Zhang 2005), linguistic context had an effect on aspiration. It supported the claim that the following vowel had a highly significant effect on VOT with longer VOTs before high vowels (Maddieson 1997). The effect of number of syllables in a word was consistent with Lisker and Abramson (1964): monosyllabic words had stops with longer VOTs than the polysyllabic ones. With bilabial stops as a default category, the effect of place of articulation was significant for velar stops and supported the universal tendency for VOT values to be longer with a further place of articulation (Maddieson 1997). Due to the nature of the naturally occurring data, the degrees of freedom suggested a large number of values to vary for most variables, except ideological orientations.

With cosmopolitans treated as a default category for ideological orientation, the model showed that cosmopolitans had the longest VOT values, in-betweens came second ($p = .0021$), while Polish Poles ($p < .001$) had the shortest VOT. The interaction between sociocultural identity and place of articulation was significant for Polish Poles suggesting that they have longer VOT values for both dental and velar stops than those reported for cosmopolitans' bilabial stops. When each stop was examined separately (Kozminska 2016), ideological orientation was always significant and cosmopolitans' VOTs were the longest for each stop. In separate models for bilabial and velar stops, cosmopolitans were followed by in-betweens, while Polish Poles came last. For dental stops, cosmopolitans had the longest VOT values, but Polish Poles came before in-betweens.

Crucially, length of stay in Britain was not significant, suggesting that longer exposure to English did not determine aspiration. With all participants reporting fairly similar contact with Polish either in offline sites in the UK or via communication technologies and with similarly international networks of cosmopolitans and in-betweens, cosmopolitans' VOTs could not be explained in terms of proficiency. Contact with English alone could not explain the differences between cosmopolitans and in-betweens. Neither did interaction between speech rate and proficiency become apparent. Rather, the use of the English feature was dependent on a dominant ideological orientation, which may influence contact with the two varieties.

Table 4.2 Mean VOT(ms), standard deviations and number of all stops for fifteen women (N=1408)

Speaker	Mean VOT (ms)	Standard deviation	Number of tokens	Speaker	Mean VOT (ms)	Standard deviation	Number of tokens	Speaker	Mean VOT (ms)	Standard deviation	Number of tokens
P2	29	13	115	I1	36	13	79	C1	45	18	99
P6	38	14	81	I2	31	16	84	C3	47	16	75
P9	31	14	155	I3	33	11	109	C4	35	11	77
P14	30	14	103	I4	33	14	40	C6	42	16	92
P16	30	17	107	I5	36	17	131	C7	46	17	61

Table 4.3 Results for significant fixed effects for all stops (N=1408); reference levels: VowelHigh, SyllablesInAWord1, PlaceOfArticulationBilabial, IdentityCosmopolitan, Cosmopolitan:Bilabial. * p≤ 0.05; ** p≤ 0.01; *** p≤ 0.001

Variable	Value	Detransformed VOT	Std.Error	DF	t-value	p-value
Intercept	4.15	64	0.24	1377	17.08	0
VowelLow	-0.26	49	0.05	1377	-5.09	0.0000***
SyllablesInAwordMoreThan2	-0.14	55	0.05	1377	-2.81	0.0051**
PlaceOfArticulationVelar	0.28	84	0.09	1377	3.16	0.0016**
IdentityIn-between	-0.27	49	0.07	10	-4.1	0.0021**
IdentityPolish Pole	-0.5	39	0.07	10	-7.72	0.0000***
Polish Pole: Dental	0.33	88	0.06	1377	5.7	0.0000***
Polish Pole:Velar	0.26	83	0.07	1377	3.82	0.0001***

The quantitative analysis suggested some dominant trends showing that the body offered particular affordances and some combinations of linguistic and sociocultural factors were more likely to result in higher VOT values. Crucially, it also suggested that although each speaker's grammatical system was different (Mufwene 2020), this feature was accessed and shared across cosmopolitan women's accounts. My close listening exercise also indicated that this was not the only feature that differed from standardized norms reported for Polish. I hence now examine how sociolinguistic and discourse analytic tools may help understand unexpected forms of knowledge production, at not only segmental but also prosodic levels.

Fall-rises

When I considered surface representations of intonational contours for all women, the corpus of declarative intonational phrases resembled other findings for Polish (Francuzik et al. 2002; Karpiński 2006) as falling intonation was the most frequent. Table 4.4 shows the number of tokens and percentages for all women.

The fall occurred in 85 per cent of all nuclei (65–97 per cent). The rises and fall-rises occurred 6–9 per cent of all tokens, respectively. As expected, rising

Table 4.4 Distribution of all intonation patterns (fall, rise, fall-rise) for fifteen women

Interview	Fall		Rise		Fall-Rise		Total
	N	%	N	%	N	%	N
P2	971	90	76	7	29	3	1076
P6	822	93	52	6	13	1	887
P9	1203	87	113	8	66	5	1382
P14	1047	88	132	11	8	1	1187
P16	881	91	36	4	55	6	972
I1	631	83	76	10	54	7	761
I2	628	82	84	11	51	7	763
I3	1069	97	24	2	9	1	1102
I4	621	89	38	5	37	5	696
I5	1304	94	38	3	51	4	1393
C1	533	65	112	14	180	22	825
C3	756	75	24	2	223	22	1003
C4	632	72	66	7	184	21	882
C6	1185	84	72	5	151	11	1408
C7	536	66	39	5	234	29	809
Total	12819	85	982	6	1345	9	15146

intonation for declaratives was observed (2–14 per cent), and there were no clear differences between the three orientations. In contrast, there was a trend for cosmopolitan women to make much greater use of the fall-rise than the others (11–29 per cent, compared to 1–7 per cent for Polish Poles and in-betweens), with most producing over 20 per cent. The raw distribution of all declaratives showed that the fall is by far the most frequent for all and rising intonation occurs at a frequency similar to that reported in other studies (Grabe and Karpinski 2002; Karpinski 2006). The occurrence of fall-rises was however new.

These percentages did not tell me much about the functions of the new intonational device employed by the female cosmopolitans. I had to look at the raw distribution of all 1345 tokens of fall-rises according to their discursive function as defined during Conversation Analysis to see whether the groups differed in their usage. Four functions are analysed in Table 4.5: emotional speech, implication, continuation of talk and 'other' (e.g. emphatic contexts). The new function, continuation of talk, occurred most frequently for all women, showing that all have picked it up. For all but two participants, the percentage of fall-rises used to project more talk to come exceeds 50 per cent (all female cosmopolitans – over 87 per cent). For female cosmopolitans, the number of tokens was also much higher than for other groups. For Polish Poles, the range

Table 4.5 Distribution of fall-rises across fifteen women according to discursive function

Interview	Emotional		Implication		Continuation		Other		Total
	N	%	N	%	N	%	N	%	N
P2	0	0	8	28	16	55	5	17	29
P6	0	0	0	0	11	85	2	15	13
P9	0	0	6	9	48	73	12	18	66
P14	0	0	1	12.5	6	75	1	12.5	8
P16	3	5	2	4	42	76	8	15	55
I1	2	4	16	30	32	59	4	7	54
I2	0	0	6	12	39	76	6	12	51
I3	1	11	3	33	4	44	1	11	9
I4	2	5	6	16	23	62	6	16	37
I5	3	6	16	31	19	37	13	25	51
C1	0	0	2	1	170	94	8	4	180
C3	0	0	0	0	222	99.5	1	0.5	223
C4	0	0	1	1	179	97	4	2	184
C6	0	0	4	3	142	94	5	3	151
C7	0	0	14	6	203	87	17	7	234
Total	11	1	85	6	1156	86	93	7	1345

was 55–85 per cent, while for in-betweens it was 37–76 per cent. All other functions displayed much lower levels of occurrence: emotional – 0–10 per cent, implication – 0–31 per cent, other – 0–25 per cent. Most notably, for all cosmopolitan women, the percentages of occurrence of all other three functions did not exceed 7 per cent. When the discursive functions were compared to the functions reported for standard Polish, all speakers employed fall-rises in a new way, i.e. to project more talk to come. However, one group, cosmopolitan women, made greater use of the new intonational device, which was manifested in both the numbers of tokens and percentages of declaratives with fall-rises used to express continuation of talk.

In line with Bucholtz and Hall (2016) and embodied cognitive science, the analysis of the two features stressed that 'linguistic knowledge is grounded in the body's perceptual and motor systems' (174). General trends suggested that standardized phonological norms dominated collected linguistic performances for all speakers. When the focus was put on material enactments, bodily transformations and movements pushed me, however, towards thinking about webs and connections in collective forms of knowledge production, and recognition that differences were sounded out in subtle, yet meaningful, ways. This in turn led me to ask how the participants were drawing on clusters of phonetic-semiotic detail to construe particular self and collective images through their stance-taking acts, and how they were entangled in the production of perspectives and formation of their subject positions in transnational space. Paying attention to the sounded differences across emerging orientations also made me acknowledge that speakers reconfigure language over particular materialities to express and negotiate intersections of positionalities and interests. The focus on material affordances of sounded signs also shed light on *connections* between the ways in which particular scalar metaphors and rhythms were becoming more dominant. I therefore decided to move towards examining how scales of relevance were reassembled through pragmatically achieved, relational sociophonetic actions and reactions in these situated public research encounters.

In the next section, I briefly introduce each dominant chronotopic frame, and analyse discursive orientations of the self towards others, time and space, foregrounding how sounded signs were affecting relationality between interlocutors, forms of knowledge and thoughts and their role in setting limits and enabling possibilities for new angles of vision. To do so, I focus on the chaining of stance configurations in the three ideological orientations: the ways in which my participants were construing images of normality, how they were scaling themselves and others in time and space, and what labelling practices and other linguistic devices were used to link selected events, actions and practices to reconstruct their experiences in transnational space. At the same time, I draw attention to the sensory experience and its role in formation of each orientation. As suggested before, I focus on dominant chronotopic frames and emerging rhythms to reveal how some practices and ways of being, acting and seeing were created, deconstructed and reclaimed to portray legitimate subject positions in these particular situated encounters. I therefore focus on fleshing out how connections were fixed through different units of comparison and how particular contrasts were highlighted and faded away through the chaining of sounded aspects of discourse. This in turn enables me to stress the political and historical relation between social and sensory orders and its impact on perceptual knowledge and mediation of the material and social worlds in transnational space.

Enregistering dominant repetitions: 'Polish Poles'

The first dominant image that I sketch in this chapter relies on an orientation invested in the ideology of authenticity. It emerged in interviews with five women and twelve men whose accounts I classified as 'Polish Poles'. In these accounts, the image of a 'real' self was defined by roots of origin rather than the immediate offline surroundings. These participants therefore presented themselves as part of the Polish nation operating in sociohistorical timespace and indexed alignment with state-level political formations. The state was also a salient means to fix connections between units of comparison used in these participants' construal of sameness and difference. This also went in line with their sensory inclination to maintain standardized patterns of pronunciation imagined as attributes of 'real' Poles. Herein, I bring together selected excerpts to flesh out how epistemological claims were made in these accounts, what units of comparison where key for self-presentation and how standardized soundings reinforced dominant cultural metaphors.

I start with excerpt (1) which demonstrates alignment with the state formation in the interview with Ela, a 25-year-old woman who had spent six years in the UK, and, at the time, was working in advertising in London.

(1) Ela (P16)[3,4]
1 KK: na czym polega ta twoja relacja /z Polską
       what does your relationship with Poland consist in?

2 P16: nie no na pewno jest ważna bo mimo że mieszkam tutaj to jestem \P(16ms)olką
no for sure it is important because even if I live here I'm Polish

3   i (.)   z (h) małymi wyjątkami   nigdy bym się tego nie \wyp(23ms)arła (.)
and (.) with small exceptions (h) I would never deny that (.)

4 KK: mhm

5 P16: jakby uważam że to JEST bardzo coś co mnie definiuje jako \osobę
like I think that that is something that really defines me as a person

6 KK: mhm

7 P16: e (0.2) jakby to jest szcze- szczególnie mieszkając za \[granicą
uhm (0.2) like esp-   especially when living [abroad

8 KK: [mhm]

9 P16: to jest BARdzo ważna cześć tego kim TY \jesteś
it's a very important part of who you are

Similarly to other Polish Poles, when the topic of the relationship with Poland emerged in discourse and I asked Ela for an explanation, she positioned herself towards the question by stressing the importance of ethnic identification for life in transnational space. Although her response began with a discourse marker *nie no* 'no [emphasis]', she immediately aligned herself with the state formation with an emphatic *na pewno* 'for sure' and evaluative adjective *ważna* 'important' (2). When construing her self-image as aligned with the Polish nation, she provided further explanation in (2) and anchored her turn in the here and now by means of deixis of place *tutaj* 'here' and present tense with one person singular marking on the verb *jestem* 'I am'. By doing so, she also made an ontological claim about herself being *Polką* 'a Pole(FEM)', which was reinforced by sounding standard in (2) and throughout the stance-act. In (5), Ela added information and repeated that ethno-racialized identification was important for self-identification, with increased volume on the existential *JEST* 'is' in the present form, indicating permanence. This was further reinforced by her adding 'especially living abroad'(7), which implied the state logic as a reference point, and was linked with the repeated content *very important*, also uttered with increased volume on a degree word *BARdzo* 'very' (9). She therefore completed her stance towards self-identification by predominantly relying on the unfolding of the propositional content, default standard Polish falling intonation on declaratives and pronunciation patterns similar to those reported for Polish.

When weaving connections between the stance-acts, Polish Poles usually explained their need for self-identification as Polish as a way to find their place in

British social structure, where others saw them as Poles/Eastern Europeans. Such strong othering UK discourses were mentioned by Marek, a 25-year-old man working in the corporate sector in London who had lived six years in Britain. In excerpt (2), he scaled himself in relation to others explicitly positioning himself towards the othering discourses after being confronted by my yes/no question about the importance of ethnic identification.

(2) Marek (P13)[5]

1 KK:	a czy to jest dla ciebie ważne że jesteś /Polakiem	
	and is it important for you that you're Polish?	
2 P13:	tak bo- ważne bo: (0.8) ciągle myślę po \p(19ms)olsku	
	yes because- important because (0.8) I still think in Polish	
3	no nie \ciągle czasami myślę po \p(19ms)olsku	
	maybe not constantly sometimes I think in Polish	
4	i- a druga rzecz to jest to że .hhh inni ludzie też cię widzą jako \Polaka	
	and- and another thing is that other people also see you as a Pole	
5 KK:	°mhm°	
6 P13:	y zawsze ktoś tam ma jakiś- asocjuje \stereot(29ms)ypy	
	uh always someone has some- associates stereotypes	
7	albo- albo przynajmniej kategoryzuje ludzi w różne \szufladki	
	or- or at least categorizes people into different boxes	
8	i- i że wiem że ludzie będą mnie widzieć jako \Polaka	
	and-and that I know that people will see me as a Pole	
9	albo kogoś z Europy \Wschodniej więc jeżeli już mnie mają widzieć jako \tak(57ms)iego	
	or someone from Eastern Europe so if they have to see me as such	
10	to powinienem e (0.2) wziąć to na własne \barki czy tam jak to się \mówi	
	then I should uh take the strain or however one says it	
11	i \żyć z tym	
	and live with it	
12 KK:	okay(h)	
13 P13:	i \nie chcę uważać się za kogoś kim nie \jestem	
	and I don't want to think I'm someone who I am not	

Marek concurred with *tak bo- ważne* 'yes because- important' (2). In the subsequent four phrases (2–3), he positioned himself towards the object of the question by listing facts: asserted that he still thought in Polish, linking the language to the self, and that others saw him as a Pole. After I signalled understanding with *mhm* (5), he used standard Polish cues for signalling continuation of talk and provided further explanation in lines (6–9). In (6), he began to situate his response within historical timespace by asserting that people *zawsze* 'always' rely on stereotypes (6) with the habitual present verb form and *stereotypy* 'stereotypes' pronounced in line with reported norms for Polish VOT and default falling intonation for declaratives. He then repeated the content with the English calque with Polish morphosyntax *asocjuje stereotypy* 'associates stereotypes' in the present form and used a bivalent verb again with Polish morphosyntax *kategoryzuje* 'categorizes' followed by the standard Polish *w różne szufladki* 'into different boxes', throughout sounding standard. In (8), he moved on to position *ludzie* 'people' in contrast to the first-person singular pronoun *mnie* 'me' who will be seen as a Pole, pointing to the unchanging character of the self as defined by origins. When positioning himself in relation to actors in social space, he therefore relied on state-level and geopolitical divisions. This was further reinforced in (9), when he referred to his unchanging Eastern European origins. When weaving connections in his account, he evaluated the content asserting that if he was to be seen as *takiego* 'such', again pronounced with standard pronunciation and followed by a standard filler *e*, he should *wziąć to na własne barki,* literally 'take it on own arms'. This way he took ownership of the stance, which he reinforced by repeating the content *żyć z tym* 'live with it'. When construing his situated self-image, he finished the turn with default falling intonation signalling definitiveness, a cue that I took up as I then uttered an established English loanword *okay* and expressed surprise with a very small burst of laughter. Marek did not pick up the non-linguistic cue, but rather provided further information aligning with the othering processes and arguing that he 'does not want to think of himself as someone whom he is not'. In his final turn, he reinforced his alignment with the initial proposition and state-level identification and projected an authentic Polish identity. Throughout the turn, he took his stance towards the question through the repetition of propositional content describing othering processes in Britain and repeatedly asserting that it was his responsibility to 'be Polish'.

Crucially, in all Polish Poles' accounts, realness and authenticity were imagined in relation to the state of origin. However, the accounts displayed a palette of degrees of ideological intensification. As suggested before, for all participants, one's identity was not static, but for Polish Poles, it was revealed through the logic of the nation-state, chronological order of one's life experiences portrayed against sociohistorical background and tightly linked to the semiotic, including linguistic, codes authenticating one's ethnicity. Operating within the logic of the nation-state, when scaling others, in the accounts, Polish Poles usually defined themselves in relation to other national groups in the UK as this contrast became more salient in these accounts than internal differences within the Polish-speaking population. In their self-presentations, they also embraced Polish culture and language, which was reflected in their high Polishness Index scores (7–9), with Polish network scores between 20 and 83 per cent.[6] Such a presentation was mostly disentangled from class distinctions, with some participants only occasionally asserting that their Polish practices were confined to particular networks and groups in the UK. They also typically explained their presence in Britain in relation to the overall socio-economic situation in Poland, mentioning young adults' difficulties in transitioning from the university to the workplace.

Such a logic was visible in Marek's account in excerpt (3). Marek was also the only self-identified gay man in my project, who was born and raised in Białystok, a city in Eastern Poland, which as suggested before, was often associated with nationalistic movements in 2010s. In the extract, we see how he imagined and negotiated realness in relation to his nonheteronormative experiences in transnational space. In (1), like other Polish Poles, he explained it in relation to the state he was born into and where he lived most of his life. In (2), he also linked it to the ability to speak Polish, stressing that these two facts defined him as Polish, and sounding standard. In (5), he then went on to question the relationship between realness and race and other factors, repeating the content with the standardized rhythm. Shortly afterwards, he linked his reflections on Polishness to the current locality by referring to London's multicultural dynamics, with which he aligned and from which he distanced himself at the same time. To do so, he first described London with an English calque *wrzący garnek* 'melting pot', providing explanation in (8) and positively evaluating it in (9) *na pewno to jest dobre* 'for sure it's good'. Relying on the unfolding of the propositional content, in line with standardized Polish norms, he maintained the floor and contrasted the positive evaluation with an emphatic prepositional phrase 'for me personally' followed by an assertion: 'it neither bothers me' 'nor attracted me' (10). Unlike in other Polish Poles' accounts, Marek's stance towards realness as a function of being part of a nation was, however, later contrasted with extreme conservatism of some parts of Polish society. In (11–13), he listed aspects of social life 'that don't suit me': independence marches, Fundacja Mamy i Taty, both associated with nationalistic and anti-LGBTQ+ rhetoric. This led him to assert that as a gay man he had 'bad memories' connected with 'some aspects of Polish politics'. However, rather than seeing homophobic aspects of public life in Poland as a factor to negate his affiliation with the state, in (15), he made an epistemological claim beginning with *wiem* 'I know' in which he asserted that his possible return to Poland would not be explained in relation to homophobic encounters. Instead, like all Polish Poles, he later explained a possible decision to return in relation to socio-economic factors and work. When taking the stance, although drawing occasionally on English morphosyntax, he completed his stance sounding standard at phonetic level and presented a less purified understanding of realness.

(3) Marek (P13)

1 P13: to że że urodziłem się i spędziłem większość swojego życia jeszcze \w Polsce
that that I was born and spent most of my life already in Poland

2 i TO że mówię po \p(bad quality)olsku to dwie dwie rzeczy pewnie
and that I speak Polish   these are the two two things that probably

3 które definiują mnie jako \Polaka według mnie-
define me as a Pole   in my opinion

4 KK: dobrze a a-
right and, and-

5 P13: nie wydaje mi się żeby to miałoby związek z genetyką rasą kolorem \skóry i tak \dalej
I don't think it's linked to genetics, race, skin colour   and so on

6 czyli równie dobrze uważam za Polaka osobę która urodziła się \w Polsce albo
so equally I see a Pole in a person who was born in Poland   or

7 przyjechała do Polski jako małe \dziecko i też tam spędziła większość \życia
came to Poland as a small child   and spent most of their life there

...

When talking about London:

8 wrzący \garnek różnych idei i kultur które tutaj \amalgamują się
a melting pot   of various ideas and cultures which amalgamate here

9 no więc tak tak na pewno to jest \dobre ale dla mnie \osobiście
so yes, yes for sure it's good   but for me personally

10 ani to nie \przeszkadza ani ani to nie jest- nie nie że mnie to \przyciągnęło \nie
it neither bothers me   nor nor it is-   no, not that it attracted me,   no

...

When talking about aspects he dislikes about Poland:

11 P13: no w Polsce nie pasuje mi pewnie-   taki prawico- skrajnie prawicowy
so in Poland what doesn't suit me probably-this right-wing-ultra-right-wing

12	konserwatyzm niektórych \ludzi prawda jakieś tam marsze niepodległości /prawda
	conservatism of some people right such independence marches right?
13	Fundacja Mamy i Taty czy jak ona się tam \nazywa
	Fundacja Mamy i Taty [foundation of Mom and Dad] or whatever it's called
14	bo ja jako- jako geja to też mam jako wiesz no- pewnie złe \wspomnienia
	because I as- as a gay man so also then have you know- probably bad memories
15	jeśli chodzi o pewne aspekty polityki \w Polsce ale wiem że to –
	when it comes to some aspects of Polish politics but I know that it-
16	jeżeli bym wrócił do \P(24ms)olski to wcale bym nie myślał całymi \dniami
	if I went back to Poland then I wouldn't think all day
17	och jak mi tutaj jest \źle
	oh how horrible it is here for me

At the other end of the continuum of ideological intensification, the realness was occasionally, however, linked not only to the state of origin, but also an explicit nationalistic stance towards Polishness, that is to say, the idea of pure Poles without any foreign traits, in line with reported preferences for purification in some parts of Polish society (Bolagun 2020). Admittedly, views linking realness to a belief in purity were very rarely exposed. Importantly, even in those situations, it was not defined as a biological essence, but rather an ideal that one chooses to believe in in transnational space. We see such an attitude in excerpt (4), when Kamil, a 27-year-old man who had lived eight years in the UK and at the time was working in the corporate sector in London, reflected on his understanding of ethno-racialized divisions and sociocultural space in Poland. Kamil first produced a negated propositional phrase beginning with *to nie jest tak* 'it's not that' (1), which enabled him to show that he was aware of the fact that Poland was not composed only of *czystych Polaków* 'pure Poles'. This was followed by my exclamation *oo* and a small gasp. Kamil did not take up the non-linguistic cue, but rather the internal variation in Poland faded away as discourse unfolded. He contrasted his assertion by means of *z drugiej strony* 'on the other hand' (3), with a propositional phrase anchored in the present by means of the present continuous verb form *trwa* 'lasts' indicating that this idea lasts 'in one's head'. To take his stance, Kamil repeated the content, evaluated it as 'perhaps fake', and produced a discourse marker 'I don't know', before asserting 'but this is an ideal I have believed in for a long time' (5). When asked for confirmation, in (7–10), he explicitly aligned with the image of a pure Pole, and linked it to 'living abroad', where the ideal guided his behaviour. While taking the stance, he sounded standard throughout the excerpt.

(4) Kamil (P3)

1 P3:   to też nie jest tak że Polska składa się z samych takich czystych \Polaków
        it also isn't so that Poland is composed of only such pure Poles

2 KK: oo (h)

3 P3:   z drugiej strony to jest jakaś idea która gdzieś tam w głowie \trwa
        on the other hand it is an idea that lasts somewhere there in one's head

4   żeby być takim czystym Polakiem bez żadnych \naleciałości
        to be such a pure Pole without any foreign traits

5   może to jest \sztuczne nie wiem   ale to jest jakiś taki ideał który mi przyświecał
        maybe it's fake   I don't know   but this is such an ideal that I have believed in

6   przez długi \czas
        for a long time

7 KK: czyli tobie przyświecał taki ideał /tak   że chciałeś tak myśleć o /sobie
        so this is an ideal you believed in, right? that you wanted to think about yourself this way?

8: P3: tak   że jestem za /granicą długi czas ale jednak jestem \Polakiem
        yes   that I've been abroad for a long time but I am still a Pole

9   reprezentuję Polskę reprezentuję polskość jakoś \t(17ms)am
        I represent Poland, I represent Polishness in a way

10   tym kim \jestem tym jak się zachowuję i co \mówię i tak \dalej
        by who I am   by the way I behave and what I say and so on

When scaling the self in relation to others, time and space, in these accounts, the construal of the images also relied on gendered distinctions. This resulted in differences in orientations to the future. Most men expressed a wish to return to Poland in the near future as international experience would allow them to find permanent well-paid employment, preferably high-rank positions in business and politics. This was not true for the gay man who expressed a wish to return in distant future. As noted in Chapter 1, women also did not express such a wish usually arguing that they enjoyed their lives in Britain. However, at the same time, women often wove their understanding of gender roles in relation to their embracing of Polish culture as a whole. This often led them to align with more traditional images of femininity and family values, and to making explicit references to differences in sociocultural expectations between the two nation-states.

Such a situated juxtaposition and comparison of gendered stereotypes was woven through standardized linguistic expression as can be seen in excerpt (5), when Ewa, a 25-year-old woman who had spent five years in the UK and at the time was working in the corporate sector in London, brought the topic of Polish traditions up. Excerpt (5) came after her assertion that she enjoyed the fact that the British value traditions and openness, which she compared to her stay in France, which she evaluated as less open towards immigrants. In the excerpt she also linked traditions to particular images of femininity and gender roles, and aligned with Polish culture and expectations and circulating images of the Mother-Pole. In excerpt (5), she listed factors important for her life-making such as attachment to traditions, with vowel lengthening at the end of *tradycji* (1), in line with standard Polish norms to maintain the floor. This enabled her to introduce the concept of 'values that guide us' in (1), maintaining the floor with rising intonation, thus sounding standard. She then scaled the values in relation not only to the Polish state, but Eastern Europe. When doing so, she relied on the first person plural 'our part of Europe', assuming uniformity, and explicitly contrasting it with *koleżanek z Anglii które są w podobnym wieku* 'female friends from the UK, same age' and their lack of consideration for marriage (4) and having a family. In (5), she contrasted the mentioned content by *a* 'but' followed by an emphatic first-person pronoun *ja* 'I' and habitual verb form *myślę* and degree word *dużo* 'I think about it a lot'. To support the claim, she provided more evidence 'I have good friends from Latvia' and aligned with them *bardziej* 'more' than with the British. Throughout her turn she construed her self-image relying on standard Polish norms, both morphosyntax and phonetic detail, and therefore aligned with dominant images of the Mother-Pole in line with dominant rhythms.

(5) Ewa (P2)

1 P2: właśnie tak jak powiedziałam przywiązanie do \tradycji: jakieś wartości którymi się /kierujemy
exactly as I've said attachment to traditions   some values that guide us

2   które wydaje mi się że-   które ludzie może nie tylko \z Polski   ale z naszej części \/Europy
     which seem to me that-   which people maybe not only from Poland but our part of Europe

3   są są do nich bardziej \przywiązani i na przykład-   chyba raczej większość moich koleżanek y:
     are, are very much attached to   and for example-   probably most of my female friends

4   \z Anglii   które są w podobnym wieku raczej nie myśli o \małżeństwie   o zakładaniu \rodziny
     from England who are the same age are not thinking about marriage   about setting up a family

5   a ja o tym myślę \dużo: nie wiem mam akurat mam dobrych przyjaciół \z Łotwy
     and I think about it a lot   I don't know I have exactly I have good friends from Latvia

6   i wydaje mi się że oni są trochę bardziej do nas \podobni
     and it seems to me that they are a bit more similar to us

When the participants were comparing entities appropriate for desired linguistic and sociocultural conduct, as mentioned earlier, in these accounts, the ability to speak standard Polish was often linked to the self and presented as a practice authenticating one's ethno-racialized identification. In the interviews, most Polish Poles claimed that they did not use too much English in their Polish. Some presented themselves as linguistic purists, which was evident even in the interview setting. For example, throughout his account, Adam, an active member of the UK Polish community organizations with an expressed intention to play an important role at the community level, repeatedly used the word *twarzoksiążka* to refer to Facebook, an English word which together with a few of its diminutive forms was usually used in Poland at the time. In one case, such an attitude expressed by Bartosz, who was also very active in the community and who by some was jokingly called 'the king of Polonia', led to his picking on my usage of *ok*, which was commonly used in Poland and asserting 'we would try not to use it'. Instead, he proposed to use *w porządku*. Such instances pointed to fractal recursivity as some Polish Poles were becoming hypercorrect. This, however, tended to be confined to lexical and phonetic levels, while syntactic influence was often evaluated as 'normal'. This is visible in a self-remark produced during the interview by Paweł, a 25-year-old man who had spent five years in the UK and at the time, was working in the corporate sector in London. In the quote, he identified one grammatical construction *powiedziawszy to* as a calque from English, which he evaluated as 'today perhaps my favourite phrase' and 'not in Polish', but pronounced in line with reported Polish pronunciation patterns.

(6) Paweł (P10)

1 P10: powiedziawszy to co jest dzisiaj chyba moim ulubionym /wyrażeniem   i też nie jest po \p(23ms)olsku
       having said that   which is today perhaps my favourite phrase   and also isn't in Polish

2   bo to jest dokładna kalka having said \that
       because it's an exact calque of having said that

Sensory inclinations verbalized in these accounts suggest that the participants' aesthetic engagement had primarily to do with the sonic dimension of discourse, where mixing at phonetic level was usually negatively evaluated. This can be seen in excerpt (7) produced by Maria, a 27-year-old Polish Pole who had spent eight years in the UK and was working in the corporate sector in London. In the interview, similarly to other Polish Poles, Maria linked speaking Polish with an English accent to pretending to be someone whom one is not (9), which echoed earlier comments about authenticity. In this excerpt, changes in the sonic aspects of discourse were selected, linked to the 'real' self and negatively evaluated through the snobbish vs. down-to-earth opposition fractally projected onto the UK Polish diaspora.

(7) Maria (P9)[7]

1 P9:	no ale po polsku- ja jestem \z Polski		
	but in Polish? I'm from Poland		

2 KK: mhm

3 P9:	więc dlaczego miałabym mieć (.) brytyjski \akcent i <też nie	
	so why should I have a British accent (.) and <I have	
4	mam dla siebie wymówki> żeby mieć angielski akcent bo gdybym mieszkała tutaj	
	no excuse for myself > to have an English accent because if I lived here	
5	/sama nie jeździła do \P(34ms)olski i nie miała polskich \znajomych	
	alone didn't go to Poland and didn't have Polish friends	

6 KK: mhm

7 P9:	to czuję że to by było bardziej <\akceptowalne> a że ja mówię po \p(25ms)olsku to ja czuję że
	I feel it would be more acceptable but because I speak Polish so I feel that I
8	no byłabym jakimś takim snobem \strasznym i strasznie arogancka jakbym nagle
	would be an awful snob and very arrogant if suddenly
9	pojechała do \P(32ms)olski i zaczęła (h) mówić <jakbym miała żabę \w buzi> i udawała
	I went to Poland and began speaking as if I had a frog in my mouth and pretended
10	że jestem z Wielkiej \Bryt(28ms)anii także mi się wydaje że to by było trochę \żałosne
	that I was from Great Britain so I think it would be a bit pathetic

Later in the interview, Maria also reflected on observed practices of other speakers of Polish and differentiated herself from such people presenting the Polish language as revealing individual character in historical timespace. To do so, she performed an act of semantic authority over the object of her answer to the question about new ways of speaking expressing seriousness and power within standard Polish norms. The extract began with a question about the difference between Maria and those sounding nonstandard, whom she had described in her previous turn.

(8) Maria (P9)[8]

1 KK:	czyli myślisz że na czym polega różnica między tobą i twoimi \znajomymi	
	so what do you think the difference between you and your friends consists in	
2	i takimi ludźmi którzy tak \robią że że z czego to /wynika	
	and such people who are doing it that that what causes this?	

3 P9:	tak jak mi się- >tak jak \mówiłam< z \sytuacji		w której się \znajdujesz
	as I- *as I said*	*on a situation*	*in which you are*
4	ile mówisz po \p(22ms)olsku		
	how much you speak Polish		
5 KK:	mhm		
6 P9:	to myślę że to jest jedna \rzecz(h) a druga to nawet nie wiem jak to \określić		
	so I think this is one thing	*and the second I don't even know how to define it*	
7	czy to jest /wychowanie	czy to jest jakiś taki /światop(27ms)ogląd	
	if it's upbringing?	*if it's such a worldview?*	
8 KK:	mhm		
9 P9:	eeem czy wła:śnie nastawienie do /języka		
	uhm or precisely an attitude towards the language?		
10	no bo mi się wydaje że właśnie ja chciałam iść na \polonistykę		
	because it seems to me that I also precisely wanted to study Polish studies		
11	też przez jakiś \czas	więc dla mnie ten polski był bardzo bliski: .hhh mojemu \sercu	
	also for some time	*so for me this Polish has been very close to my heart*	
12	więc ja nie chcę go \kaleczyć	ale jakbym miała ten język \gdzieś	
	so I don't want to barbarize it	*but if I didn't care about the language*	
13	to no jak mi łatwiej się \komunik(42ms)ować	tak będę \mówić	
	then what's easier for me to communicate	*then I'll speak like that*	

Maria began her response by producing a truncated phrase followed by a sped-up clarification. In (3–4), she linked her answer to her previous turns and listed reasons why Polish speakers acted differently in Britain: individual circumstances and contact with Polish. Each phrase finished with standard default falling intonation for declarative IPs. As I did not interrupt as the propositional content unfolded, in (6–7), Maria continued providing further reasons simultaneously disaligning from the content by asserting that she 'does not know how to define this' *nie wiem jak to określić*. When doing so, she also used rising intonation, standard Polish for questions. She then moved on to presenting changes as a result of *światopogląd* 'worldview' in (7), throughout herself sounding standard. After I signalled understanding with another *mhm* (8), Maria continued listing potential factors in (9). This led her to contrast the list pronounced with rising intonation with information about her own past, pronounced with falling intonation, which allowed her to present her stance in line with standard norms and signal definitiveness. At the same time, she deictically anchored the turn in the past, inserted an emphatic *ja* 'I', *dla mnie* 'for me' in (10, 11) and evaluated the Polish language with an affective adjectival phrase *bliski mojemu sercu* 'close to my heart'. While construing her self-image as aligned with Polish culture and language, she used the default standard fall for each IP. Finally, she concluded the turn by using a value-laden *jakbym miała ten język gdzieś* 'if I didn't care about the language' to present an alternative, negative stance towards Polish as a reason why others speak in a way that she contrasted with the not 'barbarized' language (12). Like other Polish Poles, she took the stance towards Polish relying on the unfolding of the propositional content, using Polish morphosyntax and sounding standard, which also allowed her to exercise her authority and project a 'real' Polish identity. By aligning closely with the Polish language, historical reality was also portrayed as important for her character development and similarly to other Polish Poles, linked to the true self defined by roots and origins.

In contrast, in these accounts, English was usually imagined as a separate entity, a necessary tool for communication and presented as a self-evident choice whenever there was a non-Polish-speaking person involved in multiparty conversation. However, Polish Poles did not explicitly desire speaking English to fellow Poles. This is evident in excerpt (9), where Marek, the 25-year-old man introduced earlier, compared practices observed among other national groups defined in line with the state logic, 'Germans' or 'Dutch'. In (1), Marek introduced a scenario where other nationals would speak English to one another. In (3), he contrasted this with *a* 'but' and linked the self via an emphatic *ja* 'I' to a knowledge claim 'know' in which he asserted that 'Poles will never do that'. In (5–6), he went on to repeat the assertion and provided further scenario for encounters with other speakers of Polish in line with standardized Polish norms. In (5), he evaluated the practice as *dziwne* 'weird' and in (7), concluded that 'Poles don't do that', which was reinforced by his evaluation of a person who does not conform to the norm as one with whom *coś jest nie tak* 'something is wrong' (7–8). Again, at the same time, we see that his stance was accomplished mainly by the unfolding of the propositional content, default falling intonation and standardized pronunciation patterns.

(9) Marek (P13)

1 P13: no bo właśnie nie wiem czasami jak widzisz dwóch \Niemców czy dwóch \Holendrów
    so I don't know because sometimes when you see two Germans or two Dutch people

2   w pokoju gdzie nie ma innych ludzi- oni ze sobą będą mówić po \angielsku
    in a room where there are no other people they will speak English to each other

3 a ja wiem że °Polacy° nigdy tego nie \zrobią   takie po prostu nie wyobrażam sobie że znam °kogoś°
    and I know that Poles will never do that   such I simply can't imagine that I know someone

4 i wiem że jest Polakiem-   czasami jak jestem \w sklepie   i czuję że ktoś jest \Polakiem
    and I know that he is a Pole- sometimes when I'm in a shop   and feel that someone is a Pole

5 to pytam się czy on może jest \Polakiem żeby mówić po \p(34ms)olsku bo inaczej wiem że to jest takie \dziwne
    so I ask whether he is maybe a Pole   to speak Polish   because otherwise I know that it's so weird

6 wiesz jest tutaj dwóch Polaków i próbuje ze sobą po angielsku \mówić yyy
    you know there are two Poles and they are trying to speak English to each other uhm:

7 więc Polacy tego nie \robią a jak jeden \robi to mi się wydaje że coś jest coś jest
    so Poles don't do that   and if one does   then I think there is something there is something

8 nie tak \z nim   taka moja \teoria
    wrong with him   such is my theory

The situated weaving of self and collective images presented in this section highlighted the ways in which the dominant chronotopic frame was emerging in accounts of Polish Poles through material enactments in which the self and other continued to be scaled and positioned at multiple levels. We see that in these accounts, the dominant frame organized social and linguistic experiences and practices through the ideology of authenticity, embedded in gender dynamics and highly dependent on historical and state-level ethno-racialized divisions. In these accounts, one's actions and possibilities were imagined and brought in relation to each other mostly through normative linguistic behaviour projected from the country of origin and evaluated in stark contrast to the country of residence, where othering practices and infrastructure together with its internalized ethno-racial logic facilitated acceptance of the dominant Polish-centric understanding of one's subject position, often also portrayed as in line with one's preferences. The sonic dimension of discourse also actively shaped the production of perspectives on norms and practices, where sounding standard, although replete with complex English syntactic influence, enabled one to exercise control and connect their knowledge claims to authority in line with established norms. These sensory inclinations were, however, sharply contrasted with the other end of the spectrum of ideological orientations that I collected.

Encountering new rhythms: cosmopolitans

I therefore now move on to the other end of the spectrum of emerging ideological orientations. Here I focus on the cosmopolitan accounts in which in verbalized discourse, participants distanced themselves from Polishness and rejected nationality as a basis for identity. Similarly to the previous section, I examine how this position was scaled in relation to classed, gendered and xenoracist practices and actions. At the same time, I foreground the sonic dimension of discourse and sounded differences between cosmopolitan women and men in order to flesh out how the women were construing self and collective images through embodied scale-making actions in new ways. By doing so, I want to draw the reader's attention to the role of sonic materiality in making knowledge claims and forming momentary alignments.

I start with the stance towards the relationship with the country of origin, which, in contrast to the previous section, relied on contestation of state-level ethno-racialized divisions. In excerpt (10), Natalia, a 22-year-old female graduate student and consultant from Oxford, presented such a stance-act and challenged classificatory labels associated with state-level formations. Like other cosmopolitans, she did not deny coming from Poland, but argued that it did not make her who she was. The quote is part of a longer passage in which after an emergent question about self-identification, Natalia defined herself as *człowiek* 'a human being'.

(10) Natalia (C7)[9]

1 KK: a powiedz mi na czym polega twoja /p(bad quality)olskość   bo jest jakaś polskość u /ciebie
       and tell me what does your Polishness consist in   *because there is any Polishness in you?*

2 C7: na pewno \jest   ale raczej: (0.2) nie ma żadnej świadomej krea::cji
      for sure there is   but rather there isn't any conscious creation

3 KK: mhm

4 C7: w mojej \polskości(h)
      in my Polishness

5 KK: ok

6 C7: uhm więc czuję że \/jest   ale nie: jest do końca: \/uświadomio:na
      uhm so I feel that there is   but I am not entirely aware of it

7   i raczej jest (5.0) czasami jest \/intruzem(h)   w [mojej
      and sometimes it's more an intruder   in my

8 KK: [ok]

9 C7: kreacji \/świadomej
      conscious creation

10 KK: mhm (.) to jaka jest ta twoja kreacja świadoma gdzie polskość jest /intruzem
       mhm so what is this conscious creation where Polishness is an intruder like?

11   na czym to /po<u>le</u>ga(h)
          what does it consist in?

12 C7: nie wiem-   no czuję się taka troszkę \BEZ narodowości jako /takiej
          I don't know- I feel a bit without nationality as such

Excerpt (10) began with a question about the presence of Polishness within this definition. When construing her self-image, Natalia started by concurring assertion 'for sure there is', but in (2) she disaligned from it. To do so, she relied on the unfolding of the negated propositional content 'there isn't any conscious creation' and vowel lengthening in the nucleus of the IP, resulting in my concurring *mhm* and not taking the floor. Natalia deictically positioned the object of discourse with the first-person singular possessive pronoun *mojej polskości* 'my Polishness' (4), presenting a personalized rather than traditionalist stance towards Polishness, and finished her turn with falling intonation and laughter. After I expressed understanding with the English loanword *ok*, Natalia produced an English-like filler *uhm* and continued explaining her stance arguing unlike Polish Poles, not to be consciously working on her Polishness. In (6), she produced content aligning with Polishness, but the phrase, similarly to the next two IPs, ended in a fall-rise. Like other cosmopolitan women, this way she signalled continuation of talk, in line with English, rather than Polish, interactional frameworks (Local 1992). Additionally, like other cosmopolitan women, through the fall-rise, Natalia invoked the here-and-now of the act of speaking and used the suprasegmental feature to disalign from Poland. She positioned and evaluated Polishness as the value-laden 'intruder' in her conscious creation (7–9), again pronounced with falling-rising intonation. In (10), I picked upon her signal for talk continuation, the fall-rise (9), by uttering *mhm*, but nevertheless took the floor to ask for a clarification. As a result, Natalia began with a discourse marker *nie wiem* 'I don't know' and repeated that she felt *bez narodowości* 'without nationality' (12) with an emphatic *bez* 'without', challenging established state-level categorizations. The stance rejecting nationality was accomplished by the unfolding of the propositional content and like for other cosmopolitan women, subtly signalled with a combination of phonetic features drawn from English orienting the speaker away from Polish nationality and evoking the here-and-now of the speaking situation.

In these accounts, such a position was linked to unwillingness to differentiate between people on the basis of nationality alone. The stance against ethno-racialized divisions was also most often explained in the context of discriminatory practices observed or experienced through encounters with some Polish-speaking people in the UK. Unlike in Polish Poles' accounts, the internal differences within the UK Polish population did not fade away, but rather this contrast was picked out, evaluated and compared. For example, in the interview, Kaja, a 30-year-old psychology graduate working in the education sector in East London, kept coming back to negative attitudes towards others among a group of Polish-speaking friends she used to hang out with at the beginning of her stay in the UK. This included their refusal to spend time with her friends originally from Albania or unwillingness to speak English in mixed groups with a large number of Polish-speaking people, despite the friends' working in professions that required an advanced knowledge of English and therefore, having an ability to speak English. In excerpt (11), she recalled how the friends' unwillingness to speak English negatively impacted their relationship. The turn begins with her evaluative judgement of such a practice as *bezczelne* 'shameless' (4). In (8), she produced a propositional phrase in which she linked her first relationship with an Englishman to a bivalent *problem*, which she explained in relation to the friends' unwillingness to speak English to him. After being asked for a clarification, she provided further detail, maintaining the floor by means of the new intonational device, the fall-rise, and in (13), asserting that when talking in a group, she had to persuade the Polish-speaking friends to speak English. She also asserted that the practice made her partner feel uncomfortable (15). While making the knowledge claim, she relied on multiple symbolic resources, but importantly this also involved her occasional use of palatalized fricatives (1), English-like fillers (4) and repeated signalling of more talk to come with falling-rising intonation, which actively shaped relationality between the interlocutors and the sensory experience.

(11) Kaja (C4)

1 C4: ¹że jakby jesteś w kraju w którym mówi się po angielsku /tak
      that like you're in a country where they speak English right?

2 KK: °mhm°

3 C4: więc- i są ludzie na około ciebie którzy mówią po /angielsku i nie rozumieją ciebie po \p(inaudible)olsku
      so-   and there are people around you who speak English   and don't understand you in Polish

4   to jest trochę \/bezczelnie jeżeli będziesz- jeżeli się siedzi z kimś na przykład uhm-   nie wiem jakoś tam
      it is slightly shameless   if you'll-   if you're sitting with someone for example uhm- I don't know somehow

5   w \/grupie i i są ludzie >którzy rozmawiają po angielsku i którz rozmawiają po \p(bad quality)olsku < to się
      in a group and and there are people who speak English and wh speak Polish   so one

6   wybiera jednak ten język który wszyscy \umieją
      still chooses the language that everybody knows

7 KK: a ci Polacy >z którymi na początku się zadawałaś to< mówiłaś że oni tak średnio-
      and these Poles that you would hang out with at the beginning you said that they so so-

8 C4: właśnie to było tak mój związek pierwszy który był z Anglikiem był \problem   bo-
      exactly it was so my first relationship with an Englishman there was a problem   because-

9   oni nie chcieli na przykład po angielsku rozmawiać \z nim
      they didn't want for example speak English with him

10 KK: ale oni w ogóle nie chcieli /tak
      but they didn't want at all?

11 C4: nie \nie oni po prostu naczy- coś tam jeżeli coś coś chcieli od \/niego   albo coś
      no no   they simply that is-   something if they wanted something something from him or something

12   to rozmawiali do niego po \angielsku   >ale jakbyśmy siedzieli w towarzystwie< to przeważnie właśnie
      then they would speak English to him   but if we were sitting in a group then mainly exactly

13   nie było tak że (0.1) ja musiałam przekonywać że może porozmawiamy po angielsku żeby on był jakby
      it wasn't so that   I had to persuade them that maybe we'll talk in English so that he like

14   się czuł-   ale zawsze jak się do mnie zwracali z \/czymś   to po polsku /mówili
      would feel- but always when they talked to me about something   then they spoke Polish

15   i on nie rozumiał \nic   i on się głupio \czuł
      and he didn't understand anything   and he felt awkward

In these accounts, not entirely denying the importance of historical consciousness, the participants oriented themselves and explained their actions and plans predominantly in relation to the here and now. They often aligned with Britain, but did not identify as British. Rather they presented the reality from a global scale where they positioned themselves against classificatory national labels describing Britain as a place that at the time allowed them to be 'who they want to be', although awareness of othering discourses was also present and the participants often did not limit their future to the UK. For example, when considering her future plans, in excerpt (12), Kaja described her recent reflections on a possible European referendum, pointing to her awareness of strong anti-European discourses in the UK already in 2013. In (1-2), she introduced the idea of the poll in the current locality, with a VOT of 30ms in the word *europejskie*, with propositional content anchored in the here and now, and repeated in (2) by uttering a deictic expression *tutaj* with this time a more English-like VOT of 37ms. She then introduced a possible scenario of being thrown out of the UK in case Britain decided to leave Europe (3), which was followed by an emphatic first-person pronoun *ja*, a present verb form *mówię* and a question *jak to?* expressing surprise. She then went on to evaluate the scenario as 'weird', which she pronounced with a fall-rise (4). This enabled her to maintain the floor and produce repeated content 'being thrown out' (5). Positioning herself towards the other, the British authorities who can come and send one home, she drew attention to the current anxiety, which may result in nullification of her UK experience and education. While producing the phrase, she anchored her turn again in the here and now, producing a deictic expression *tutaj* with an English-like VOT of 40ms (10). As the discourse unfolded, she continued to reflect on her multiple allegiances fixing connections in the here and now. In (15), she asserted that her 'home is here in England', which was immediately followed by *mój dom jest w Polsce* 'my home is in Poland'. When mentioning 'in Poland', she produced a fall-rise (15), which enabled her to maintain the floor. This was immediately followed by a clarification 'or more my parents' home'. The stance towards one's home was further negotiated in (17–19), as Kaja repeated that she saw home in both the UK and Poland. When doing so, whenever she aligned with the here and now, she relied on the new devices: *tutaj* 'here' was repeatedly pronounced with English-like VOTs (21, 24), while in (21), when aligning with current affairs in the UK, she maintained the floor by means of a fall-rise. Finally, in (24), Kaja provided further explanation linking 'family' to 'here and here', anchoring her proposition in Britain and Poland at the same time. In this example, we see that rather than relying on static sound systems, Kaja creatively moved along the continuum of variation to position herself towards the talk itself. By doing so, she accomplished her cosmopolitan stance refusing to confine herself to either state-level formation.

(12) Kaja (C4)

1 C4: nawet jeż¦eli ja- teraz dostaliśmy jakieś listy z głosowania: że w Anglii też jest jakieś głosowanie
        even if I-   we've just received some polling cards that in England there are some European

2 \europ(30ms)ejskie też jest Parlament \Europ(bad quality)ejski referendum europejskie \t(37ms)utaj
        elections   there is also the European Parliament   European referendum here

3 tak się zastanawiałam czy jeżeli Anglia wyjdzie \z Europy to nas \wyrzucą (h)
        I was thinking whether if England leaves Europe   then they will throw us out

4 ja mówię jak /t(bad quality)o ale to jest właśnie takie \/dziwne bo tak się zastanawiałam że-
        I say how come?   but it's exactly so weird   because I've been thinking that-

5 to co mnie /wyrzucą   to co nie wiem-   przyjdą do mnie do \domu   i powiedzą nie jesteśmy
        so what will they throw me out? so what I don't know- they'll come to my place   and tell me we're

6 już w /Europie   byłaś tutaj dziesięć [lat ale-
        no longer in Europe?   you've been here ten years but-

7 KK: [((inaudible))]

8 C4: no \dokładnie co mi [powiedzą że-
 exactly what will they tell me that-

9 KK: [czy zostać tu-]
 or stay here

10 C4: no ale to ty się tak \zastanawiasz to co nagle skasują twoje dziesięć \lat całą twoją edukację \t(40ms)uta
 but you're thinking so what will they suddenly cancel your ten years your whole education here

11 KK: mhm

12 C4: powiedzą nie czy powinnam zrobić ten paszport angielski bo /może (h)
 will they say no or should I have this English passport because maybe

13 KK: ((inaudible))

14 C4: no bo tak no bo to by zmieniło moje życie \pewnie
 yes because yes because this would change my life probably

...

15 jak mówiłam mój dom jest tutaj \w Anglii mój dom jest \/w Polsce raczej bardziej moich rodziców \dom
 as I was saying my home is here in England my home is in Poland or more my parents' home

16 KK: a twój dom jest tu /tak
 and your home is here right?

17 C4: naczy moich rodziców \dom ale to jest też mój \dom i bardziej to jest mój dom \t(37ms)utaj
 that is my parents' home but it is also my home and more my home is here

...

18 jakby czuję się uh częścią \Anglii ale na pewno rzeczy które się dzieją w Anglii tak samo
 like I feel uh part of England but for sure things happening in England equally

19 mnie \/dot(39ms)yczą i y jakby tak- z rzeczami które się dzieją \w Polsce
 concern me and like so- with things happening in Poland

20 KK: mhm

21 C4: bo tak naprawdę moje życie się może zmienić jeżeli coś sie stanie \/t(34ms)utaj
 because really my life can change if something happens here

22 moje życie się może zmienić jak coś się stanie \z Polską
 my life can change if something happens to Poland

23 KK: mhm

24 C4: bo mam rodzinę tutaj i \/t(38ms)utaj jakby bliskich dla \siebie
 because I have family here and here like my loved ones for me

25 uhm jakby w tym samym momencie mnie to jakby \dotknie
 uhm like in the same moment it'll affect me

In these accounts, the self's positioning in relation to anti-migration sentiments observed in Britain at the time was also evident in other interviews. The practices and actions were therefore situated and evaluated in relation to resurging discourses on national identity in the current locality. For example, throughout the interview, Iza, a 30-year-old social media employee, strongly aligned herself with the current locality and explicitly repeatedly pointed to her preference for multicultural dynamics in London rather than other parts of the UK and Poland, which she associated with less diversity. Such a positive stance towards multiculturalism was expressed in all cosmopolitan accounts, but for one participant London's size and diversity were contrasted with the preferred state in Oxford (Natalia), pointing to individual preferences. The quote begins after Iza contrasted lack of diversity in Poland with the current place of residence portraying its multicultural dynamics as a desired state. In (1), she linked the self through a prepositional phrase *dla mnie* 'for me' to a positive evaluation of diversity. While doing so, she produced a series of prolonged vowels in both nuclear and final positions, which together with the unfolding of the propositional content enabled her to maintain the floor. In (1–2), she pointed to anti-migration discourses in the UK at the time of speaking 'what annoys many English people at this moment', pronounced with a fall-rise and burst of laughter to downplay the seriousness of the situation, and clarified by 'that there are so many people here'. While doing so, she produced an English-like VOT in *tutaj* 'here', which enabled her to index the here and now of the speaking situation. In the following phrase, she then contrasted the general moods with *a* 'but', first-person pronoun *mi* 'I' and aligned with the aforementioned content. The final *podobało* 'I liked' was produced with vowel lengthening, echoed in the next phrase in which she repeated the content. Repeating the content yet again *ludzie zjeżdżają z całego świata* (3) and maintaining the floor with a fall-rise, she finally evaluated it as 'interesting' positively aligning with the current locality (3). As the discourse unfolded, we learned that the anti-migration sentiments, however, affected her everyday life in complex ways. In (4–6), she introduced new information that she had an English boyfriend, whose whole family were English. While doing it, she maintained the floor with fall-rises (4, 6) and recalled that sometimes they forgot that she was Polish. Here, we see that rather than aligning with the current locality, Iza pointed to her ethnic classification and produced a standard Polish VOT in *Polką* (26ms) in (7), which enabled her to position herself away from negative experiences and practices in the UK. As she provided clarification 'such taunts' and repeatedly referred to negative attitudes towards migrants (8–9), her rhythm was different from that of Polish Poles: she used vowel lengthening in consecutive syllables in *Londynie* and falling-rising intonation (8, 9). In final lines, we see that the negotiation and downplaying of anti-migration sentiments was also quite complex, with Iza first producing a general claim about the English treating immigration *bardzo w porządku* 'very all right', aligning with circulating images of Polish migrants taking the jobs from the Brits, but eventually contrasting those alignments with references to exploitation *Polacy są tutaj taką tanią siłą roboczą* (15). We see that similarly to Polish Poles' accounts, the othering discourses also came up in cosmopolitan accounts. However, unlike in Polish Poles' accounts, the difference was negotiated in relation to actions and events in the here and now rather than permanent characteristics. They were also enacted by means of clusters of phonetic detail that actively participated in positioning of the self towards others in time and space.

(13) Iza (C3)

1 C3: to dla mnie wiesz to było \/pozyt(48ms)ywne to co dużo Anglików wkurza w tym \/momencie (h)
    so for me you know it was positive   what many Englishmen are now annoyed by in this moment

2   że że jest tylu ludzi \t(45ms)utaj   a mi się akurat to \podoba:ło: że jest taki tygiel \kultura:lny:
    that that there so many people here but I actually liked it   that there is such a cultural melting pot

3   że ludzie zjeżdżają z całego \/świata   i no że jest \ciek(bad quality)awie
    that people are coming from the whole world and that this is interesting

...

4   ja na przykład mam Angli- chłopaka \/Anglika
    I for example have an Engli- an English boyfriend

5 KK: mhm

6 C3: i cała jego rodzina jest \/Anglików także czasami słyszę- nawet oni zapominają że ja jestem
    and his whole family are English   so sometimes I hear- they even forget that I am

7   \P(26ms)olką i czasami to jakiś na przykład jakiś-   i byliśmy na jakiś yyy \świętach
    a Pole   and sometimes then some for example some-   and we came for some holidays

8   i jakieś były takie docinki że pełno ludzi \w Londy:nie::   pełno \/imigrantów
    and there were some taunts that there are many people in London many immigrants

9   że że powinna Anglia jakoś reagować \na /to
    that that England should react somehow to that

...

10   no ale generalnie mi się wydaje że- (0.3ms) Angli:cy:- odnoszą się tak bardzo w porządku do /emigracji
    but in general it seems to me-   the English- they treat emigration in a very all right manner

11	chociaż no na pewno jest-	na pewno jest tak- em:	dużo ludzi mówi że pracę \zabie<u>ra</u>my
	although there is for sure-	*for sure there is-*	*uhm many people are saying that we're taking jobs*
12	i tak \<u>da:</u>le:j	no i pewnie jakaś jest w tym \<u>pra:</u>wda:	ale z drugiej strony
	and so on	*and probably there is some truth in it*	*but on the other hand*
13	też są jakieś pozyty:wne: ekonomiczne \/re<u>a</u>kcje		nie reakcje tylko jakieś nie wiem-
	there are also some positive economic reactions		*not reactions but some I don't know-*
14	dużo się \<u>dzie</u>je	mi się wydaje że ciężko byłoby im znaleźć tylu \/pracow<u>ni</u>ków
	a lot is happening it seems to me that it would be difficult to find so many employees
15	Polacy są tutaj taką tanią siłą roboczą tutaj \<u>trochę</u>
	Poles are here such a cheap labour force here a bit

As shown earlier, similarly to all cosmopolitan accounts, the previous excerpt also points to awareness of classed differences. Such an awareness is also visible in an extract from an interview with Paulina, a 23-year-old law graduate student living in London. In excerpt (14), Paulina began her answer by asserting that it was *oczywista rzecza* 'an obvious thing' that all or as she immediately corrected herself most *kelnerek* 'waitresses', pronounced with a prolonged vowel on the nucleus, were *Polkami* 'Polish' (1–2).[10] Providing further evidence for the presence of Polish migrants in low-paid jobs, in (2), similarly to Natalia, she asserted that all cleaning ladies in her college were Polish, as expected, pronounced with *k* within norms for both languages. When discussing horizontal differences within the Polish-speaking population, Paulina also mentioned that often these were her British friends who drew her attention to other Polish migrants, which also contributed to the formation of a classed perspective. In (5), she listed possible scenarios, *załatwić z kelnerką* 'dealing with a waitress' pronounced with a prolonged vowel on the nucleus, or being in a hotel, which also ended in a prolonged vowel, enabling the speaker to maintain the floor and link it to the quote 'there is no shampoo'. Here when recounting the past event, Paulina also relied on an English-like VOT on *szamponu* (68ms) in (6). She then used the passive voice in the present tense *jestem wysyłana* 'I am being sent' to negotiate with 'the people' who were seen by others as Poles. Here *Polakami* 'Poles' was pronounced with a longer VOT on the velar stop (70ms), enabling her to align with the context of speaking. Paulina then went on to list other scenarios for encounters with other Polish-speaking migrants, drawing on English-like fall-rises to maintain the floor and confirming that the stereotype of a Polish migrant associated with low-paid jobs existed. Finally, in (9), she offered an evaluation of the stereotype as 'not negative', pronounced again with a fall-rise, which resulted in me not taking the floor (10), but uttering a concurring *mhm*, and Paulina repeating the content about lack of overtly negative statements about Polish migrants among her non-Polish friends. The self's positioning was therefore negotiated through a number of English-like devices that enabled Paulina to align with the local context and differentiate herself from other Polish-speaking migrants. However, the final phrases also enabled her to downplay the difference by evaluating the classed stereotype as 'not negative'.

(14) Paulina (C1)

1 C1: na pewno to znaczy- oczywistą rzeczą jest to że każda- nie każda- ale większość kelne:rek jest
      for sure that is-   it is an obvious thing that every-   not every- but most waitresses are

2   \Pol<u>k(60ms)</u>ami u mnie w collegu wszystkie sprzątaczki były \Pol<u>k(50ms)</u>ami
     Poles   in my college all cleaning ladies were Polish

3 KK: mhm

4 C1: em i hmm to znaczy na pewno był-   to taki stereotyp że na przykład wszystkie moje koleżanki na
      uhm and hmm that is for sure there was- such a stereotype that for example all my friends for

5   \<u>przy</u>kład jak ktoś coś chciał załatwić \z kel<u>ne::</u>rką   albo jak jestem w \ho<u>t(34ms)</u>elu:: ii nie ma
     example when someone wanted to arrange something with a waitress or when I'm in a hotel   and there is

6   \szam<u>p(68ms)</u>onu zawsze ja jestem wysyłana żeby negocjować z tymi \lu<u>dź</u>mi bo wiadomo że oni
     shampoo   always I am being sent to negotiate with these people   because one knows that they

7   pewnie są \/Pola<u>k(70ms)</u>ami i [Paulina] się dogada /tak   albo jak zamawiam w barze drinka to zwykle
     are probably Poles   and [Paulina] will get along right? or when I order a drink at a bar then usually

8   barmanami też są \/Pol<u>a</u>cy i też⌋ ja załatwię dwa dodatkowe drinki za \<u>da</u>rmo   albo coś \takiego   także na
     bartenders are Polish   and also I will arrange two additional drinks for free   or something like this so for

9   pewno ten stereotyp \/<u>jest</u> aczkolwiek ja nie jestem pewna czy to jest \nega<u>t(30ms)</u>ywny /stereotyp
     sure there is this stereotype but I am not sure if this is a negative stereotype

10 KK: mhm

11 C1: przynajmniej nie zetknęłam się z czymś takim żeby ktoś mi powiedział że o ci Polacy o \<u>e:</u>
      at least I didn't come across such a situation that someone would tell me oh these Poles oh ugh

In these accounts, the presence in Britain was also explained in relation to the local economy and social norms in Poland, where Polish society was imagined as lacking the same range of suitable social positions that allowed being financially independent. This was especially visible in women's accounts, where lack of opportunities and desirable lifestyles often came up as in excerpt (15). Cosmopolitan women repeatedly disaligned themselves from stereotypical gender norms, for example, the image of the Mother-Pole, and aligned with job opportunities and norms observed in Britain. For example, after being asked about her preference for staying in the UK/return to Poland, Iza, a 30-year-old woman who had spent seven years in the UK and, at the time, was working in social media in London, produced a long stretch of discourse in which she positioned herself away from life in Poland and aligned with staying in the UK. To do so, she deictically anchored her turn in the present with first-person singular (1) and negatively evaluated a series of factors that she associated with Poland. The quote began with Iza linking 'her generation' with 'suffering from the post-communist mentality', uttered with a fall-rise that enabled her to maintain the floor (1) and contrast it with younger generations and their way of looking at the world. While doing so, her rhythm was characterized by vowel lengthening in consecutive syllables and further fall-rises (1–3). Having evaluated younger generations as 'more cheerful' and 'ambitious', she provided further explanation about her generation. Again, while making her claim, she repeatedly used vowel lengthening and English-like VOT in *negatywni* (58ms) in (6), which, at the same time, enabled her to disalign herself from the image of her peers. She then went on to contrast the lifestyle of Londoners with that of her medium-sized city in central Poland, where she 'lacked anonymity', linking it also to differences in gendered practices and norms. In (11), she described English 30-year-olds as 'those who still go out'. In (14), Iza contrasted the information that she had given about British 30-year-olds with the life of Polish 25-year-olds, pointing to reported differences in societal expectations between the two states. As the propositional content unfolded, in line with English, rather than Polish, interactional frameworks, she relied on repeated vowel lengthening and fall-rises in (11–16). In (14), she asserted that Polish 25-year-olds closed themselves at home, which she evaluated negatively with a negated content and an indefinite pronoun *I nic się nie dzieje w ich życiu* 'nothing happens in their lives' and a palatalized fricative in *życiu* (15–16). In (16), she provided further clarification with reference to gender norms. When making a negatively evaluated generic claim about all 'women putting on weight' (16), she produced an aspirated stop in *tyją*, a disyllabic verb with a dental stop followed by a high vowel [ɨ]. The VOT was 63 ms, radically diverging from reported Polish norms. She then continued to negatively evaluate men with generic *faceci* in (16) and after listing a few other gender and generational differences, when confronted with a yes/no question about her preference for staying in the UK, concurred with *tak* 'yes'.

(15) Iza (C3)

1 C3: też mi się wydaje że moje \pokole:nie: jest   jeszcze cierpi na tą postkomunistyczną \/ment(37ms)alność
it also seems to me that my generation   still suffers from this post-communist mentality

2 i dopiero podejrzewam że:: na przykład moje dzieci- albo nawet bo mam dziesięcio::
and I suspect that only for example my children-   or even because I have ten-

3 dwudziestoletniego \brata dziesięć lat \/młodszego   i nawet już jego pokolenie jest trochę \inne
a twenty-year-old brother   ten years younger   and even his generation is a bit different

4 już jest takie trochę bardziej \pogo:dne: inaczej patrzą na \życie::   są bardziej tacy \ambitni:
they're already a bit more cheerful   they look at life differently   they're more ambitious

5 moje pokolenie jeszcze: dużo czerpie: z pokoleń naszych \rodzi:ców   którzy żyli w \komuniźmie:
my generation still draws a lot on our parents' generations   who lived in communism

6   i byli tacy \/negat(58ms)ywni
and were so negative

...

7 czas na mieszkanie w Polsce będzie fajny może za jakieś nie wiem dziesięć \la:t
time to live in Poland will be great maybe in I don't know ten years

...

8 bo ja mieszkam w takim średniej wielkości w Polsce \/mieście brakowało mi że nie miałam
because I live in a medium-sized city in Poland   I missed that I didn't have

9 właśnie tej \anonimowości:
precisely this anonymity

...

10 i czegoś takiego-   nie wiem też ludzie w moim wieku:: już-   tutaj jest zupełnie \inaczej
and something such- I don't know that people my age already-   here it's entirely different

11 ludzie którzy mają trzydzieści \la:t   cały czas jeszcze nie wiem chodzą na \imprezy
people who are thirty years old   all the time still I don't know go to parties

12 na przy:kła::d albo albo-
for example or or-

13 KK: ((inaudible))

14 C3: no a w Polsce to jest tak że nie wiem od dwudziestu pier- dwudziestego piątego roku \życia
and in Poland it's so that I don't know twenty-one- twenty-five-year-old

15 ludzie mają dzieci rodziny i po prostu zamykają się \/w domu   i nic się nie dzieje
people have children families and simply close themselves at home   and nothing happens

16 w ich \/życiu   i kobiety tylko \/t(63ms)yją   i faceci tylko brzuchy im \rosną
in their lives   and women only put on weight   and guys their bellies only grow

As the stance towards ethno-racialized divisions was made in relation to gender distinctions, attention was also drawn to different actions and images. In women's accounts, the topic of misogynist actions and practices among other UK Polish migrants was often brought up. In excerpt (16), after being asked about stereotypes of Poles in the UK, Natalia, a 22-year-old graduate student who had spent three and a half years studying at Oxford, began her answer by linking it to the current locality, and the presence of a classed stereotype of 'Polish cleaning ladies' (1). This was pronounced with a fall-rise, which enabled Natalia to maintain the floor and immediately provide additional information pronounced with decreased volume on *taki* 'such'. After I picked on the stereotype and the non-linguistic cue, and explicitly asked whether it was 'not nice', Natalia positioned herself towards the question by first aligning with the evaluation, and then, providing additional information: stating that most of her friends talk to their cleaning ladies, pronounced with a fall-rise, and immediately followed by an assertion that showed awareness of deskilling in the UK 'many of the cleaning ladies graduated from university in Poland'. As the conversation unfolded and I asked about instances of feeling ashamed of being Polish, Natalia began with a negative *nie chyba* 'no probably', again pronounced with a fall-rise, which this time enabled her to show hesitancy and at the same time resulted in me not taking the floor. Natalia then provided explanation marked with colloquial *naczy* 'that is' as she recounted an incident at her dojo practice in Oxford, where two younger Polish-speaking men had mistreated an older woman. As she took her stance, she heavily relied on the new intonational device (6,8,10,12) to introduce new content and maintain the floor. While doing so, she provided more detailed information about the men, listing their jobs and at the same time, making a classed distinction. Finally, in (12), she pointed to their misogynist behaviour. To do so, she produced a velar stop within Polish and English norms, as expected, and maintained the floor by means of the new intonational device. After I expressed understanding, Natalia repeated the propositional content explicitly labelling the practice as 'chauvinistic' (14). As she put actions and people in relation to each other, she stressed one individual's behaviour and evaluated the manner in which both Polish men in the practice behaved as 'jarring'. As the discourse unfolded, she kept maintaining the floor with fall-rises (16–17) and pointed to the subsequent evaluation of Polish migrants by English-speaking people present in the dojo practice by providing an English-sounding quote 'shit another Polish guy'. In (21–27), she repeated her evaluative stance towards the propositional content and provided more information about a particular situation, where an elderly woman was mistreated and suffered verbal abuse from the Polish men. While scaling herself in relation to others, Natalia repeatedly relied on falling-rising intonation, English-like fillers ('uhm') and direct quotes in English, which enabled her to animate forms of resistance towards gendered actions of others falling under the same ethnic label and echo cosmopolitan discourses that stress the commitment to people one does not know.

(16) Natalia (C7)

1 C7:   jeśli chodzi o O:ksford ponieważ jest tyle polskich \/sprząt(bad quality)aczek   to jest jeszcze °taki°
        when it comes to Oxford because there are so many Polish cleaning ladies   so there is also such

2 KK: /sprząt(bad quality)aczki i to jest /niefajne
        cleaning ladies? and it's not nice?

3 C7:   no \niefajne   naczy większość moich znajomych rozmawia ze swoimi \/sprzątaczk(bad quality)ami
        yes not nice   that is most of my friends talk to their cleaning ladies

        i dużo tych sprzątaczek skończyło studia \w Polsce
        and many of these cleaning ladies graduated from university in Poland

. . .

4 KK: (h) ok ok powiedz mi czy zdążyło ci się czy zdążyły ci się jakieś sytuacje w których y już niekoniecznie-
        ok ok and tell me whether you've had any situations in which you maybe not necessarily

5   że się wstydziłaś-   ale że nie chciałaś się przyznać że jesteś /z Polski
        that you were ashamed but that you didn't want to admit that you were from Poland?

6 C7:   \nie /chyba naczy-   pamiętam że no no wstydziłam się trochę-   i cały czas trochę się \/wstydzę
        no I guess that is-   I remember that I was ashamed a bit-   and I am a bit ashamed all the time

7 KK: mhm

8 C7:   w moim dojo jest kilku \/Polaków
        in my dojo practice there are a few Poles

9 KK: mhm

10 C7: uhm którzy- nie są studentami ani nie są \/profesorami   jeden jest \port(bad quality)ierem
        uhm who-   they aren't students nor professors   one is a porter

11 KK: acha

12 C7: drugi \elektrykiem   em nie zawsze się dobrze zachowywali w stosunku do \/k(45ms)obiet
        the other an electrician   uhm they didn't always behave well towards women

13 KK: acha ok

14 C7: bardzo szowinistycznie się \/zachowyWAli szczególnie jeden \z NICH
       they behaved in a very chauvinistic way   especially one of them

15 KK: ok i to wte-
       ok and then-

16 C7: i wszyscy byli bardzo pewni \/SIEbie   w RAżący \/SPOsób   i pamiętam że jak przyszedł kolejny
       and all were very self-confident   in an jarring way   and I remember that when another Pole

17   \/P(28ms)OLak- to on wtedy powiedział shit another Polish \guy
       came-   then he said shit another Polish guy

18 KK: oo (h) i jak ty się wtedy /czujesz
       oh and how do you feel then?

19 C7: em °kiepsko° no jest mi trochę \wstyd   bo panowie się zachowywali \/niemiło
       uhm poorly I'm a bit ashamed   because the men didn't behave in a nice way

20 KK: mhm

21 C7: em włączając w to to jak się zachowywali w stosunku do pani która mogłaby być ich \mamą
       uhm including in it that how they behaved towards a woman who could have been their mum

22 KK: ok

23 C7: to są młodzi chłopcy uhm: dwadzieścia kilka \/lat
       these are young boys uhm twenty something years old

24 KK: mhm

25 C7: a pani jest pięćdziesięciokilkuLETNIA która ma DZIEci w ich \wieku
       and the woman is fifty something years old who has kids their age

26 KK: no tak

27 C7: uhm a któryś z nich potrafi jej powiedzieć \shut up   kiedy ona jest-   no nie no po prostu zachowanie
       uhm and one of them can tell her to shut up   when she is-   no just the behaviour

28   Polaków w dojo-   to chyba wtedy miałam najwięcej do czynienia \z Pola[k(45ms)ami]
       of Poles in dojo-   this is perhaps when I had most contact with Poles

29 KK: [ok]

30 C7: bo z nimi \trenuję
       because I train with them

31 KK: mhm ok czyli to nie-
       mhm ok so it not

32 C7: \bezczelne
       shameless

In their self-presentations, cosmopolitans presented low Polishness Index scores (0–3), their networks were more international than Polish Poles (14–50 per cent), and they related Polishness to childhood memories and their families, linking it with private, rather than public and collective life. However, women and men relied on different linguistic devices when sharing their situated logics. This is clearly seen in an excerpt from an interview with Jacek, a 32-year-old man who had spent six years in the UK and, at the time, was working in the corporate sector. In the quote, similarly to cosmopolitan women, he did not mobilize the discourse of national identity, but evaluated his practices in relation to the personalized self operating in the here-and-now. At the same time, he relied predominantly on standardized means of expression. In the excerpt, he positioned himself towards selected cultural symbols as in a preceding turn, he had denied the presence of Polish food in his life. Excerpt (17) begins after his wife, present in the house, asked about a Polish soup *chłodnik*.

(17) Jacek (C5)[11]

1 C5: lubię jakieś tam \po<u>tra</u>wy naczy pewnie dla każdego KRAJ to w sumie bardziej to .hhh
I like some dishes   I mean probably for anyone a country is in fact more about

2 jakie tam dzieciństwo przeżyli i tak \<u>da</u>lej   tak pozostaje to \<u>ra</u>czej
what childhood they had and so on   this stays more

3 KK: mhm

4 C5: trudno to nazwać \narodowo<u>ści</u>owe   po prostu z dzieciństwa dobrze się każdemu
it's difficult to call it national   it's just that almost everyone has good

5 prawie \ko<u>ja</u>rzy   jeżeli było dobre (h) \dzie<u>ciń</u>stwo
associations with childhood   if it was a good childhood

6 KK: hmm (h)

7 C5: więc to są takie sentymenty z dzieciństwa bardziej niż takie \narodowo<u>ści</u>owe
so these are such sentiments from childhood more than national

8 °wydaje mi się°
it seems to me

9 KK: acha czyli to to \<u>ok</u>
aha so this then ok

10 C5: a że W MOIM DOMU nie było jakiejś obse:sji: z \pol<u>sko</u>;ścią   to tak jej nie \<u>mam</u>
and because in my home there was no obsession with Polishness   so I don't have it

Line (1) comes as a response to the wife's turn as Jacek agreed that he enjoyed some Polish dishes. In the next IP, however, he linked the answer to his previous turns and evaluated the fact in relation to one's childhood. While doing so, his declarative phrases finished with the default standard fall, standard alveolar fricatives, no vowel lengthening. To take his stance, he rather used an indefinite pronoun *każdego* 'anyone' and linked *kraj* 'country' to childhood memories. In line with standard cues including non-linguistic ones, I did not take the floor (3) and uttered concurring *mhm* to signal understanding. Jacek continued and evaluated the fact using a value-laden adverb *trudno* 'difficult' to question its national character. He further evaluated childhood as a source of positive associations and specified its type *dobre* 'good'. While doing that, he used another generic pronoun *każdemu* 'everyone' and ended the IP with standard falling intonation and a burst of laughter. I expressed alignment by producing *hmm* (6) and barely audible laughter. Jacek then concluded with a predicate aligning with childhood sentiments and made a scalar distinction explicitly contrasting them with national sentiments (7–8). I expressed approval with *ok*, but my turn first displayed a level of hesitation with *czyli* 'so' implying a request for further clarification in 'standard' Polish. As a result, Jacek provided his final turn linking the general remarks from earlier turns to his own experience. He uttered a minor IP with the first-person possessive pronoun *moim* 'my' relatively louder to the surrounding talk when linking it to his *domu* 'home' in Poland and deictically anchoring the utterance in the past in order to produce a negated phrase 'there was no obsession with Polishness'. Occasional vowel lengthening in word stressed positions occurred, but the turn concluded with standard norms with Jacek aligning through the propositional content with his home practices rather than the national sentiments that he had mentioned before. Similarly to the other cosmopolitan man, his talk about and alignment with specific chronotopes was hence enacted by means of different contrastive features from those deployed in women's performances. This created a different communicative effect in which authority was accomplished in line with the sensory and social order the men knew from Poland.

The gendered differences can be explained in relation to differences in partners: both men, like almost all men in the project had Polish-speaking partners; most women and all cosmopolitan women had international partners. As cosmopolitans explicitly asserted that they did not intend to return to Poland, in their accounts, all linked their future more to English and global economy. They often aligned with English and multilingual practices explicitly arguing for multilingualism to be positive and enabling a better understanding of the world. They asserted that they did not mind language mixing; however, women and men differed in ways in which they explicitly positioned themselves towards compartmentalizing their resources. As all reported speaking English to fellow Poles, the two men expressed less positive attitudes to translanguaging practices at the sentence level. In contrast, changes in salience of linguistic resources led women to take a positive stance towards reassembling Polish and English resources at the phonetic level. Women therefore accepted or even liked the changes as an expression of their new positioning. At the same time, this did not, however, mean that they accepted all kinds of differences as some ways of speaking were explicitly named as not desirable, pointing to the classed differences in linguistic constructions and word choices (this can be observed across the three orientations).

As suggested earlier, in these accounts internal variation within Polish-speaking population did not fade away and connections were fixed through units of comparison focusing on actions and events rather than permanent characteristics. Class differences were acknowledged, rather than erased, but at the same time new observations and conjunctures about such fixing regimes were also made as seen in excerpt (18). In (1), Maja asserted that she 'values various things in Poland and the Polish language', making repeated use of English-like devices, which also enabled her to position herself towards the here and now of the speaking situation. In (2), she contrasted the previous content with *ale* 'but' making an ontological claim 'I am a free spirit', which she unpacked in (4–5). Again, when doing so, she made use of new devices including maintaining the floor with a fall-rise (5). In (7), she provided further clarification by linking the assertion with her previous comments in which she critiqued the Polish class system. While doing so, she relied mostly on the unfolding of the propositional content in which using the state logic as a reference point, she introduced new information: 'everybody wants to show off, prove something', 'judge others', 'compare'. She then disaligned from it in (10–11), linking 'being abroad' with 'feeling free'. As the discourse unfolded, she listed changes in her Polish and when confronted with a question about her feelings towards them, aligned with the practice. To do so, she increased the volume, produced a truncated phrase, followed by an assertion 'I don't care', linking it to the evaluation 'I like feeling from abroad', at the same time connecting the change in language to her critical comments about class.

(18) Maja (C6)

1 C6: cenię sobie: bardzo wiele rzeczy \w Polsce   i i i w polskim \języ:ku   uh nie wiem i \humor
I value many things in Poland a lot   and and and in the Polish language uh I don't know and humour

2   i róż^jne inne \rzeczy   ale- ale gdzieś nie wiem-   ja jestem wolnym \duchem
and various other things   but- but somewhere I don't know-   I am a free spirit

3 KK: mhm

4 C6: i czuję ż/e że lubię lubię być tą osobą zza \granicy   lubię być tą osobą która czasem
and I feel that that I like like being this person from abroad   I like being this person who sometimes

5   \/wpada i po prostu-
comes and just-

6 KK: mhm

7 C6: ale /jednocześnie- która nie musi się- ja się \męczę   w tym środowisku gdzie wszyscy
but at the same time- who doesn't have to- I get tired   in such an environment where everybody

8   wciąż chcą sobie jeszcze coś \poK(bad quality)Azać   \udowodnić
still wants to show off   prove something to others

9 KK: mhm

10 C6: oceniają się względem \innych \porównują mnie to \męczy bo ja- ja w czymś takim nie umiem
judge themselves against others compare   this makes me tired because I-I cannot function in something

10   \funkcjonować   i i czuję się WOLna za \granicą
like this   and and I feel free abroad

...

11 KK: a jak się czujesz jak ktoś powie że masz bardziej melodyjny czy że mówisz z
and how do you feel when someone tells you that you have a more melodic or that you speak with an

       /akcentem jak ci z tym   czy to wogle cie-
accent?   how are you feeling about it   does it at all-

12 C6: JAKOŚ WIESZ CO jakoś nie- specjalnie mnie to nie \/obchodzi   jakoś tak y: w sumie gdzieś-
somehow you know somehow no- I'm not especially concerned about that   somehow so somewhere-

13   ja się lubię tak czuć tak zza granicy jakoś \tak
I like feeling this way from abroad somehow

As shown earlier, when engaged in a conversation with me, similarly to other participants discussed so far, women drew on a wide range of symbolic resources, but the sounded experience was not the same. We see that at the phonetic level, typified by the participants and linked to qualities associated with members of the UK Polish diaspora, unlike the two men, cosmopolitan women reassembled their Polish and English resources in new ways. While motivated by discursive function and circumstances of production, selected repetitive combinations of phonetic detail were used by the women to index disalignment from Poland-related issues or alignment with the local context. The accumulation of signs and movement along a continuum of variation enabled the women to position themselves within the narrating event producing relevant distinctions within specific emerging and locally valid orders of indexicality. While nested within the stability of the dominant linguistic expression, these subtle repetitive soundings indexically located cosmopolitan women within a matrix of domination and served to animate forms of resistance linking them to circulating images of independent 'global girls' (McRobbie 2009) who constantly resist dominant positioning. A close examination of soundings and resoundings enables us to see how phonetic detail participated in the formation of knowledge claims and subject positions, showing that these were combinations of symbolic resources that enabled the dynamic construal of self images, where articulation of speech sounds, rhythms and vibrations actively shaped the sensory encounter and relationality. These sounded differences and repetitions, never static, were open to the dynamic interplay of embodied material combinations enacted in a world of power relations, and, at the same time, enabling emancipatory practices to be articulated.

Recognizing multiple logics: in-betweens

Finally, I turn to the third ideological orientation, which is markedly different from the other two positions in terms of dominant chronotopic frames, yet its rhythm is similar to Polish Poles. In these accounts, the self-presentation predominantly relies on images of evolving private selves operating within stable, but contrasting timespaces. The label, as suggested before, is my own invention at the time and should not be confused with in-betweenness as hybridity or language mixing used in other studies of migrants (e.g. Li and Zhu 2013). Like all participants, these five women and one man rather present their hybrid positioning in a particular way in these situated events. The label is used to suggest in-betweenness between the two extreme explicit positions towards sociocultural identification.

As in other accounts, the positioning of the self towards the country of origin and Polishness emerged as a unit of comparison to be highlighted and explained. In these accounts, the women and the man still identified as Polish, but oriented towards the world and Britain. To do so, they deployed images of the personalized self that moved between relatively stable timespaces. Such an act of identification is visible in excerpt (19), which comes from an interview with Edyta, a 27-year-old head-hunter who had spent eight years living and working in Greater London. In the extract, Edyta defined herself as an international *Polka* 'Pole', pronounced with a bilabial voiceless stop with an English-like VOT and default standard falling intonation. After my concurring *ok*, in (3), Edyta evaluated such a definition as potentially inadequate, sounding standard. In (4–5), I asked for a clarification, producing a standard unaspirated stop in *polskość* 'Polishness'. Edyta began her next turn aligning with being Polish as she asserted that she 'still feels Polish'. This was also reinforced by *Polka* 'Pole' pronounced with much lower VOT and again, falling intonation. As I relied on standard cues and did not take the floor, in (8–11), Edyta continued and positioned herself towards the question by contrasting facts from her own life abroad with life of Poles in Poland. To do so, she first deictically anchored her turn in the present with first-person singular marking on *mieszkam* 'I live' and then switched to first-person plural to refer to her and her international partner's travels, which she had mentioned before. When invoking the international character of her relationship, unlike cosmopolitan women, she maintained standard Polish means of expression. She then presented the timespaces as unchanging and herself as successfully evolving when she juxtaposed her 'approach to the world' with that of all her peers in Poland in lines (10–11). Each consecutive phrase ended with the default standard Polish fall for declaratives, Edyta used standard fricatives, no dark l, no vowel lengthening. Only, in line with tendencies for in-between women to use longer VOTs than Polish Poles, but shorter than cosmopolitans, she produced a slightly longer VOT in *kultury* (11) 'culture' disaligning herself from Poland. When comparing herself with 'Poles who stayed in Poland', she negatively evaluated them as a uniform whole, a group that were *mniej otwarci* 'less open', and accomplished her stance through the unfolding of the propositional content and standard means of expression.

(19) Edyta (I3)[12]

1 I3: nie wiem- międzynarodowa \P(50ms)olka
      I don't know- an international Pole

2 KK: ok

3 I3: ale nie wiem czy to jest wiesz (.) odpowiednie \określenie
      but I don't know you know if that's an appropriate term

4 KK: yyy dobrze to powiedz mi na czym polega ta twoja międzynarodowa /p(19ms)olskość
uhm ok so tell me what does your international Polishness consists in

5 °w takim razie°
then?

6 I3: w sensie że (.) nadal się czuję \P(30ms)olką
in that that I still feel like a Pole

7 KK: mhm

8 I3: ale mieszkam już tak długo za \granicą (laughter)
but I've lived abroad for so long

9 i wiesz i tyle żeśmy \jeździli
and you know and we've travelled so much

10 że wydaje mi się że jakby mam- mam trochę inne podejście do (.) \świata
that it seems to me that like I have- have a bit different approach to the world

10 niż Polacy którzy zostali \w Polsce   w tym samym \wieku
than Poles who stayed in Poland   the same age

11 którzy powiedzmy mniej \zobaczyli   czy są mniej otwarci na inne \kult(38ms)ury
who let's say have seen less   or are less open to other cultures

As shown earlier, in these accounts one's positioning was repeatedly linked to openness, which echoed cosmopolitan accounts. However, unlike cosmopolitans, in-betweens stressed that Polishness defined as cultural heritage was included in this definition, what they intended to keep when living abroad. Such an orientation is shown in excerpt (20), which comes from an interview with the only 32-year-old in-between man who had spent eight and a half years in the UK and worked as an advisor in the public sector closely cooperating with the European Union. In (1), he linked the self via a noun phrase *całe moje życie* to the European Union, an important part of his identity. While orienting himself towards 'Europeanness', he first aligned with the EU's practices, then critiqued them to finally evaluate this aspect of public life as *rzecz pozytywna że Europejczycy się zbierają do kupy i robią coś wspólnie* 'a positive thing that Europeans come together and do things together'. As the discourse unfolded, he relied on standardized Polish norms and finished taking the stance by admitting in (10) that Polishness was important to him, repeating the content that he introduced earlier and thus, completing his stance.

(20) Adrian (I6)

1 I6: prawie całe moje życie międzynarodowe związane jest z Unią \Europ(bad quality)ejską
    almost my whole international life is connected to the European Union

2   i dla mnie to jest też ważny element mojej \tożsa<u>mo</u>ści
    and for me this is an important element of my identity

3   \europ(24ms)ejskość   oraz to że ta europejskość się wyraża przez organizację
    Europeanness   *and that that this Europeanness is expressed through an international*

4   międzynarodową która według mnie robi dużo \do<u>bre</u>go
    organisation which is in my opinion doing a lot of good

5   też sporo złego albo robi to \źle
    also a lot of bad or does it wrong

6   jest to dla mnie rzecz pozytywna że Europejczycy się zbierają do \k(50ms)upy
    this is a positive thing to me that Europeans come together

7   i robią coś \wspólnie
    and do something together

...

8   to pewnie by się najpierw określił jako \czło<u>wie</u>ka
    so I would probably call myself a human being first

9   potem jako \Europej<u>czy</u>ka   a potem jako \Po<u>la</u>ka
    then a European   *and then a Pole*

10 dla mnie ta polskość jest na pewno \<u>wa</u>żna i może ważniejsza niż bym chciał to \<u>przy</u>znać
    for me this Polishness is for sure important and perhaps more important than I would like to admit

In these accounts, the personalized self was also scaled in relation to the othering discourses in the UK, but unlike in other accounts, such discourses were downplayed. In excerpt (21), Daria, a 23-year-old graduate student living in South-east England for three and a half years, admitted that the stereotype of an immigrant in the current locality, pronounced with an English-like rise-fall and vowel lengthening, was directed at Poles (1). In (2), she provided background information to support the claim 'Polish is the second language in the UK' and 'everybody is aware of the Polish presence'. She then recalled a recent scandal when the British Prime Minister called Poles 'a destructive element' (6). Relying mainly on the unfolding of the propositional content, she contrasted the introduced content with her evaluation *ale myslę że to było przypadkowe użycie* 'but I think it was a random usage' (6). After my concurring *mhm*, Daria went on to explain Cameron's position 'as not directed' at Poles, which was supported by the presence of positive opinions circulating in Britain: Polish migrants as hard-working, educated. To accomplish her stance, Daria sounded quite standard, although following the trend for all women, she used some fall-rises to maintain the floor.

(21) Daria (I4)

1 I4: myślę że ten stereotyp /\imigranta: jest trochę skierowany do \Polaków
I think that this stereotype of an immigrant   is somewhat directed at Poles

2   polski jest oficjalnie drugim najczęściej używanym językiem \w Anglii
     Polish is officially the second most used language in England

3   więc jakby wszyscy są świadomi tej obecności \Polaków
     so like everybody is aware of this presence of Poles

4   ale myślę że jednak nie ma takich strasznie negatywnych \skojarzeń
     but I think that there are no such horribly negative associations

5   no jakby ostatnia była ta afera z Cameronem który podał no- Polaków
     like recently there was this scandal with Cameron who used-   Poles

6   jako ten dystruktywny \element   ale myślę że to było przypadkowe \użycie
     as a destructive element   but I think it was a random usage

7 KK: mhm

8 I4: jakby tego \narodu   jakby to nie było do końca \skierowane   no bo jednak
      like this nation   like it wasn't directed   because still

9   dużo się czyta o \t(26ms)ym   że pracodawcy chwalą \Polaków   mówią że są
      one reads a lot about the fact   that employers command Poles   say that they are

10   bardzo ciężko \pracujący   i chwalą to że jednak dosyć wykształceni ludzie
      very hard-working   and command that still pretty educated people

11   przyjeżdżają tutaj \pracować   i że często jakby to jest dla nich właśnie
      come here to work   and that often like this is for them precisely

12   takie pozytywne doświadczenie zatrudnienie \/Polaka no bo on lepiej wykona
      such a positive experience to employ a Pole   because he will work better

13   pracę niż ktokolwiek \inny
      than anyone else

Unlike in other accounts, such practices were also repeatedly linked to education and knowledge. When Edyta, the 27-year-old head-hunter from Greater London introduced earlier, reflected on the stereotype of Eastern Europe as 'a less developed' region, similarly to other in-betweens, she recalled repeatedly countering the idea. To do so, she used a habitual verb form *tłumaczyłam*

'I was explaining', which she complemented with an evaluative claim *wcale aż tak źle nie jest* 'it's not that bad at all' (1). In (1–2), she contrasted the claim with an event in which her English-speaking partner's sister exhibited lack of knowledge about the presence of shopping malls in Poland. When introducing the event, she relied on the unfolding of the propositional content which ended in deixis of place *do Polski*, anchoring the event in the Polish state. While doing so, in line with a trend for in-betweens to use some aspirated stops similarly to cosmopolitan women, she produced an English-like VOT. While providing further detail, she described the sister as 'educated' (3). In (3), she projected more talk to come with a fall-rise and immediately provided more specific information about the sister's university studies and intelligence. Using direct quotation of the partner's assertion that he was unable to talk when in the shopping mall, she then quoted the sister's remark in (6), which she also mitigated for with a burst of laughter. She evaluated the content repeating the claim about the sister's perceived openness to internationalisms and contrasted it with the attitudes of 'the English who do not travel and all' (8). While taking the stance towards the object of talk, she occasionally relied on the new devices, but mostly followed standardized means of expression, which enabled her to complete her stance.

(22) Edyta (I3)

1 I3: wiesz no tłumaczyłam że może wcale aż tak źle nie\jest
   you know I was explaining that maybe it's not that bad at all

2 ale siostra [imię]-   jak [imię] po raz pierwszy przyjechał do \P(40ms)olski
   but [husband name]'s sister   when [husband's name] came to Poland for the first time

3 ona miała wtedy osiemnaście \lat   wiesz wyedukowana \/dziew<u>cz</u>yna
   she was eighteen years old then   you know an educated girl

4 em poszła też na bardzo dobre \st<u>u</u>dia   także \inteligentna \bystra   to \wiesz
   uhm she also studied for a very good degree   so intelligent   sharp   you know

5 [imię] powiedział nie mogę teraz z tobą \rozmawiać   jesteśmy w centrum
   [husband's name] said I can't talk to you right now   we're in a shopping

6 \hand<u>lo</u>wym powiedziała oni mają centra handlowe /w Polsce (h)
   mall   she said do they have shopping malls in Poland?

7 także- wiesz i to jest osoba która jest otwarta na międzynarodowe \wiesz
   so-   you know and this is a person who is open to international you know

8 także możesz sobie \wyob<u>ra</u>zić   co normalnie Anglicy myślą którzy nie jeżdżą i \w ogóle
   so you can imagine   what normally the English who don't travel and all think

At the same time, education and knowledge were also linked to in-betweens' repeated explicit disassociations from images of working-class Poles, echoing Polish public discourses linking racism and homophobia to the working classes. We see this in excerpt (23), a quote from the interview with Adrian, the only in-between man introduced earlier, who reflected on the presence of the stereotype of a Polish construction worker (1), which, as he mentioned before, as a man he had to frequently position himself towards in everyday life in Britain. When defining the presence of the stereotype with an English *implicit* (2), asserting that he had never personally experienced it, an attitude that he linked to his work environment. In (3–5), he introduced the image of a Pole who was not open. Relying on the standardized means of expression, he introduced a hypothetical scenario in which he acknowledged that he positioned himself towards others' assumptions about his ethnic background in Britain. As the discourse unfolded, he repeated lack of face-to-face confrontations with the stereotype, countered it with a possibility of circulating unspoken assumptions (11), and repeated the content asserting lack of face-to-face encounters (12). The repeated content combined with default linguistic norms enabled him to take a stance towards the object of talk, and make a knowledge claim divergent from that of Polish Poles, although similarly sounding.

(23) Adrian (I6)

1 I6: ze stereotypem z którym się spotykałem to głównie ten stereotyp /budow<u>la</u>ny
a stereotype that I've encountered is mainly the stereotype of a construction worker

2 czasami w mojej \p<u>ra</u>cy ale to jest takie bardziej \impl<u>i</u>cit nigdy tego nie
sometimes at work   but this is such more implicit   I've never

3 doświadczyłem na przykład \oso<u>bi</u>ście bo ja się zajmuję sprawami dialogu
experienced this for example personally   because I deal with matters related to intercultural

4 międzykulturowego rasizmu czy stosunków \wielokultu<u>ro</u>wych   Polacy z otwartości
dialogue racism or multicultural relations   Poles are rather

5 raczej na tym odcinku nie-
for openness at this interval not-

6 KK: nie słyną
not famous

7 I6: nie \s<u>ły</u>ną   więc ja na przykład pracuję \gdz<u>ieś</u>   i wypowiadam się na temat równości
not famous   so I am for example working somewhere   and talking about racial

8 \ra<u>so</u>wej   czy czy praw \czło<u>wie</u>ka   to zakładam że część osób na widowni
equality   or or human rights   then I assume that part of the audience

9 z którymi do których /mó<u>wię</u>   może mieć jakieś \stereot(27ms)ypy
with whom to whom I'm speaking   can have some stereotypes

10	ale nigdy mi tego nie powiedziano \wprost na temat tego że mogę być		
	but no one has ever said it to me directly that I can be		
11	rasistą i \homofobem	może tak oni \myślą	ale nigdy mi nikt tego
	a racist or a homophobe	*maybe they think like that*	*but no one has ever told me this*
12	w twarz nie \powiedział		
	to my face		

In these accounts, the images of 'violent' or 'drunk' working classes were also often mobilized to justify perceptions of the British public and its othering practices. In excerpt (24), Agata, the thirty-year-old scientist introduced earlier, recalled an encounter with another Polish migrant during her visit in a supermarket on Cowley Road in Oxford, stressing differences within the Polish-speaking population, which diverged from cosmopolitans' mitigating practices when discussing class differences. In the excerpt, we learn that Agata was raised with an ideal that when abroad, one must 'present oneself in the best way' (3), which set the scene for her recounting of the past encounter. As Agata provided background information, maintaining the floor with standardized norms, she went on to introduce the complicating action of meeting another Pole, labelling the other migrant with value-laden *straszny facet* 'an awful man', describing qualities of character, rather than focusing on actions alone, and *pijaczyna* 'drunkard' who *wydziera się pół po polsku pół po angielsku ale raczej po polsku* 'shouts half Polish half English but mostly in Polish' (6), pointing to lack of desired knowledge and quality. As she recounted subsequent actions, we learn that the shop assistant refused to sell him alcohol and Agata intervened, all pronounced in line with standardized norms, no fall-rises to maintain the floor, no aspiration in *po polsku* and so on. Agata eventually recalled asking the man to leave the supermarket and provided an explanation for her behaviour in (15–16). Using the first-person singular marking on the verb *chciałam* 'wanted', she explicitly asserted that she wanted to demonstrate the existence of 'different profiles' and counter the stereotype of a working-class Pole.

(24) Agata (I1)

1 I1:	moi rodzice zawsze wpoili mi takie \przekonanie	że być może jestem jedyną
	my parents have always instilled in me a conviction	*that maybe I'm the only*
2	Polką którą dane osoby \poznają	w związku z tym powinnam prezentować
	Pole that the given people will get to know	*so I should present*
3	się że tak powiem na tle kraju jak \najlepiej	i miałam taką
	myself so to speak against the background of the country in the best way	*and I had this*

4	jedną sytuację w sklepie na \Cowley		stoję sobie w supermarkecie w kolejce	
	one situation in a shop in Cowley		*I'm standing in a supermarket in a queue*	
5	przede mną taki straszny \facet	taki \pijaczyna	\z Polski	wydziera się
	in front of me such an awful man	*a drunkard*	*from Poland*	*is shouting*
6	pół po polsku pół po\ angielsku		ale raczej po \p(22ms)olsku	
	half Polish half English		*but mostly in Polish*	
7	że że chce kupić \alk(31ms)ohol		a sprzedawca mu go nie \sprzeda	
	that that he wants to buy alcohol		*and the shop assistant that he won't sell it to him*	
8	bo jest \pijany	zgodnie \z prawem	no i \podchodzę	bo było nas tylko \dwoje
	because he is drunk	*according to law*	*and I come closer*	*as there were only the two of us*
9	w tej \kolejce	właśnie ten pijaczek i \ja	i się pytam \sprzedawcy	
	in this queue	*just this drunkard and me*	*and I ask the shop assistant*	
10	taki młody \chłopak	nie bardzo wiedział jak sobie z tą sytuacją \poradzić		
	such a young guy	*he didn't really know how to deal with this situation*		
11	pytam się sprzedawcy czy pomóc \może		i sprzedawca mówi no nie chyba że	
	I ask the shop assistant whether I can help		*and he says no only if you*	
12	pani mówi po \p(28ms)olsku	ja mówię \tak	mówię po \p(bad quality)olsku	
	you speak Polish	*and I say yes*	*I speak Polish*	
13	i wyprosiłam tego pijaka ze sklepu po \p(15ms)olsku		bo chyba po angielsku	
	and I made this drunkard leave the shop in Polish		*because I guess in English*	
14	nie \rozumiał	i załatwiłam \sprawę	oczywiście mogłam się nie przyznać	
	he didn't understand	*and I dealt with the matter*	*of course I could've not admitted*	
15	do tego że jestem \P(26ms)olką		ale chciałam po prostu pokazać temu sprzedawcy	
	that I am a Pole		*but I just wanted to show this shop assistant*	
16	że są ludzie o różnych profilach z naszego \kraju		przynajmniej nie będzie	
	that there are people of different profiles from our country		*at least he won't*	
17	miał już tego przeświadczenia że Polacy przychodzą po pijaku i robią burdy \w sklepach			
	be convinced that Poles come drunk and make brawls in shops			

She then went on to share her reflections on different members of the Polish diaspora, where similarly to other in-betweens, she construed an image of an evolving self operating in relatively stable, but contrasting timespaces, associated with particular qualities of character and practices. Having described Poles in Argentina, when asked about the UK, she described Poles as 'toned down, maybe a little more polite' (10). This was, however, contrasted with 'at the same time Poles in the UK are a different race' (11). Relying on the unfolding of the propositional content as a way to maintain the floor, she introduced the idea of those 'who have been here for quite a few years' (12) as those who 'take on English features' (14), implying assimilation as a desired state. When clarifying differences between migrants, similarly to cosmopolitans, she signalled disalignment also by means of an English-like VOT (15). She described the newly arrived as 'rebellious' (18) and 'very revolutionary' (21). She evaluated their practices as positive, but immediately contrasted them with the English features as those one acquires in chronological, linear order when becoming a UK Pole. We see that when construing a desired image of UK Poles, Agata made use of standardized means of expression, with only occasional use of aspiration, overall achieving a different communicative effect from cosmopolitan women.

(25) Agata (I1)
1 I1: takie spostrzeżenia że zawsze jak się spotyka
such observations that always when one meets

2 ludzi polskiego \pocho<u>dze</u>nia
people of Polish origin

3 KK: mhm

4 I1: czy Polaków w różnych \kra̲jach to widzi się te cechy różnych
or Poles in various countries   then one sees features of various

5 innych narodów \w Pol<u>a</u>kach
other nations in Poles

6 KK: mhm

7 I1: no nie wiem Polacy z Argentyny są bardzo tacy głośni i \żywio<u>ło</u>wi
I don't know Poles in Argentina are very loud and frolic

8 i ((inaudible)) bardzo \spo<u>k(63)o</u>jni
and ((inaudible)) very calm

9 KK: to jacy są Polacy /<u>z Ang</u>lii
so what are the Poles in England like?

10 I1: y- \stono<u>wa</u>ni   tacy troszeczkę uprzejmiejsi \<u>mo</u>że: m: jednocześnie
uhm toned down   slightly more polite maybe   at the same time

11 Polacy w Anglii to jest troszeczkę inna \ra̲sa
Poles in England are a slightly different race

12 bo tacy Polacy którzy są tutaj już dobre kilka \<u>lat</u>
because Poles who have been here quite a few years

13 KK: mhm

14 I1: czy kilkanaście \nawet   przejmują te cechy \angielskie
       or a dozen even   take on English features

15   natomiast Polacy którzy przyjechali tutaj ze dwa trzy lata \t(37ms)emu
       but Poles who came here two three years ago

16   są nastawieni trochę na \walkę   bardzo często zaczynali od \zera
       they are oriented toward a fight they often started from zero

17   mimo że mieli kwalifikacje które były uznawane \w Polsce
       despite the fact that in Poland their qualifications were recognised

18   i mają taką troszeczkę buntowniczą \duszę   i wydaje mi się że po
       and they have slightly rebellious souls   and it seems to me that after

19   kilku /latach   to to podejście troszeczkę \okrzepnie
       a few years   this attitude will calm down

20   i staną się troszeczkę bardziej \angielscy   ale na początku są tacy
       and they'll become more English   but at the beginning they are so

21   bardzo bardzo \rewolucyjni   bo to oni zakładają związki zawodowe
       very very revolutionary   because that's them who set up trade unions

22   w różnych fabrykach gdzie \pracują   bo to oni są zainteresowani
       in various factories where they are working   because that's them who are interested

23   powstawaniem polskich \szkół   i oni zaczynają się domagać różnych \praw
       in setting up Polish schools   and who start demanding various rights

24   co jest bardzo dobre i bardzo \fajne   ale z kolei Polacy takiego nie wiem
       which is very good and very nice   but on the other hand Poles of such I don't know

25   powiedzmy drugiego pokolenia w Anglii przypominają
       let's say second generation in England resemble

26   bardziej Anglików niż \Polaków
       the British more than Poles

Additionally, in these accounts, mobility was desired and perceived as enabling opportunities and personal growth. Unlike cosmopolitans, in-betweens did not explicitly exclude a possibility of going back to Poland, but rather evaluated it as highly unlikely. Such an alignment with opportunities was visible when Adrian, the only in-between man introduced earlier, talked about his acceptance to a postgraduate degree at the University of Cambridge, which he was able to attend thanks to a full scholarship provided by the Polish state. In the quote, he compared the situation to *złapałem pana Boga za nogi*, an idiom that could be loosely translated into 'having a chance once in a life time'. Not long afterwards, he began his turn with 'at that stage' which he immediately linked to *teraz* 'now', the self *mi* and personal philosophy (5) to pursue 'various opportunities' that life brings or that he creates for himself (6–7). We see that to construe his self-image, Adrian did not employ any of the new devices and like speakers of 'standard' Polish predominantly relied on the unfolding of the propositional content and default pronunciation.

(26) Adrian (I6)
when talking about his acceptance to Cambridge
1 I6: ale myślałem że jak mi już zaproponowali w pełni płatne \styp(bad quality)endium
 but I thought that if they offered a fully funded scholarship

2 KK: nie no \tak (h)
 no right (h)

3 I6: to co ja jeszcze innego mogę /robić wydawało mi się że złapałem pana Boga
 so what still other can I do? *it seemed to me that I had a chance once*

4 za \nogi i \pojechałem
  in a lifetime *and I went*

...

5 na tym etapie zwłaszcza do teraz mi się nie zmieniła filozofia \życiowa
 at that stage especially till now my life philosophy hasn't changed

6 że raczej podążam za różnymi możliwościami czy \szansami które mi
 that I rather follow various opportunities or chances that

7 życie stwarza albo które sobie sam \stwarzam
 life creates for me or that I create for myself

As suggested earlier, class distinction was also reflected along gendered lines. This was clearly seen in women's repeated alignment with images of 'educated women' rather than the traditional Mother-Pole. For example, in excerpt (27), we see Agata, the thirty-year-old scientist from Oxford, positioning herself against classed images of Eastern European women as searching for Western husbands by referring to her doctoral degree. To construe a desired gendered image, Agata first introduced a scenario where she was faced with consequences of circulating stereotypes about Eastern European women as a whole. In (2), she recalled her visits to Australia, her partner's state of origin, where as she reported, she had been frequently interrogated at the airport. In (5), she provided explanation for bringing the encounter up by explicitly linking the authorities' practice to her region of origin. As the discourse unfolded, she used existing standardized devices to maintain the floor (rise in 5, 6), and connected the experience to anti-migration sentiments present worldwide. Finally, pointing to variation within the ethnic category, in (9–10), she introduced her Oxford degree to counter the logic of the encounter and accomplished her stance mainly in line with Polish standardized norms.

(27) Agata (I1)

1 I1:	czasami bycie Polką jest może troszeczkę \trud<u>nie</u>jsze		bo ma się te	
	sometimes being a Polish woman is slightly more difficult		*because you have these*	
2	problemy z wizami \cza<u>sa</u>mi	albo nie wiem na lotnisku w Australii		
	problems with visas sometimes	*or I don't know at the airport in Australia*		
3	zawsze mnie \przepyt(30ms)ują	°jakbym nie wiem co im \zro<u>bi</u>ła°		
	they always interrogate me	*as if I did I don't know what to them*		
4 KK:	/naprawdę			
	really?			
5 I1:	tak tak bo jak się jest z Europy /Wschod<u>n</u>iej		i się ma te dwadzieścia kilka /lat	
	yes yes because when you are from Eastern Europe		*and are twenty something years old*	
6	i się nie ma \<u>mę</u>ża	to znaczy że w tym raju na /<u>Zi</u>emi		którym jest \Aus<u>tra</u>lia
	and you don't have a husband	*this means that in this paradise on Earth*		*which is Australia*
7	i się zostanie na \zawsze i się zaraz złapie jakiegoś \Australij<u>czy</u>ka			
	and you'll stay forever	*and you'll catch an Australian man*		
8 KK:	no \<u>tak</u> (h)			
	oh yes			
9 I1:	i będzie się miało obywat(27ms)elstwo	i co Australia zrobi z doktorem		
	and you'll have the citizenship	*and what will Australia do with a PhD*		
10	z [dziedziny] z /Oks<u>for</u>du			
	in [field] from Oxford?			
11 KK:	(h)			
12 I1:	bo przecież trzeba nie wiem emigrantów /pogonić			
	because nevertheless immigrants need to, I don't know, be chased off			

Similarly to other accounts, in-betweens also linked the evolving self to their perception of desired ways of speaking. Here, the knowledge of English was usually defined as reflecting ambition, respect and learning skills, which also echoed cosmopolitan accounts. Such a logic can be found in excerpt (28), when Iwona, a 27-year-old scientist who had spent eight years in the UK and was working at Oxford, expressed her wish to speak English without a Polish accent (1). In (5), she provided explanation for her stance towards the English language: 'to show respect' and 'that I am able to learn'. This was contrasted with a way of speaking that made 'your hair stand on end' (6), with only one fall-rise on the final *dęba*, and completing her stance mainly in line with the norms reported for Polish.

(28) Iwona (I5)

1 I5: mnie by bardzo przeszkadzało mieć polski \akcent
   it would bother me a lot to have a Polish accent

2 naczy wiadomo że trochę go \mam
   that is it's obvious that I have it a bit

. . .

3 ja na przykład zawsze uważałam za taką ambicję \moją
   I for example always found it such my ambition

4 że chcę mówić dobrze po \angielsku   bo po pierwsze chcę pokazać że
   that I want to speak English well   *because first of all I want to show*

5 szanuję ten \język   po drugie chcę pokazać że umiem się \nauczyć
   that I respect the language   *secondly I want to show that I am able to learn*

6 a nie że będę \mówić   no tak że po prostu wszystkim włosy stają \/dęba
   and not that I'll be speaking   *in a way that makes one's hair stand on end*

Unlike Polish Poles, in-betweens also did not take a traditionalist stance towards the Polish language, but mixing was explained in relation to particular activities and having an accent, portrayed as less desired, 'a matter of bad taste', and again lack of education. In excerpt (29), Adrian provided such argumentation by linking Polish to his private self for whom the standard language signalled one's education and professionalism, at the same time linking his sensory preferences to previous comments.

(29) Adrian (I6)[13]

1 I6: >bo chciałbym mówić po \p(bad quality)olsku<
   because I would like to speak Polish

2 bo jest to język w którym mi się wydaje wciąż jestem najbardziej \sprawny
   because it seems to me that it is a language which I'm still most able to speak

3 KK: mhm

4 I6: jeśli zsumować \wszystko ymm angielski   >głównie ze względów \zawodowych<
   to sum it all up   *uhm English*   *mainly for professional reasons*

5 bo wiem że mi się angielski bardziej \przyda   >przydaje mi się z resztą< \t(26ms)eraz
   because I know that I'll use English more   *I'm actually using it now*

6		i bardziej mi się przyda w przyszłości niż \p(19ms)olski	>ponieważ tak jak powie<u>dzia</u>łem<
		and I'll be using it in the future more than Polish	*because as I said*
7		nie wiążę \z Polską	ani z \językiem polskim
		I don't bind with Poland	*nor with the Polish language*
8		>bo to też nie to< /<u>sa</u>mo	
		because it's also not the same	
9	KK:	mhm	
10	I6:	y:: y:m swojej przyszłości \zawo<u>do</u>wej	>gdybym pracował tutaj w jakiejś firmie<
		uh uhm my professional future	*if I worked here in a consulting*
11		\do<u>rad</u>czej i >analizował na co dzień< stan polskiej \gospo<u>da</u>rki	
		company and analysed the state of the Polish economy every day	
12		>to może miałoby to dla mnie również< znaczenie \zawo<u>do</u>we	
		then maybe it would also have professional meaning for me	
13	KK:	mhm	
14	I6:	jak ten polski \<u>znam</u>	\NIE >ma to dla mnie wielkiego znaczenia<
		if I know this Polish	*it doesn't have much meaning for me*
15		więc ten polski jest dla mnie teraz tylko- >przynajmniej w większości teraz< językiem	
		so this Polish is for me now only at least most of the time now a private	
16		\pry<u>wat</u>nym	
		language	
17	KK:	ok i nadal w tym [dla-	
		ok and still in this for-	
18	I6:	[>w tym języku prywatnym< jest to dla mnie \<u>waż</u>ne	
		in this private language it is important to me	
19	KK:	[ok	
20	I6:	[\<u>tak</u> >wydaje mi się że jest to dla mnie< \<u>waż</u>ne	
		yes it seems to me that it is important to me	
21		chociaż głównie to wynika z tej ogólnej \zasady	że że że jak się mówi w jakimś \języku
		although it mainly results from this general principle	*that that that if you speak a language*
22		>jak się mówi w nim <u>płyn</u>nie<	to >powinno się mówić \po<u>praw</u>nie<
		if you speak it fluently	*then you should speak properly*

In (1), Adrian asserted that he intended to speak Polish with a verb with first-person singular marking *chciałbym*. He then positioned himself towards Polish by calling it 'a language which I'm still most able to speak', ending in the default standard fall through which he signalled definitiveness and exercised authority. I expressed an understanding in (3) and Adrian continued listing further arguments for both languages. In (4–5), he produced a series of consecutive IPs following standard norms deictically anchored in the present in which he linked English to 'professional reasons' and the public life. In (5), while deictically anchoring his turn in the future and using first-person pronoun, he evaluated that English would be more useful for him. He then immediately positioned the object also in the present and reiterated its current usefulness (5). In (7), he explicitly asserted that he did not bind his future neither to Poland nor to Polish, disaligning from the country of origin. At the same time, both voiceless stops in onsets of nuclei in (5) and (6) were uttered with standard VOTs. In (10–12), he provided an alternative scenario to emphasize the point that Polish was not important in his professional life, sounding standard. In (14), after producing a loud negative particle *NIE* 'no', he used a prepositional phrase with first-person singular pronoun *dla mnie* 'for me' and evaluated Polish as a private language. When I picked upon the content and uttered a truncated phrase finishing in *w tym dla* 'in this for' (18), Adrian did not allow me to finish and continued repeating the propositional content explicitly asserting that it was important to him to speak Polish. I tried to express understanding, but it overlapped with Adrian's next turn in which he provided the final clarification about a general rule to speak any language well (21), a common rationale presented by in-betweens in which standard language was not linked to true selves, but disclosed level of education and professionalism. To do so, he shifted the scale to any language by using the indefinite *jakimś* 'a', and impersonal verb form in third-person singular *powinno się* 'should', throughout sounding standard.

In these accounts, we see yet another image emerging. Similarly to Polish Poles, the dominant frame in these encounters was mostly construed by means of standardized linguistic behaviour. However, for in-betweens, the self was personalized and not portrayed as part of a state-level formation. At the same time, rather than operating in the here and now similarly to cosmopolitans, it was evolving and moving through relatively unchanging timespaces, where connections were fixed through pointing to particular character attributes and valued types of knowledge. Finally, instead of rejecting nationality, in this section, we see an orientation in which ethno-racialized identification was embedded in being international and mobile, and where cultural heritage was understood usually in relation to ideals of 'high' culture portrayed as desired and maintained. In these self-presentations, the dominant frame of representation and enactment resulted in a predominantly classed orientation, where education and knowledge explained difference and helped navigate the contradictions of transnational space, heavily relying on rather than downplaying horizontal differences within the Polish-speaking population. In these situated encounters, such a reasoning also often enabled one to explain othering practices and contrast the assimilating and evolving self moving in chronological timeframe with racist, homophobic and violent recently arrived 'masses'. This went in line with imagination of language as in these accounts, speaking properly was portrayed as adding value and indexing one's professionalism and education. We see that the verbalized sensory inclinations made the participants pick out and negatively evaluate the changes in the sonic dimension of discourse, which echoed Polish Poles' evaluation, but was explained in relation to different actions and attributes. This in turn points to the multiplicity of logics contributing to emerging epistemologies of purification caused by sonic recontextualization.

5

Redefining Sociolinguistic Listening

Renegotiating our relationship with history through sensorial transformations

This book was devoted to the study of the ways in which time- and place-making processes were linked to subject creation through the chaining of signs at times of radical change. It focused on the situated production of perspectives on norms and practices, and how it was entangled in specific histories and concrete situations. It investigated the distribution of spaces, times and forms of engagement in relation to sensorial modes and bodily automatisms. Ethnographically locating relevant modalities of signification, it examined how the practice of sociolinguistic listening may be reused to understand how people on the move reconfigure their relation to circulating images of normality in the context of multipresence in various sites and extended capabilities of action enabled by the changing material and sociocultural infrastructures of the globalised world. By focusing on embodied material performances and dynamics of expert knowledge production, it aimed to trigger a conversation about the ways in which we experience history and come to recognize the emerging multiplicities of figuration. By tracing emerging sensory inclinations and examining how sounded signs lent themselves to participation, the book fleshed out the processes through which multilayered messages presented themselves to the senses. Considering connections between social and sensory orders, it tried to refocus the debate onto modes of transformation of categories in transnational space and material possibilities for action. Recognizing various perceptual knowledges and changing culturally constituted nature of the sensorium, it argued that a move away from the discourse-materiality dichotomy may help unpack how communities on the move come to reproduce systems of exclusion and inequality, how simultaneously, alternative visions emerge that challenge such systems and how this may unsettle the processes of parcelling relations of domination.

To do so, I started my investigation by bringing the reader closer to the unequal structuring of public subjectivities in a world that is always problematic (Haraway 1988). To explore how subject positions may be inhabited, contested or transformed in public research encounters in transnational space, I first introduced possible bodies and meanings relevant for the studied context. To do so, I walked the reader through the history of Polish and Eastern European migrations, dynamics of open European borders, commonalities and differences between the Polish and British states, and their entanglement in colonial history and legacy. An emerging picture pointed to complexities, contradictions and parallel realities. We saw how the state perspective enabled the emergence of dominant images of normality, in both states historically built on the White, upper and middle class, male heteronormative able-bodied citizen's gaze and perspective. A closer examination of the particular apparatuses of such a vision's production helped us see, however, that the focus on differences in these machineries enables the means for understanding the unsettling tensions resulting from forced one-to-one translations. Gradually moving away from the state perspective, I aimed to situate these processes of assembling categories in relation to contemporary politicization of movement in time and space. I pointed to dominant metaphors historically used to frame migrations, their resulting othering processes in the UK and contradictions of the simultaneous history of nesting orientalism in Eastern Europe. Such a global overview enabled me to argue that fixed soundings and appearances result from historical struggles over the production of ethno-racial and linguistic authority in which modernity/coloniality's insistence on linear social progress built in universal time continues to erase coexistent temporalities and spatial realities.

Following sensory inclinations relevant for the studied context, I wanted to show that sociolinguistic listening could be productively used to challenge sedentary logics and colonial definitions of culture (e.g. Das 2016; Eisenlohr 2007) and to move towards the study of processes of diaspora formation and emerging transformations of collective memory in contemporary mass-mediated society. Pointing out how standard register formation participates in the processes of demarcation of power and domination, I decided to examine how frames of representation were linked to frames of performance in my situated encounters with UK-educated Polish-speaking young adults in South-east England. By doing so, I wanted to draw the reader's attention to sociolinguistic listening's capacity to shed light on contemporary carthographies of communicability and materiality's role in empancipatory practices. I therefore investigated how my interlocutors positioned themselves towards social images associated with standardized Polish speech. My analysis of the local production of perspectives on norms and practices revealed three dominant ideological orientations that relied on different time-space-personhood configurations: from Polish Poles navigating the demands of the transnational space through the narrative of the real self operating in sociohistorical timespace, through in-betweens whose dominant chronotopic frame relied on presentation of the evolving self moving through stable, contrasting timespaces, to globalist cosmopolitan selves in the here and now. The juxtaposition of differing knowledge claims revealed that despite sharing social background, experiences and position, the participants scaled the self in relation to others, time and space in multiple ways, pointing to simultaneity of heteroglossic (Bakhtin 1981) interpretations and polycentricity of language norms.

The analysis focusing on emergent discourses of normality aimed to foreground the potential and force of the *fragment* in a never finished process of weaving self and collective images. Beginning with 'strange' or 'weird' diasporic soundings, which, for many, still threaten the social order, I wanted to see how chronotopic analysis of contradictory logics and rhythms may elucidate the ways in which the self constantly repositions itself in relation to altering constellations of power and how refocusing the debate onto the sounded experience, with its potential to link across singular subjectivities, may enable new angles of vision on 'bodies in process' (Bennett 2010). Tracing emerging cartographies of knowledge (Briggs 2007) in conjunction with sounded actions and reactions, I aimed to see how my participants navigated the demands of the global culture that forces ever-changing configurations, unsettles narratives of origins and produces fragmented 'unhomely' (Bhabba 1992) subjectivities, still located within particular structures and means of control. The comparison of accounts highlighted the dominance of some scalar metaphors (Hill and Mannheim 1992) and standardized linguistic forms, pointing out how scale-making practices may 'problematically fix one's view and limit imagination' (Carr and Lempert 2016). At the same time, it reminded us that scaling is 'discursively forged, pragmatically achieved, relational,' continually changing and potentially transforming.

The juxtaposition of different knowledge claims, scaled in relation to particular things, events and actions, also brought us closer to pluriversal alternatives and emerging vulnerabilities, always embedded in intersectional struggles and never theorized in detachment. We see that the processes of assembling scales of relevance at particular intersections of positionalities and interests were embedded in the constant co-constitution of elite and non-elite global modernities, nations and empires, where fears surrounding legal status, othering and competition between categories enabled particular ordering practices in which all 'objectif[ied] dimensions of time and space through the use of scalar metaphors' (Das 2016). Formed in the context of specific possibilities of access and privilege, the emerging accounts pointed to a continuum of ethno-racialized identification produced and recorded in situated research encounters. A close examination of material-discursive moves and countermoves demonstrated that all participants, prompted by the researcher, actively engaged in the re-appropriation of signifiers and all made judgements about aspects worth being reproduced. In line with the logic of global capitalism, difference was therefore continually exploited at multiple levels in the ongoing process of situated self-presentation, where fine-grained oppositions used to rationalize one's positioning echoed narratives of modernity built on contrast between the mind and body, reason and affect, experience and institution, society and nature, science and tradition, educated and primitive, female and male, civilized and violent, urban and rural, and so on (Das 2016).

Discourse analysis of the accounts pointed to the emerging complex concepts of the social self, where ethno-racialized, classed or gendered distinctions were made in relation to particular histories of collective images, memories, cultural symbols and constant processes of connecting beyond territorial lines challenging the relevance of a single metric. Continually scaling the self in relation to these multiple others that are always nearby (LaBelle 2018), we see overlapping histories of encounters with particular fixing regimes: from the receiving state's othering discourses and processes through gendered differences in life strategies to recognition and reproduction of class differences. The chronotopic analysis, however, foregrounded a more nuanced understanding of situated perspectival formation that enabled different possibilities of action (Woolard 2013). It also stressed the contested and ideological dimension of scale-making, suggesting divergent forms of engagement in public space and use of available resources.

At the same time, I wanted to draw attention to the significance of aesthetic judgements for the ways in which the senses mediated social worlds. I therefore decided to study the changing perceptual knowledges and role of sonic recontextualization in processes of authentication and purification. Similarly to other projects (e.g. Woolard 2016; Das 2016), my analysis revealed that there was no predictable correlation between the studied positioning and preference for linguistic purity. What was, however, visible was that in these accounts, standardized language was embedded in the politics of cultural imagination and long-distance nationalism that unfolded rapidly in time and space. Here again there was no uniformity: I had to recognize that the standard itself was imagined via various metaphors. For Polish Poles, it was a source of authenticity, for in-betweens, a sign of professionalism. Additionally, despite positive alignment with mixing practices, ideals of classed purity also emerged in the cosmopolitan accounts, where particular stigmatized constructions and lexical choices were still regarded as of lesser value. The participants' orientation towards standardized norms enabled the domination of ideals of linguistic purity, located in and mediated through sonic materiality. At the same time, the verbalized ideals of the self and the life in transnational space stood 'in tension with notions of what [was] practically achievable' (Carr and Lempert 2016). When sign material was thoroughly examined, we saw that English infiltrated the performances in convoluted ways: from occasional English-influenced grammatical constructions in the speech of Polish Poles, through sporadic use of new devices by in-betweens, to hybridized phonetic practices of cosmopolitan women. This in turn made visible that all boundary projects 'shift from within' (Haraway 1988) as interlocutors constantly redefine 'the partners in exchange, the objects of exchange and the very concept of exchange' (Sansi 2018: 123).

Closely examining surface representations of signs of migrations, my analysis also pointed to sociolinguistic listening's capacity to shed light on the body's affordances (Bucholtz and Hall 2016) for scale-making: how it was assembled, recognized and linked to particular images of time-space-personhood. Focusing only on one sense of scale, soundings and resoundings, I drew on an existing body of knowledge to use it as a proxy for understanding the emerging matter-energies and interdependencies that participated in the construal of these situated self-presentations. Building on circulating metacommentary linking sounded differences to people, I wanted to examine how sociolinguistic and phonetic tools could be used to investigate unexpected processes of embodied knowledge production. My analysis pushed us towards recognizing how linguistic production was embedded in complex perceptual and motor systems, but also to note that people *do* things with sounds and semiotics of the voice relies on non-uniformly distributed sociolinguistic knowledge. Collecting accounts of cosmopolitan women enabled me to think with the materiality of the code to see what is known, and what is missing, what beginning with the particular tells us about the larger vision, and what this in turn tells us about conditions for being heard.

While the cosmopolitan women's use of selected segmental and prosodic features was embedded in linguistic context like in other projects (e.g. Zhang 2005, Mendoza-Denton 2008), the features, performing selected discursive functions, participated in the construal of stances, positionalities and role alignments and depended on dynamic relationality. Similarly to Podesva (2016), the findings highlight that components of multilingual repertoires are best seen as 'resources for taking stances' about ethno-racial classification and othering issues. Following Mufwene (2020), I want to suggest that the collective soundings do not necessarily indicate shared grammars. 'More realistic is the assumption that [the interlocutors] communicate successfully with one another simply because their respective idiolectal grammars can process all their various utterances successfully most of the time' (Mufwene 2020) and repeated experience and engagement with certain soundings leads to reorganization of expected patternings. The collective soundings, however, enable us to see how emerging images of person types unsettle the sociolinguistic landscape through their very interactional moves and countermoves.

We cannot be, however, misled. My analysis was based on highly institutionalized encounters, produced under particular conditions of relationality, proximity, forces of control and surveillance. It was also conducted among participants who could be seen as fairly privileged, operating in a Western capitalist political economy, able to raise their voice to make knowledge claims in an academic project. Despite focusing on nuances, the project therefore built into the tradition of privileging elite experiences. It could be also argued that such an encounter is unusual and in the everyday life, we rarely explicitly position ourselves towards these images. What the analysis shows, however, is that even in such designed, one-to-one encounters, *imperfection* is key to understand how people relate to one another, how they make their talk heard and understood across different scales and whose voice and knowledge get to be institutionalized and become dominant. The focus on the sounded experience therefore enables us to move away from the perspective purely built on visual semiotics, with its potential to steer us towards rational objectivity, and towards the politics of the spoken word which relies on continual negotiation of forms and meanings. A close analysis of scale-making practices in relation to shifting infrastructures of sociocultural space in the globalised world may thus enhance the processes of figuration of new political subjectivities and emerging economies of attention, moving beyond colonial logics and subjects. Acknowledging that transience of linguistic performances is shaped through neoliberal pressures as well as changing *democratic* opportunities, we must also recognize its potential in making counter-narratives key for emerging communities of movement (Stavrides 2016) and reordering of the public for radical compassion and sharing.

Foregrounding that *sound is movement* (LaBelle 2018), my analysis also enables us to recognize the *transient* and *unexpected* as a productive position. We see that when called into being through an academic project, the relation to the dominant otherness is made and remade, interrupted and redirected through the constant transformation of self and collective images. The movements and explorations, through their embodied character, continually reinforce, but also challenge the stabilizing forces and the grid of what is expected. After Rosa and Flores (2017), we could argue that 'no embodied form is inherently racialized nor is any linguistic form discretely classifiable in relation to a named language'. Rather gradient linguistic forms are dynamically used as pragmatically salient indexes of subjectivity similarly to other projects (Mendoza-Denton 2008; Woolard 2008). At the same time, the analysis enables us to see that individual embodiments are always situated in relation to structures of power, which in turn may push us to analytical changes required to understand contemporary language data and phenomena. The emerging verbal gestures could be therefore seen as moments and forms of critical engagement and creative togetherness, where living with uncertainty, hybridity and intercultural confrontation generate multi-dimensional meanings and readings, while rhythming and sensing enable becoming conscious of *varied energies* and *complex solidarities*, with their challenges and opportunities.

Such a recognition may in turn help us understand and *craft* new ways of imagining self and collective images emerging in transnational, digitally mediated timespace, which in the everyday life spans across multiple situations, contexts, participation frameworks and materialities. Closely focusing on sensorial modes and their role for individuals and communities may help us see how the perception of the relationship between the self, others, time and space is changing and at the same time, remains embedded in the politics of accessibility and availability. As further ethnographic fieldwork, conducted for the Family Language Policy project in the Greater London area between 2017 and 2019, shows, emerging images of Polish-speaking migrants in the UK are rather always entangled in *complex, never complete* and *contradictory* embodied practices of being and living with others. At the same time, the emerging logics of repetition and renewal are expressed through multiple combinations of verbal and non-verbal signs. In our project post the Brexit vote, we demonstrate a plethora of ethno-racialized orientations and practices, always embedded in personal histories, history of power relations between and within communities at a particular time, situated configurations of human and non-human entities, communicative and bonding needs, access to material resources, prior multilingual experiences or legal arrangements. A fine-grained intersectional analysis enables us to show that contrary to portrayals of working classes circulating among participants whose accounts are analysed in this book, the continuum from national to cosmopolitan is actively exploited at multiple intersections.

The often massified working classes may therefore rely heavily on the narrative of the timeless Polish nation, but they may also disalign from state-level formations and align with ideals of global citizenship. Long-term ethnographic fieldwork at both community and family levels enables us to observe that discourses of linguistic authenticity and anonymity (Woolard 2016) impact orientation and practice in intricate ways. For example, when I talked about multilingual practices and contact with local authorities and social workers with working-class mothers in Haringey, London, discourses of realness were mobilized to mitigate for fears of not having the right to speak proper English. In the everyday life of some working-class families I worked with over the period of two years, I saw that such discourses, together with struggles for employment and housing as well as being at the receiving end of anti-migration sentiments, may lead to racist, homophobic and nationalistic displays. However, as my participants reminded me, there are generational and individual differences even within single families, which lead to constant negotiation of such positionings and practices. Importantly, the working classes also mix beyond the ethno-racial divide, which often enables new 'spaces of creativity and power' (bell hooks 1991) to emerge. This is perhaps most visible in the case of a two-parent non-heteronormative family with a history of transracial adoption (Kozminska and Zhu Hua 2021), where experiences of non-hegemonic masculinities, political economic subordination together with bonding needs and experts' advice led to continuous alignment with cosmopolitan values. In the everyday life, similarly to other contexts, elites and non-elites hence engage in creative tensions between demand and desire, necessity and opportunity, often 'refus[ing] the ideological dichotomy that has sustained language hierarchies in the modern period' (Woolard 2016: 304).

The focus on *enactment*, which is always situated, embedded, embodied and extended, may therefore help unpack how politics is negotiated, what possible contextual meanings of the orientations and practices may be identified and desirable norms and images perpetuated. It may also push us towards asking what different types of records may illuminate. By doing so, it may therefore help us understand how the old is brought into the new, how stories live on and reawaken different senses to imbue landscapes and timescapes with their own memory. Finally, it may help us see that 'human values are developed through the experience of listening' (Oliveros 2022: 2022) and sensing. This may enable us to move towards examining how political economic forces work and how individuals and communities re-establish their relationship with these forces. This in turn will highlight how 'values of care', which constitute 'qualitative, cultural and ethical foundations' for building 'radically caring societies' (Hall and Silver 2020), haunt the quantifiable economic 'dominance of capitalist logics of value'. Finally, such processes of unpacking how domination is produced may lead us to new forms of reflection and prioritizing collective action to renegotiate our relationship with history.

Expanding our tools to practise healing: Sociolinguistic listening as curatorship and radical openness

This book was written in the context of the ongoing 'crisis of care' (Fraser 2016), where 'the labour that builds the foundations of society goes both unrecognised and undervalued' (Hall and Silver 2020). Building on migratory matter produced by fairly privileged participants, I tried to devise an approach to tune into the web of interconnected thoughts, observations and feelings, and relations between them. The recent years and the specificity of the current historical conjuncture have taught me not to offer predictions and one-to-one explanations. In 2022, my participants from both projects were still in the UK. Estimates of Polish population suggested that in June 2021, the number dropped to second after India in terms of 'countries of birth for the foreign-born', but Poland was 'still the top country of citizenship of foreign citizens (696,000), accounting for 12% of non-UK citizens living in the UK' (https://migrationobservatory.ox.ac.uk/resources/briefings/migrants-in-the-uk-an-overview/). Some of my participants had also moved, to Poland or elsewhere, which included some cosmopolitan women. Additionally, some set up families, some changed their jobs and still others moved within the UK. The reader cannot therefore expect a set conclusion and there will be no attempt to imagine what the participants' social histories and life trajectories may be. These findings have also prompted multiple forms and interpretations, only highlighting that 'scale never means one thing' (Carr and Lempert 2016). The moment-by-moment heterogeneous processes bringing my participants' accounts into new webs and connections foregrounded the complexities of a changing social world, where no truth is absolute, but 'the rules that determine what counts as truth mean that some truths count more than others' (Collins 2019).

In this book, I have therefore attempted to focus on the interconnections between situated research actions, processes of knowledge production and communication. I aimed to investigate 'why some truths are present [...] while others remain neglected, as well as whose truths are believed and whose are dismissed' (Collins 2019). To do so, I approached my data as a means to generate new knowledge about adjustments that must be made to make sense of emerging transnational cultures and projects. In others words, I aimed to explore what 'can be opened up, conceptually and practically, whilst things are closed down', 'what can be thought differently' (Hall and Silver 2020) to make our tools more relevant to contemporary social transformations. My text and juxtaposition of rhythms and logics served to show that all time-space-personhood images are built through relations with other time-space-personhood images and it is materiality and aesthetic judgements that mediate the relation between them. To grasp what counts as normal in transnational space and imagine how better futures might be woven, I chose to let the data guide me towards processes of weaving that generate different realities. Moving beyond reflexive acknowledging of my position, which risks sociolinguists and anthropologists often 'coming to understand themselves', following Tinius and Macdonald (2020) and Ndikung (2021), I explicitly focused instead on *recursivity*, that is 'recursive sequence of revelation', an 'ongoing mutually-affecting relationality between things, people, thoughts, and forms of knowledge' (42). By doing so, in line with the material semiotic turn in humanities and social sciences, I wanted to investigate how politics of the *how* can push us towards asking why fragile webs and connections in objects of knowledge do not fall apart, how they overlap, impact one another and what combinations and relations produce what effects. I wanted to see what new routes for exploration and experience may be triggered by encounters with 'normality' and 'weirdness', when approached with wonder and without fear. I was curious to see how weirdness and sensory inclinations 'loop[] and weave[themselves] into our experience of reality' and what this enables us to learn about 'the limits of our own selves' and 'entangled colonies of consciousness' (Pilkington 2021: 67).

Developing my approach in the context of discourses of normality among fairly privileged positionalities and interests, I decided to focus on the emergence of the *dominant* scale: what regulatory mechanisms make it work and at *whose* expense. Focusing on embodied enactments and sensory experience, I explored how in situated accounts, different realities were woven through different material-discursive moves and countermoves, at the same time, stressing how difficult and time-consuming it may be to undo the domination of some scalar metaphors and rhythms. Having put different forms of language against one another, I would like to suggest that my analysis, however, urges us to move away from turning complex linguistic practices into objects with delimited and fixed boundaries, towards dynamic systems and processes shaped by evanescent and long-lasting explorations of possibilities and movements, constantly in search and done with others. My analysis made visible that nothing is connected to everything, but linguistic boundaries are best understood as 'interior routes of modernity/coloniality and global linear thinking' (Mignolo and Walsh 2018) that are continually reinforced, contested, disrupted and transformed.

The focus on the materiality of the code and its affordances aimed to highlight the ways in which people 'make signs in the context of interpersonal and institutional power relations to achieve specific aims' (https://multimodalityglossary.wordpress.com). By doing so, I wanted to draw the reader's attention to the ways in which situated epistemological claims were made through senses and how we come to hear each other in transnational space. By using phonetic tools in conjunction with discourse analysis, I focused on the ways in which heterogeneous knowledge projects emerged through the collaborative work between my participants and me. This enabled me to highlight the importance of interactions of sound relationships and their role in shaping modes of attention and consciousness. By doing so, I aimed to emphasize the processes contributing to the ways in which selective attention may pick out qualities and through actions and reactions link them to guesses about the signs' meanings (Gal and Irvine 2019). The analysis suggested that sounded differences would be best understood as interactionally developed scalar connections that in conjunction with other material–semiotic signs make value effects in the world. The focus on the consequences of particular soundings and resoundings also led me to 'an all-embracing perspective on an ever-expanding field' (Oliveros 2022: 51), where going beyond my own imagination I chose to shift assumptions to describe language phenomena that I encountered.

Remembering that sounds are partial in meaning-making and that these material events like all events may be taken up differently by others, I also wanted to show how sociolinguistic knowledge may be used not to make distinctions between the physical and the mental, but to flesh out how the focus on bodies situated in moments in history helps see how language is placed in the 'ideational-mental realm' where specific knowers learn off each other and through expressive forms 'convey objects of thought' (Gal and Irvine 2019). The detailed material–semiotic analysis aimed to draw the reader's attention to processes through which existing logics and rhythms continue to be evoked, rejected or transformed to produce new conjunctures and observations. Focusing on acts in the sensuous world, I flagged up how bodily response shapes and is shaped by the making and remaking of subjectivities in transnational timespace, where *all* bodies 'never leave[] the place of [their] production' (Inoue 2003: 165). I chose to listen to 'more than one reality simultaneously' (Oliveros 2022: 30), to reveal how 'what is heard is changed by listening and changes the listener' and how 'through training and experience' listening 'produces culture' (Oliveros 2022: 29). Building on the migratory sensorial matter produced by the privileged, I would finally like the reader to consider the findings' contribution to *undoing* dominant logics and carving a way to start imagining the form of the *underheard* and *silenced*: how new metric standards and parameters may be established when bodies open themselves up 'in order to survive' (LaBelle 2018: 68) and live with others, and how this in turn only underscores the 'inherent violence that fundamentally underpins the social order' (69).

It has been argued that 'we interpret what we hear according to the way we listen' (Oliveros 2022: 38). In her discussion of the 'strange' and 'unpleasant' speech of schoolgirls associated with lower classes in Japanese society in the nineteenth and twentieth centuries, Inoue (2003) argued further that 'the perception (whether auditory or visual) is never a natural or unmediated phenomenon but is always already a social and nationality', 'an effect of a regime of social power, occurring at a particular historical conjuncture, that enables, regulates, and proliferates sensory as well as other domains it, in turn, informs' (157). Discussing conditions of possibility for schoolgirls' speech to be heard, she notes the profound importance of the category of a *woman* for the social order and its deviation from the norm as a precondition to be perceived as 'a problem' or threat. We learn that schoolgirls' linguistic production and reception were entangled in the formation of the listening subject – the male intellectual and state authorities deeply engaged in the formation of 'modern' Japan built around ideals of autonomy and purity, where contaminated women's and girls' voices constituted a possibility for Japan 'to be held up to Western standards of modernity' (161). Inoue argues that schoolgirls' speech functioned as an 'acoustic mirror', where 'female-and-yet-modern' indexes inauthenticity and illegitimacy and at the same time, expresses Japanese male modernity, dislocated as peripheral and behind the 'authentic and original' Western modernity. She argues that the auditory emergence of the register only illuminates how 'the subject is inherently split and insufficient and that the wholeness of the subject [. . .] is an impossible ideal' (178). After Spivak (1988), she also reminds us that not all others can 'constitute themselves' and 'speak for themselves' in similar ways to those in dominant positions, and their possibilities of agency might, as in the case of Japanese schoolgirls from lower classes, lie precisely in the moments in which their voices 'arrest' others, challenging the liberal notion of the speaking subject (Bhabha 1994) and uncovering the auditory making of modernity.

We see that modernity is both seen and heard through particular historicities of telling and institutionalizing stories and subjects, which stresses the existence of competing modernities with 'their own dynamics, contradictions and syntheses' (Inoue 2003: 179). Inoue proposes that the violence of linguistic modernity lies not necessarily in erasing the other, but in excluding 'what the other is saying about what he or she said' (161). Working in the context of post-apartheid South Africa, Williams and Stroud (2015) propose to challenge the exclusion of feelings and reactions of the disenfranchised groups towards institutionally legitimized linguistic forms by paying close attention to the politics of everyday life and ways in which non-dominant groups articulate their multiple claims over various *senses of scale* in various 'zones of encounters'. Differentiating between private, parochial and public zones, with their blurred boundaries and overlapping domains, they point to the importance of often non-referential linguistic detail embedded in particular participation frameworks that involve chronotopic linkages between time-space-personhood and their specific combinations. Stressing that politics is often enacted in less research-like environments such as bars or pubs, they demonstrate how the stand-up comedy performances they analysed heavily relied on metapragmatic awareness of the crowd involved, hence their dynamic 'enregistering of linguistic features, and their subsequent uptake' (33). Drawing attention to the different ways in which sounds are pronounced, and code-mixing or pragmatic features of delivery are used, they point out their constitutive part in habitual choices that people make to express their voice (Stroud 2009). Moving away from static understandings of citizenship, they suggest to resist explanatory reductionism and refocus the debate onto 'acts of citizenship', which rely on their varied semiotics and rhetorical devices to make 'claims for justice'.

In his analysis of the creation of extreme locality among youth participating in cipha battles in South Africa, Williams (2016) further notes that grassroots multilingual practices and 'entextualization of the local' may create favourable conditions 'for expression of marginalised racial and ethnic identities', increasing potential for their agency. He reminds us that in some contexts 'the creation of extreme locality is necessary' as particular ways of speaking, like Cape Afrikaans, may be stigmatized across social space continually preventing its speakers from accessing spaces of power and upward mobility. Similarly to other projects on global hip-hop (e.g. Alim 2006), he shows how the youth engage in creative and strategic use of English, Cape Afrikaans, Sabela and African American English resources continually testing the limits of racialized varieties and forming new registers that challenge both inferiority of Cape Afrikaans and stigmatized portrayals of its speakers as 'unintelligent, lazy and criminal'. We see different ways of engaging with particular features and recontextualizing local and global resources in conjunction with local proxemics and dialogue with particular audiences. Crucially, Williams points out that the youth 'do so with the knowledge of the history of racial subjugation that has provided them the conditions to enregister such stereotypes since its creation in colonialism and transformation in apartheid', reminding us that we never act in a vacuum or, to paraphrase Eribon, we 'don't find a new form for ourselves coming out of nothing' (2019: 200).

Highlighting 'destabilizing hegemonic and oppressive processes of [ethno-] racial categorization' (Alim 2016), these projects and many other recent projects focusing on the relationship between language, race and ethnicity rather aim to push academic debates forward and critically disrupt ontologies on which these definitions are based and in relation to which insistent readings and impositions are done by others. When discussing 'the transracial subject as one who knowingly and fluidly crosses borders while resisting the imposition of racial categories', Alim points to the importance of 'push[ing] back against the need to know' who one 'really' is, at the same time fleshing out that to start undoing the dominant logics, 'a *collective* process of social transformation' [emphasis added] is needed. He argues further that the 'dialectic of positionality', rather than being about linear translation, consists of processes 'imbued with *active* choices' [emphasis added] and their political effects that are multidirectional and transgressive as they unpack the misconceptions of dominant imagination and practice. As part of mutual education and a way to understand how people navigate between resisting and strategically employing categorization in everyday life, the practice of sociolinguistic listening could be therefore reused to 'strengthen the possibilities and responsibilities of a public-facing academia' (Hall and Silver 2020). By putting the voices of those positioned as marginal as central, it may help confront our histories with honesty as we get to know each other in transnational space, and unpack the construction of the imagined whiteness and its links to linguistic imagination and practice.

In order for 'those categories, which were meant to define and control the world for us' not to continue to 'boomerang[] us into chaos' (Baldwin 1955), we must therefore let weirdness probe our own beliefs and acknowledge that 'the irreducible price of learning is realising that you do not know' (Baldwin 2018). This in turn may push as away from asking 'what counts as x' to exploring relations that make x through material–semiotic webs and weaves that come in different forms and styles and their subsequent consequences. This may help understand how 'stories justify and authorize the distinction among signs' (Gal and Irvine 2019: 275) and redirect previous flows of power. To do so, we must therefore offer a redefinition of sociolinguistic listening for unsettling systems of domination. Stressing the urgency of the calls for *participation* (e.g. Li Wei 2018), I would like to propose that the practice would be better off when seen as a form of curatorial authority and openness in which the researcher is 'invested in the project and opens their expertise up to the world' (Hicks 2020). If the reader like me finds rescue in the art world, they will note that curatorship involves acts of selecting and arranging as well as acts of control and use. Ndikung (2021) reminds us that it is also about '*caring* and *healing*' in the 'state of perpetual change' adjusting itself to time and space (49). It is therefore a practice 'malleable in form' and 'multiplicity of existences' that must care about the artist, the art as well engage in a deep understanding of the audience, extending in time and space, that is before, during and after the actual exhibition. Given the aforementioned, 'the curator has to be flexible' (Obrist 2014: 110).

Like curatorship, sociolinguistic listening is an embodied and affective practice in the process of knowledge production, where bonds of trust and opportunities for connections between multiple actors and mediation between various worlds are continually forged, 'creating the conditions for triggering sparks between them' (Obrist 2014: 154). Discussions on curatorship in the context of indigenous art often further question a possibility of a neutral presentation of knowledge where works are 'merely observations that relate to a particular experience within a particular context' (Flynn 2020: 181). I want to second this by arguing that sociolinguistic listening, like exhibition making, prevents us from the divorce of form from content, highlighting the impossibility of separating *social* and *aesthetic* forms. At the same time, my analysis of momentary stance-taking acts has put the spotlight onto the researcher's constant gaze and role in tracking and narrating the shared understandings and enactments of the participants' social worlds, reminding the reader of the dialectics and relationality of both scale-making projects and research production. Following Flynn, we must therefore recognize that both social and aesthetic forms influence both what *type* of knowledge and what its *articulation* may be. Turning away from unmediated accounts or disembodied research practices towards notions of epistemology of partial perspectives (e.g. Haraway 1988), we must recognize that all practices are situated along colonial matrices of power (Mignolo 2018) and as 'how we listen depends on our consciousness' (Oliveros 2022: 56), all impact the repository of collective memory.

We cannot therefore shy away from critically engaging with our own method and practice, perhaps not always acting against them, but participating in radical transformation of social matrix that guides our decision-making (Hicks 2020). To do so, we must take action against seeing our data as end points, not ongoing processes, as permanent forms, not multiple diverse materials. We must act against fixed formats that lack 'innovation in either a spatial or temporal dimension' (Orbist 2014:168) to change the rules of the game and create a ground for developing new ideas for conceptualizing the co-constitutive relation between flexible yet rooted in experience and recognizable, mobile yet emplaced, multiple yet singular subjects and their momentary material–semiotic attempts to hang together a sense of self and other in transnational timespace. By exploring edges of perception, we may be able to sense change, while perceiving the whole and highlight the interdependence of all beings and things. It is here hoped that sociolinguistic listening could help account for 'slight differences in perception, their interaction and effect' (Oliveros 2022) and help us navigate between the demands of the global cultures and multipresence in various sites with our senses.

Finally, if the collected soundings and resoundings could be compared to art, it might be also helpful to remind the reader that artistic practices, are 'ways of doing and making' which, to paraphrase Rancière (2013), intervene in the social world: in the organization of dominant and non-dominant 'ways of doing and making' (8) and in the relations that uphold dominant ways of being and being seen and heard. Hence, 'the exhibition is not an illustration. That is, it does not, ideally, represent the thing it purports to be "about"' (Orbist 2014: 167–8). Perhaps sociolinguistic listening could then centre around enabling better futures through the emergence of 'spaces of *care*' and opening up conversations, where *relationality* between perspectives and rhythms may become 'more than its parts' and generate *socioeconomic exchange* (Ndikung 2021). The conversations must not supplement action, and coalition-building, that is 'a vision wherein many people can see their interests identified and come together for a common good' (Dabiri 2021: 26), could benefit from links and connections emerging from sociolinguistic encounters in transnational space. Eleey (2015) adds that for an exhibition to be of high quality, 'something always needs to be put at risk', perhaps in the case of sociolinguistic listening, it might be worth putting at its heart 'a more *holistic* notion of *healing* that refers to the roots of our societal concerns and troubles' (Ndikung 2021).

Notes

Chapter 1

1 In this book, the term 'Eastern European' is used rather than East Central European or Central and East European. Ideological tensions surrounding the significance of the terms exist. However, no tensions were observed among my participants and Eastern European is a term commonly used in Britain.
2 This content was previously presented in Kozminska and Zhu Hua (2021).
3 A community of practice is defined by mutual engagement, a joint enterprise and a shared repertoire. The term was originally coined by Lave and Wenger (1991).
4 The term comes from Stavrides and LaBelle's work focusing on the emergence of new expressions of social solidarity, e.g., the movement of the squares. It highlights 'connective thresholds, commoning practices, and networks of care'.

Chapter 2

1 A subfield of sociolinguistics which studies the production and perception of linguistic variation.

Chapter 3

1 Parts of this section were previously discussed in Kozminska (2021) and Kozminska and Zhu Hua (2021).
2 With comments suggesting shared ownership.
3 Most content in this section was previously presented in Kozminska (2021).
4 Some studies Studies did not report correlation for gender (Ryalls et al. 1997; Syrdal 1996) and age (Petrosino et al. 1993; Neiman et al. 1983). Also, Lisker and Abramson (1964) did not report a correlation between VOT and speech rate.
5 Most of the content in this section was previously presented in Kozminska (2019).

Chapter 4

1. The stats were previously presented in Kozminska (2019, 2021).
2. Tests for men can be found in Kozminska, K. (2016).
3. This extract was previously presented in Kozminska (2021).
4. All names are pseudonyms. P- Polish Pole, I- in-between and C- cosmopolitans, ranked by Polishess Index scores.
5. This excerpt was previously presented and discussed in Kozminska (2020).
6. 12 of 17 Polish Poles had network scores ≤50 per cent, for 1, it approximates 50 per cent (46 per cent). Three male speakers with lower network scores are: Daniel – the only person who attended a British high school; Bartosz – an ethnic broker (had many Polish contacts, while reaching out to international contacts); Marek – the only overtly gay speaker (due to traditionally conservative character of Polish culture, he might have developed his social networks also outside of the Polish community). As women were developing different strategies to adjust to living in the UK, it may be reflected also in their social networks.
7. This excerpt was previously presented in Kozminska (2021).
8. This excerpt was previously presented and discussed in Kozminska (2020).
9. This excerpt was previously presented and discussed in Kozminska (2020).
10. Here, in line with lack of differences between the two language varieties in terms of velar stops, the VOT falls within the range of both varieties (60ms).
11. This excerpt was previously presented and discussed in Kozminska (2020).
12. This excerpt was previously presented and discussed in Kozminska (2020).
13. This excerpt was previously presented and discussed in Kozminska (2020).

References

Abdhullahi, S. and Li Wei (2021) 'Managing Language Shift Through Multimodality: Somali Families in London', in L. Wright and C. Higgins (eds), *Diversifying Family Language Policy*, London: Bloomsbury Academic.

Adichie, C. (2009) 'The Danger of a Single Story', https://www.ted.com/talks/chimamanda_ngozi_adichie_the_danger_of_a_single_story?language=en

Agha, A. (2003) 'The Social Life of Cultural Value', *Language and Communication* 23 (3–4): 231–73.

Agha, A. (2007a) *Language and Social Relations*, Cambridge: Cambridge University Press.

Agha, A. (2007b) 'Recombinant Selves in Mass-Mediated Spacetime', *Language and Communication* 27: 320–35.

Agha, A. (2009) 'What do Bilinguals do? A Commentary', in A. Reyes and A. Lo (eds), *Beyond Yellow English: Toward a Linguistic Anthropology of Asian Pacific America [Electronic Resource]*, 1–11, Oxford: Oxford University Press [Oxford Scholarship Online].

Alim, H. (2002) 'Street-conscious Copula Variation in the Hip Hop Nation', *American Speech* 77: 288–304.

Alim, H. (2006) *Roc the Mic Right: The Language of Hip Hop Culture*, London: Routledge.

Alim, H. (2016) 'Introducing Raciolinguistics: Racing Language and Languaging Race in Hyperracial Times', in H. Alim, J. Rickford, and A. Ball (eds), *Raciolinguistics: How Language Shapes Our Ideas About Race*, 1–30, Oxford Academic [online].

Allen, J. S., J. Miller, and D. David (2003) 'Individual Talker Differences in Voice-onset-time', *Journal of Acoustic Society of America* 113 (1): 544–52.

Anderson, B. (2006) *Imagined Communities: Reflections on the Origin and Spread of Nationalism*, London: Verso.

Anderson, B. and S. Blinder (2019) 'Briefing: "Who Counts as a Migrant? Definitions and Their Consequences"', https://migrationobservatory.ox.ac.uk/resources/briefings/who-counts-as-a-migrant-definitions-and-their-consequences/, accessed in 2020.

Anthony, L. (2015) *Antconc 8.5.9*, Tokyo: Waseda University.

Anzaldua, G. (2012 [1985]) *Borderlands: La Frontera: The New Mestiza*, San Francisco: Aunt lute Books.

Arendt, H. (1998) *The Human Condition*, Chicago, IL: University of Chicago Press.

Atkinson, P. (2014) *For Ethnography*. London: SAGE Publishing.

Austin, J. (1962) *How to do Things With Words: The William James Lectures*, Second Edition, Oxford: Oxford University Press.

Awan, S. and C. Stine (2011) 'Voice Onset Time in Indian English-accented Speech', *Clinical Linguistics & Phonetics* 25 (11–12): 998–1003.

Bajerowa, I. (2012) 'Język Ogólnopolski XX Wieku', in J. Bartmiński (ed.), *Współczesny Język Polski, Wydanie IV*, 23–49, Lublin: Wydawnictwo Uniwersytetu Marii Curie-Skłodowskiej.

Baker, P., C. Gabrielatos, and T. McEnery (2013) *Discourse Analysis and Media Attitudes: The Representation of Islam in the British Press*, Cambridge: Cambridge University Press.

Bakhtin, M. (1981) *The Dialogic Imagination*, Austin: University of Texas Press Slavic Series.

Baldwin, J. (2017 [1955]) *Notes of a Native Son*, London: Penguin UK.

Baldwin, J. (2018) *Dark Days*, Milton Keynes: Penguin Classics.

Balogun, B. (2020) 'Race and Racism in Poland: Theorising and Contextualising "Polish Centrism"', *The Sociological Review* 68 (6): 1196–211.

Barad, K. (2003) 'Posthumanist Performativity: Toward an Understanding of How Matter Comes to Matter', *Signs* 28 (3), https://doi.org/10.1086/345321.

Baugh, J. (2003) 'Linguistic Profiling', in S. Makoni, G. Smitherman, A. Ball, and A. Spears (eds), *Black Linguistics: Language, Society, and politics in Africa and the Americas*, 155–63, New York: Routledge.

Bauman, R. (2004) *A World of Others' Words*, Malden, MA: Blackwell Publishing.

Bauman, R. and C. Briggs (2003) *Voices of Modernity: Language Ideologies and the Politics of Inequality*, Cambridge: Cambridge University Press.

Bennett, J. (2010) *Vibrant Matter: A Political Ecology of Things*, Durham, NC: Duke University Press.

Betasamosake Simpson, L. (2011) *Dancing on Our Turtle's Back: Stories of Nishnaabeg Recreation, Resurgence and a New Emergence*, Winnipeg, Manitoba: ARP Books.

Bhabha, H. (1992) 'The World and the Home', *Social Text, 31/32 Third World and Post-Colonial Issues*, 141–53.

Bhabha, H. (1994) *The Location of Culture*, New York: Routledge.

Bidzińska, B. (2016) 'Debunking the Myth of Poland's Monoculturality', in V. Regan, C. Diskin, and J.Martyn (eds), *Language, Identity and Migration: Voices From Transnational Speakers and Communities*, 53–81, Oxford: Peter Lang.

Biedrzycki, L. (1972) *Polnische Aussprache*, Warszawa: Wiedza Powszechna.

Błasiak, M. (2011) *Dwujęzyczność i Ponglish. Zjawiska Językowo-Kulturowe Polskiej Emgiracji w Wielkiej Brytanii* [Bilingualism and Ponglish. Linguistic and Cultural Phenomena among Polish Immigrants in the UK], Kraków: Collegium Columbinum.

Blommaert, J (2007) 'Sociolinguistic Scales', *Intercultural Pragmatics* 4 (1): 1–19.

Blommaert, J. (2015) 'Chronotopes, Scales and Complexity in the Study of Language in Society', *Annual Review of Anthropology* 44: 105–16.

Blommaert, J. (2019) 'Sociolinguistic Scales in Retrospect', *Tilburg Papers in Culture Studies*, Paper 225.

Blommaert, J. and A. de Fina (2016) 'Chronotopic Identities: On the Timespace Organization of Who we are', https://biblio.ugent.be/publication/8552817/file/8552818.pdf.

Bobako, M. (2018) 'Semi-peripheral Islamophobias: The Political Diversity of Anti-Muslim Discourses in Poland', *Patterns of Prejudice* 52 (5): 448–60.

Boersma, P. and D. Weenink (2012) *Praat:* doi*ng Phonetics by Computer. Version 5.4.04*, http://www.praat.org/, accessed from April 2012 onwards.

Bourdieu, P. and L. Boltanski (1975) 'Le fétichisme de la langue', *Actes Rech. Sci. Soc.* 1: 2–32.

Bourdieu, P. (1977) 'The Economics of Linguistic Exchanges', *Social Science Information* 16 (6): 645–68.

Bourdieu, P. (1985) 'The Social Space and Genesis of Groups', *Social Science Information* 24 (2): 195–220.

Bourdieu, P. (1989) 'Social Space and Symbolic Power', *Sociological Theory* 7: 14–25.

Bourdieu, P. (1994) *Language and Symbolic Power*, Cambridge, MA: Harvard University Press.

Bren, P. and M. Neuburger (2012) 'Introduction', in P. Bren and M. Neuburger (eds), *Communism Unwrapped: Consumption in Cold War Eastern Europe*, New York: Oxford University Press.

Briggs, C. (2007) 'Anthropology, Interviewing, and Communicability in Contemporary Society', *Current Anthropology* 48 (4): 551–80.

Brown, K. (2003) *The Past in Question: Modern Macedonia and the Uncertainties of the Nation*, Princeton, NJ: Princeton University Press.

Brubaker, R. (2005) 'The "Diaspora" Diaspora', *Ethnic and Racial Studies* 28 (1): 1–19.

Bryan, B., S. Dadzie and S. Scafe (2018 [1985]) *Heart of the Race: Black Women's Lives in Britain*, London: Verso.

Bucholtz M. (1996) 'Geek the Girl: Language, Femininity and Female Nerds', in N. Warner, J. Ahlers, L. Bilmes, M. Oliver, S. Wertheim, M. Chen (eds), *Gender and Belief Systems*, 119–31, Berkeley, CA: Berkeley Women Lang.Group.

Bucholtz, M. (2000) 'The Politics of Transcription', *Journal of Pragmatics* 32: 1439–65.

Bucholtz, M. (2009) 'From Stance to Style: Gender, Interaction, and Indexicality in Mexican Immigrant Youth Slang', in A. Jaffe (ed.), *Stance*, 146–71, Oxford: Oxford University Press.

Bucholtz, M. and K. Hall (2005) 'Identity and Interaction: A Sociocultural Linguistic Approach', *Discourse Studies* 7: 4–5.

Bucholtz, M. and K. Hall (2016) 'Embodied Sociolinguistics', in N. Coupland (ed.), *Sociolinguistics: Theoretical Debates*, 173–97, Cambridge: Cambridge University Press.

Burrell, K. (2006) *Moving Lives: Narratives of Nation and Migration Among Europeans in Post-War Britain*, Aldershot: Ashgate.

Butler, J. (1990) *Gender Trouble: Feminism and the Subversion of Identity*, London: Routledge.

Butler, J. (1993) *Bodies That Matter: On the Discursive Limits of Sex*, London: Routledge.
Byrd, D. (1993) '54 000 American Stops, UCLA Work. Pap', *Phonetics* 83: 97–116.
Cameron, D. (2001) *Working with spoken discourse*, London: Sage.
Cameron, D. (2014) 'Gender and Language Ideologies', in S. Ehrlich, M. Meyerhoff, and J. Holmes (eds), *The Handbook of Language, Gender and Sexuality*, 281–96, Malden, MA: Blackwell Publishing.
Cameron, D. (2018) *Feminism*, London: Profile books.
Carby, H. (2019) *Imperial Intimacies: A Tale of Two Islands*, London: Verso.
Carr, E. Summerson (2010) 'Enactments of Expertise', *Annual Review of Anthropology* 39: 17–32.
Carr, E Summerson and M. Lempert (2016) *Scale: Discourse and Dimensions of Social Life*, Berkeley: University of California Press.
Central Statistical Office (2007) 'Women in Poland', http://stat.gov.pl/en/topics/other-studies/otheraggregated-studies/women-in-poland,2,1.htm, accessed March 2015.
Cheshire, J. (2020) 'Taking the Longer View: Explaining Multicultural London English and Multicultural Paris French', *Journal of Sociolinguistics* 24 (3): 308–27.
Cheshire, J., P. Kerswill, S. Fox, and E. Torgersen (2011) 'Contact, the Feature Pool and the Speech Community: The Emergence of Multicultural London English', *Journal of Sociolinguistics* 15: 151–98.
Chłopicki, W. (2002) 'Język Trzeciego Tysiąclecia II', in W. Chłopicki (ed.), *Polszczyzna a Języki Obce: Przekład i Dydaktyka, Tertium, Język a Komunikacja 2*, Kraków: Tertium.
Chun, E. (2001) 'The Construction of White, Black, and Korean American Identities Through African American Vernacular English', *Journal of Linguistic Anthropology* 11 (1): 52–64.
Clothier, J. and D. Loakes (2018) 'Coronal Stop VOT in Australian English: Lebanese Australians and Mainstream Australian English', in J. Epps, J. Wolfe, J. Smith, and C. Jones (eds), *Proceedings of the Seventeenth Australasian International Conference on Speech Science and Technology*, UNSW, Sydney, Australia.
Clyne, M. (1991) *Community Languages: The Australian Experience*, Cambridge: Cambridge University Press.
Collins, P. (1990) *Black Feminist Thought: Knowledge, Consciousness and the Politics of Empowerment*, Boston: Unwin Hyman.
Collins, P. (2015) 'Intersectionality's Definitional Dilemmas', *The Annual Review of Sociology* 41: 1–20.
Collins, P. (2019) *Intersectionality as Critical Social Theory*, Durham, NC: Duke University Press [ebook].
Condee, N. (2006) 'The Anti-imperialist Empire and After: In Dialogue With Gayatri Spivak's 'Are You Postcolonial?', *PMLA* 121 (3): 829–31.
Connerton, P. (1989) *How Societies Remember*, Cambridge: Cambridge University Press.

Couper-Kuhlen, E. and M. Selting (1996) *Prosody in Conversation: Interactional Studies*, Cambridge: Cambridge University Press.

Cowan, L. (2021) *Border Nation: A Story of Migration*, London: Pluto Press.

Cruttenden, A. (1995) 'Rises in English', in J. Windsor Lewis (ed.), *Studies in General and English Phonetics. Essays in Honour of Prof. J. D. O'Connor*, 155–73, London: Routledge.

Dabiri, E. (2021) *What White People Can Do Next: From Allyship to Coalition*, Dublin: Penguin Random House Ireland.

Das, S. (2016) *Linguistic Rivalries: Tamil Migrants and Anglo-Franco Conflicts*, New York: Oxford University Press.

Datta, A. (2007) 'East European Builders in London: Everyday Cosmopolitanism in Everyday Places of the Global City', Paper presented at the RGS-IBG Annual Conference, 28 August.

Davies, N. (2015) *Trail of Hope: The Anders Army, an Odyssey Across Three Continents*, Oxford: Osprey Publishing.

Dębski, R. (2009) *Dwujęzyczność Angielsko-Polska w Australii: Języki Mniejszościowe w Dobie Globalizacji i Informatyzacji. [Polish-English Bilingualism in Australia: Minority Languages in the Times of Globalization and Informatization.]*, Kraków: Wydawnictwo Uniwersytetu Jagiellońskiego.

DeGraff, M. (2001) 'On the Origin of Creoles: A Cartesian Critique of Neo-Darwinian Linguistics', *Linguistic Typology* 5 (2–3): 213–310.

DeGraff, M. (2020) 'Toward Racial Justice in Linguistics: The Case of Creole Studies', *Language: Journal of the Linguistic Society of America* 96 (4): e292–e306.

de Jong, N. and T. Wempe (2014) 'Praat Script Syllable Nuclei', https://sites.google.com/site/speechrate/Home/praat-script-syllable-nuclei-v2, accessed December 2014.

de Leeuw, E. (2014) 'Maturational Constraints in Bilingual Speech', in E. Mon Thomas and I. Mennen (eds), *Advances in the Study of Bilingualism*, 25–41, Bristol: Multlilingual Matters.

Deumert, A., A. Storch, and N. Shepherd (2020) *Colonial and Decolonial Linguistics: Knowledges and Epistemes*, Oxford: Oxford Scholarship Online.

Diskin, C. and V. Regan (2017) 'The Attitudes of Recently-Arrived Polish Migrants to Irish English', *World Englishes* 36 (2): 191–207.

Dmitrieva, O., A. Jongman, and S. Joan (2010) 'Phonological Neutralization by Native and Non-native Speakers: The Case of Russian Final Devoicing', *Journal of Phonetics* 38: 483–92.

Docherty, G. (1992) *The Timing of Voicing in British English Obstruents*, New York: Foris Publications [Electronic Resource].

Docherty, G., W. Dominic, L. Carmen, D. Hall, and J. Nycz (2011) 'Variation in Voice Onset Time Along the Scottish-English Border', in *Proceedings of the 17th International Congress of Phonetic Sciences*, 591–4.

Domański, H. (2015) *Czy są w Polsce Klasy Społeczne?* Warszawa: Wydawnictwo Krytyki Politycznej.
Dorling, D. (2019 [2014]) *Inequality and the 1%*, London: Verso.
Dorling, D. and S. Tomlinson (2019) *Rule Britannia: Brexit and The End of Empire*, London: Biteback Publishing.
Doroszewski, W. (1952) *Podstawy Gramatyki Polskiej*, Warszawa: PWN.
Drinkwater, S., J. Eade, and M. Garapich (2006) 'Poles Apart? EU Enlargement and the Labour Market Outcomes of Immigrants in the UK', in *IZA Discussion Paper Number 2410*. Bonn: The Institute for the Study of Labor (IZA).
Drummond, R. (2012) 'The Manchester Polish STRUT: Dialect Acquisition in a Second Language', *Journal of English Linguistics* 41 (1), 65–93.
Drummond, R. (2018) 'Maybe it's a Grime [t]ing: TH-stopping Among Urban British Youth', *Language in Society* 47 (2): 171–96.
DuBois, J. (2007) 'The Stance Triangle', in R. Englebretson (ed.), *Stancetaking in Discourse: Subjectivity, Evaluation, Interaction*, 139–82, Amsterdam: John Benjamins.
Duranti, A. (1997) *Linguistic Anthropology*, Cambridge: Cambridge University Press.
Duszak, A., (2002) *Us and Others: Social Identities Across Languages, Discourses and Cultures*, Amsterdam: John Benjamins.
Eade, J., S. Drinkwater, and M. Garapich (2007) *Class and Ethnicity: Polish Migrant Workers in London – Full Research Report*, Swindon: Economic and Social Research Council.
Eckert, P. (1989) 'The Whole Woman: Sex and Gender Differences in Variation', *Language Variation and Change* 1: 245–67.
Eckert, P. (2012) 'Three Waves of Variation Study: The Emergence of Meaning in the Study of Sociolinguistic Variation', *The Annual Review of Anthropology* 41: 87–100.
Eisenlohr, P. (2007) *Little India: Diaspora, Time and Ethnolinguistic Belonging in Hindu Mauritius*, Berkeley and Los Angeles: University of California Press.
Eleey, P. (2015 [2013]) 'What About Responsibility?' in W. Beshty (ed.), *Ethics*, 195–201, London: White Chapel Gallery.
Eribon, D. (2019) *Powrót do Reims [Returning to Reims]*, Kraków: Wydawnictwo Karakter.
Errington, J. (2001) 'Colonial Linguistics', *Annual Review of Anthropology* 30: 19–39.
Errington, J. (2008) *Linguistics in a Colonial World: A Story of Language, Meaning and Power*, Malden, MA: Blackwell Publishing.
Fabiszak, M. (2007) 'Migration as Schooling, Migration as Holidays', Paper presented at 'New Europeans under Scrutiny: Workshop on State-of-the-Art Research on Polish Migration to the UK', University of Wolverhampton, 2 February.
Fanon, F. (2021 [1952]) *Black Skin, White Masks*, English translation. Penguin Modern Classics.
Faudree, P. (2012) 'Music, Language and Text: Sound and Semiotic Ethnography', *Annual Review of Anthropology* 41: 519–36.

Fidelis, M. (2020) 'Gender, Historia i Komunizm', in K. Stańczyk-Wiślicz, P. Perkowski, M. Fidelis, and B. Klich-Kluczewska (eds), *Kobiety w Polsce 1945-1989: Nowoczesność, Równouprawnienie, Komunizm*, 25–45, Universitas.

Flege, J. (1987) 'The Production of New and Similar Phones in a Foreign Language: Evidence for the Effect of Equivalence Classification', *Journal of Phonetics* 15: 47–65.

Flege, J. (2007) 'Language Contact in Bilingualism: Phonetic System Interactions', in J. Cole and J. Hualde (eds), *Laboratory Phonology 9*, 353–83. Berlin: Mouton de Gruyter.

Flege, J. and W. Eefting (1987) 'Cross-language Switching in Stop Consonant Perception and Production by Dutch Speakers of English', *Speech Communication* 6: 185–202.

Flynn, A. (2020) 'The Curator, the Anthropologist: "Presentialism" and Open-ended Enquiry in process', in R. Sansi (ed.), *The Anthropologist as Curator*, 173–95, London: Bloomsbury Academic.

Fomina, J. and J. Frelak (2008) *Next Stopski London: Public Perceptions of Labour Migration Within the EU. The Case of Polish Labour Migrants in the British Press*, Warsaw: Institute of Public Affairs.

Fox, J. and M. Mogilnicka (2017) 'Pathological Integration, or, How East Europeans Use Racism to Become British', *The British Journal of Sociology* [published online], 70 (1): 5–23.

Fox, J., L. Morosanu, and E. Szilassy (2012) 'The Racialisation of the New European Migration to the UK', *Sociology* 46 (4): 680–95.

Francuzik, K., M. Karpiński, and J. Kleśta (2002) 'A Preliminary Study of the Intonational Phrase, Nuclear Melody and Pauses in Polish Semi-Spontaneous Narration', Paper presented at Speech Prosody 2002, International Conference, CNRS, Aix-en-Provence.

Francuzik, K., M. Karpiński, J. Kleśta, and E. Szalkowska (2005) 'Nuclear Melody in Polish Semi-Spontaneous and Read Speech: Evidence From the Polish Intonational Database PoInt', *Studia Phonetica Posnanensia* 7: 97–128.

Fraser, N. (2016) 'Contradictions and Crisis of Care', *New Left Review*, https://newleftreview.org/issues/ii100/articles/nancy-fraser-contradictions-of-capital-and-care.

French, B. (2012) 'Semiotics of Collective Memories', *Annual Review of Anthropology* 41: 337–53.

Gago, V. (2020) *Feminist International: How to Change Everything*, London: Verso.

Gal, S. (1998) 'Multiplicity and Contention Among Language Ideologies: A Commentary', in B. Schieffelin, K. Woolard, and P. Kroskrity (eds), *Language Ideologies*, 317–32, Oxford: Oxford University Press.

Gal, S. (2016) 'Scale-Making: Comparison and Perspective as Ideological Projects', in Summerson Carr and Michael Lempert (eds), *Scale: Discourse and Dimension of*

Social Life, University of California Press [ebook], https://www.luminosoa.org/site/books/10.1525/luminos.15/read/?loc=016.xhtml.

Gal, S. and J. Irvine (2019) *Signs of Difference: Language and Ideology in Social Life*, Cambridge: Cambridge University Press.

Gal, Susan and Gail Kligman (2000) *The Politics of Gender After Socialism*, Princeton, NJ: Princeton University Press.

Garapich, M. (2008) 'Odyssean Refugees, Migrants and Power: Construction of the "Other" and Civic Participation Within the Polish Community in the United Kingdom', in D. Reed-Danahay and C. Bretell (eds), *Citizenship, Political Engagement and Belonging: Immigrants in Europe and the United States*, 124–43, New Brunswick, NJ: Rutgers University Press.

Garapich, M. (2016) *London's Polish Borders: Transnationalizing Class and Ethnicity Among Polish Migrants in London*, Stuttgart: Ibidem-Verlag.

Garcia, O., N. Flores, K. Seltzer, Li Wei, R. Otheguy, and J. Rosa (2021) 'Rejecting Abyssal Thinking in the Language and Education of Racialized Bilinguals: A Manifesto', *Critical Inquiry in Language Studies* 18 (3): 203–28.

Garner, S. (2009) 'Home Truths: The White Working Class and the Racialization of Social Housing', in K. P. Sveinsson (ed.), *Who Cares about the White Working Class*, 45–50, London: Runnymede Trust.

Gdula, M. and P. Sadura (2012) *Style Życia i Porządek Klasowy w Polsce*, Warszawa: Wydawnictwo Naukowe SCHOLAR.

Gellner, E. (1983) *Nations and Nationalism*, Malden, MA: Blackwell Publishing.

Gershon, I. and P. Manning (2014) 'Language and Media', in N. Enfield, P. Kockelman, and J. Sidnell (eds), *The Cambridge Handbook of Linguistic Anthropology* [online], 559–76, Cambridge University Press.

Gilroy, P. (2004) *After Empire*, London: Routledge.

Goffman, E. (1983) 'The Interaction Order', *American Sociological Review* 48: 1–17.

Gopal, P. (2019) *Insurgent Empire: Anticolonial Resistance and British Dissent*, London: Verso.

Grabe, E. and M. Karpiński (2002) 'Universal and Language-Specific Aspects of Intonation in English and Polish', Paper presented at 15th ICPhS Conference, Barcelona.

Grabe, E., G. Kochanski, and J. Coleman (2005) 'The Intonation of Native Accent Varieties in the British Isles - Potential for Miscommunication?', in K. Dziubalska-Kolaczyk and J. Przedlacka (eds), *English Pronunciation Models: A Changing Scene*, Linguistics Insights Series, Peter Lang.

Graff, A. (2001) *Świat bez Kobiet: Płeć w Polskim życiu Publicznym*, Warszawa: Wydawnictwo W.A.B.

Graff, A. (2008) *Rykoszetem: Rzecz o Płci, Seksualności i Narodzie*, Warszawa: Wydawnictwo W.A.B.

Graff, A. and E. Karolczuk (2022) *Anti-gender Politics in the Populist Moment*, London: Routledge.

Gramsci, A. (1971) *Selections From the Prison Notebooks*, New York: International Press.

Grybosiowa, A. (2003) 'Modern Polish', in A. Grybosiowa (ed.), *Język wtopiony w rzeczywistość*, 197–202, Katowice.

Gumperz, J. and N. Berenz (1993) 'On Data Collection', in J. Edwards and M. Lampert (eds), *Talking Data: Transcription and Coding in Discourse Research*, 91–121, Hillsdale, NJ: Erlbaum.

Gussenhoven, C. (1984) *On the Grammar and Semantics of Sentence Accents*, Dordrecht: Foris.

Guy, G., B. Horvath, J. Vonwiller, E. Daisley, and I. Rogers (1986) 'An Intonational Change in Progress in Australian English', *Language in Society* 15: 23–52.

Halej, J. (2014) *Other Whites, White Others: East European Migrants and the Boundaries of Whiteness*, PhD thesis School of Slavonic and East European Studies UCL.

Hall, S. (1975) 'Africa is Alive and Well and Living in the Diaspora', Unpublished paper given at UNESCO conference.

Hall, S. (1977) 'Culture, Media and the Ideological Effect', in J. Curran et al. (eds), *Mass Communication and Society*, 315–48, Beverly Hills, CA: SAGE Publications. First published 1952.

Hall, S. (1995) 'Cultural Identity and Diaspora', in B. Ashcroft, G. Griffiths, and H. Tiffin (eds), *Post-Colonial Studies Reader*, 435–9, London: Routledge.

Hall, S. (2015) 'Super-diverse Street: A 'Trans-ethnography' Across Migrant Localities', *Ethnic & Racial Studies* 38 (1): 22–37.

Hall, S. and D. Silver (2020) 'Radical Care as the Foundation for a Better World' [online], *The Sociological Review Magazine*, 16 March. https://doi.org/10.51428/tsr.clmd4093.

Hanks, W. (1996) *Language and Communicative Practice*, Boulder, CO: Westview.

Haraway, D. (1988) 'Situated Knowledges: The Science Question in Feminism and the Privilege of Partial Perspective', *Feminist Studies* 14 (3), 575–99.

Haraway, D. (2006) *When Species Meet*, Minneapolis, MN: University of Minnesota Press.

Harris, R. (2006) *New Ethnicities and Language Use*, Basingstoke: Palgrave Macmillan.

Hebdige, D. (1979) *Subculture: The Meaning of Style*, London: Routledge.

Heller, M., S. Pietikäinen, and J. Pujolar (2018) *Critical Sociolinguistic Research Methods: Studying Language Issues That Matter*, London: Routledge.

HESA (2014) www.hesa.ac.uk/content/view/1897/239, accessed in 2015.

Hicks, D. (2020) *The Brutish Museums: The Benin Bronzes, Colonial Violence and Cultural Restitution*, London: Pluto Press.

Hill, J. (2008) *The Everyday Language of White Racism*, Chichester: Blackwell Publishing.

Hill, J. and B. Mannheim (1992) 'Language and World View', *Annual Review of Anthropology* 21: 381–406.

Hill, J. and O. Zepeda (1993) 'Mrs. Patricio's Trouble: The Distribution of Responsibility in an Account of Personal Experience', in J. Hill and J. Irvine (eds), *Responsibility and Evidence in Oral Discourse Studies in the Social and Cultural Foundations of Language*, Series Number 15, Cambridge: Cambridge University Press.

Hobsbawm, E. (1990) *Nations and Nationalism Since 1780*, New York: Cambridge University Press.

hooks, bell (1991) *Yearning: Race, Gender and Cultural Politics*. London: Turnaround.

hooks, bell (2015) *Talking Back: Thinking Feminist, Thinking Black*, London: Routledge.

House of Commons (2016) 'Briefing Paper no CBP7660 Polish Population of the United Kingdom', https://www.google.com/url?sa=t&rct=j&q=&esrc=s&source=web&cd=&ved=2ahUKEwjtbjD88HvAhXMilwKHRc6CowQFjAAegQIARAD&url=https%3A%2F%2Fcommonslibrary. parliament.uk%2Fresearch-briefings%2Fcbp7660%2F&usg=AOvVaw12azeerfsq0Bvqt_lbZwMe, accessed in August 2020.

Howes, D. (1991) *Varieties of Sensory Experience: A Sourcebook in the Anthropology of the Senses*, Toronto and Buffalo: University of Toronto Press.

Hudley, C., C. Mallinson, and M. Bucholtz (2020) 'Toward Racial Justice in Linguistics: Interdisciplinary Insights Into Theorizing Race in the Discipline and Diversifying the Profession', *Language* 96 (4): e200–e235.

Inoue, M. (2003) 'The Listening Subject of Japanese Modernity and His Auditory Double: Citing, Sighting, and Siting the Modern Japanese Woman', *Cultural Anthropology* 18 (2), 156–93.

Inoue, M. (2011) 'Stenography and Ventriloquism in Late Nineteenth Century Japan', *Language and Communication* 31: 181–90.

Irvine, J. (2001) '"Style" as Distinctiveness: The Culture and Ideology of Linguistic Differentiation', in P. Eckert and J. Rickford (eds), *Style and Sociolinguistic Variation*, 21–43, Cambridge: Cambridge University Press.

Irvine, J. (2008) 'Subjected Words: African Linguistics and the Colonial Encounter', *Language and Communication* 28: 323–43.

Irvine, J. (2016) 'Afterword: Materiality and Language, or Material Language? Dualisms and Embodiment', in J. Cavanaugh and S. Shankar (eds), *Language and Materiality: Ethnographic and Theoretical Explorations*, Cambridge: Cambridge University Press.

Irvine, J. and S. Gal (2000) 'Language Ideology and Linguistic Differentiation', in P. Kroskrity (ed.), *Regimes of Language: Ideologies, Polities and Identities*, 35–84, Santa Fe: School of American Research Press.

Jacquemet, M. (2019) 'Beyond the Speech Community: On Belonging to a Multilingual, Diasporic and Digital Social Network', *Language and Communication* 68: 46–56.

Jakobson, R. (1960) 'Linguistics and Poetics', in T. A. Sebeok (ed), *Style in Language*, 350–77, Cambridge, MA, MIT Press.

Janik, J. (1996) 'Polish Language Maintenance of the Polish Students at Princes Hill Saturday School in Melbourne', *Journal of Multilingual and Multicultural Development* 17 (1): 3–16.

Jassem, W. (2003) 'Polish', *Journal of the International Phonetic Association* 33 (1): 103–7.

Jassem, W. and P. Łobacz. (1971) 'Analiza fonotaktyczna tekstu polskiego', Prace Instytutu Podstawowych Problemów Techniki PAN nr 62.
Johnson, K. (2003) *Acoustic and Auditory Phonetics*, Oxford: Blackwell Publishing.
Johnstone, B. (2016a) 'The Sociolinguistics of Globalization: Standardization and Localization in the Context of Change', *Annual Review of Linguistics* 2: 349–65.
Johnstone, B. (2016b) 'Enregisterment: How Linguistic Items Become Linked With Ways of Speaking', *Language and Linguistics Compass* 10: 632–43.
Kącki, M. (2015) *Białystok: Biała Siła, Czarna Pamięć [Białystok: White Power, Black Memory]*, Wołowiec: Wydawnictwo czarne.
Karimzad, F. (2020) 'Metapragmatics of Normalcy: Mobility, Context, and Language Choice', *Language and Communication* 70: 107–18.
Karpiński, M. (2002) 'The Corpus of Polish Intonational Database', *Investigationes Linguisticae* VIII: 24–5.
Karpiński, M. (2006) *Struktura i Intonacja Polskiego Dialogu Zdaniowego*, Poznań: Uniwersytet im. Adama Mickiewicza.
Keating, E. (2005) 'Homo Prostheticus: Problematizing the Notions of Activity and Computer-mediated Interaction', *Discourse Studies* 7 (4–5): 527–45.
Keating, P., M. Mikos, and W. Ganong III (1981) 'A Cross-language Study of Range of Voice Onset Time in the Perception of Stop Consonant Voicing', *Journal of Acoustical Society of America* 70 (5): 1260–71.
Keenen, E. (1974) 'Norm-makers, Norm-brakers: Uses of Speech by Men and Women in a Malagasy Community, in R. Bauman and J. Sherzer (eds), *Explorations in the Ethnography of Speaking*, 125–43, Cambridge: Cambridge University Press.
Kelley, R. (2002) *Freedom Dreams: The Black Radical Imagination*, Boston, MA: Beacon Press.
Kenney, P. (1997) *Rebuilding Poland: Workers and Communists, 1945–1950*, Ithaca, NY: Cornell University Press.
Kent, S. (1999) *Gender and Power in Britain, 1640–1990*, London: Routledge. [e-book].
Kępińska, E. (2004) 'Recent Trends in International Migration. The 2004 SOPEMI Report for Poland', University of Warsaw Centre for Migration Research Working Paper Number 29/87. Warsaw: University of Warsaw Centre for Migration Research.
Kessinger, R. and S. Blumstein (1997) 'Effects of Speaking Rate on Voice-Onset Time in Thai, French, and English', *Journal of Phonetics* 25: 143–68.
Khan, K. (2020) 'What Does a Terrorist Sound Like? Language and Racialised Representations of Muslims', in S. Alim, A. Reyes, and P. Kroskrity (eds), *The Oxford Handbook of Language and Race*, 398–422, Oxford Academic [ebook].
Kiełkiewicz-Janowiak, A. (2019) 'Gender Specification of Polish Nouns Naming People: Language System and Public Debate', *Slovenščina 2.0* 7 (2), 141–71, https://doi.org/10.4312/slo2.0.2019.2.141-171.

Kiesling, S. (1998) 'Men's Identities and Sociolinguistic Variation: The Case of Fraternity Men', *Journal of Sociolinguistics* 2 (1): 69–99.

Kiesling, S. (2019) *Language, Gender and Sexuality: An Introduction*, London: Routledge.

Kircher, R. and S. Fox (2019) 'Multicultural London English and its Speakers: A Corpus-informed Discourse Study of Standard Language Ideology and Social Stereotypes', *Journal of Multilingual and Multicultural Development* 42 (9): 792–810.

Klatt, D. (1975) 'Voice Onset Time, Frication and Aspiration in Word-initial Clusters', *Journal of Speech and Hearing Research* 18: 686–705.

Kobiałka, E. (2016) 'Language, Identity and Social Class Among Polish Migrants in Ireland', in V. Regan, C. Diskin, and J. Martyn (eds), *Language, Identity and Migration*, Oxford: Peter Lang [ebook].

Kołodziejek, E. (2008) 'Nowa Jakość Polszczyzny: Zagrożenie czy Szansa?', in Z. Cygal-Krupa (ed.), *Perspektywy, Zagrożenia, Współczesna Polszczyzna*. Kraków-Tarnów: Państwowa Wyższa Szkoła Zawodowa w Tarnowie.

Konert-Panek, M. (2009) 'The Impact of English on Polish: Can Our Pronunciation Also Change?', *Zeszyty Naukowe* WSE-I 23: 109–15.

Kontra,M., M. Sloboda, J. Nekvapil, and A. Kiełkiewicz-Janowiak (in press) 'Sociolinguistics in East Central Europe', in Martin Ball (ed.), *Sociolinguistics Around the World*.

Kopczyński, A. (1977) *Polish and American English Consonant Phonemes: A Contrastive Study*, Warszawa: Państwowe Wydawnictwo Naukowe.

Korcz, P. and M. Matulewski (2006) 'Wpływ globalizacji na powstawanie polsko-angielskiego pidżynu zawodowego', *Język, Informacja i Komunikacja* 1: 77–90.

Kordasiewicz, A. and P. Sadura (2017) 'Migrations, Engagement and Integration of Poles in the UK and in London Borough of Lewisham: Research and Data Review Within the Londoner-Pole-citizen Project', CMR working Papers 100/158.

Korys, I. (2004) 'Migration Trends in Selected Applicant Countries. Volume III – Poland', In *Dilemmas of a Sending and Receiving Country*. Vienna: International Organization for Migration, https://publications.iom.int/system/files/pdf/migrationtrends_eu_3.pdf.

Kozminska, K. (2016) *Language and Identity in a Transnational Context: A Sociophonetic Study of the Polish of a Group of Migrants Living in the UK*, DPhil thesis, University of Oxford.

Kozminska, K. (2019) 'Intonation, Identity and Contact-Induced Change Among Polish-speaking Migrants in the UK', *Journal of Sociolinguistics* 23 (1): 29–53.

Kozminska, K. (2020) 'Sounding Out Difference: Polycentricity of Ideological Orientations Among Polish-speaking Migrants in Transnational Timespace', *Journal of Linguistic Anthropology* 30 (3): 412–37.

Kozminska, K. (2021) 'Scaling Diasporic Soundings: A Study of Polish Stops in the UK', *Language and Communication* 77: 17–34.

Kozminska, K. and Zhu Hua (2021) '"Dobra Polska Mowa": Monoglot Ideology, Multilingual Reality and Polish Organisations in the UK', *International Journal of Sociology of Language* 269: 73–98.

Kress, G. (2010) *Multimodality: A Social Semiotic Approach to Contemporary Communication*, London: Routledge.

Kress, G. and T. van Leeuwen (1996) *Reading Images: The Grammar of Visual Design*, London: Routledge.

Kroskrity, P. (1998) 'Arizona Tewa Kiva Speech as a Manifestation of a Dominant Language Ideology', in B. Schieffelin, K. Woolard, and P. Kroskrity (eds), *Language Ideologies*, 103–22, New York: Oxford University Press.

Kroskrity, P. (2018) 'On Recognizing Persistence in the Indigenous Language Ideologies of Multilingualism in Two Native American Communities', *Language and Communication* 62(B): 133–44.

Kroskrity, P. (2021) 'Language Ideological Assemblages Within Linguistic Anthropology', in A. Burkette and T. Warhol (eds), *Crossing Borders, Making Connections: Interdisciplinarity in Linguistics.* Berlin, Boston: De Gruyter Mouton.

LaBelle, B. (2018) *Sonic Agency: Sound and Emergent Forms of Resistance*, London: Goldsmiths Press.

Labov, W. (1966) *The Social Stratification of English in New York City*, Washington, DC: Center for Applied Linguistics.

Labov, W. (1972) *Sociolinguistic Patterns*, Philadelphia: University of Pennsylvania Press.

Ladd, D. (1996) *Intonational Phonology*, Cambridge: Cambridge University Press.

Ladefoged, P. (2012) *Vowels and Consonants*, Malden, MA: Blackwell Publishing.

Lave, J. and E. Wenger (1991) *Situated Learning: Legitimate Peripheral Participation*, New York: Cambridge University Press.

Law, J. (2019) 'Material Semiotics', www.heterogeneities.net/publications/Law2019MaterialSemiotics.pdf, accessed January 2023.

Leder, A. (2014) *Prześniona Rewolucja: Ćwiczenie z Logiki Historycznej [Sleepwalking the Revolution: An Exercise in Historical Logic]*, Warszawa: Wydawnictwo Krytyki Politycznej.

Lefebvre, H. (2013) *Rhythmanalysis: Space, Time and Everyday Life*, London: Bloomsbury Academic.

Lefebvre, H. (2014) *Critique of Everyday Life*. London: Verso.

Lemon, A. (2002) 'Without a "Concept"? Race as Discursive Practice', *Slavic Review* 61 (1): 54–61.

Lempert, M. and S. Perrino (eds) (2007) 'Temporalities in Text', *Language and Communication* 27 (3): 205–336.

Lennes, M. (2002) 'Cutting Long Sound Files', http://www.helsinki.fi/wlennes/praatscripts/public/save_labeled_intervals_to_wav_sound_files.praat, accessed December 2014.

Levon, E. (2014) 'High Rising Terminals in London: Gender, Ethnicity and Interactional Meaning', *UI Chicago/Urbana-Champagne*.

Levon, E. and S. Fox (2014) 'Social Salience and the Sociolinguistic Monitor: A Case Study of ing and TH-fronting in Britain', *Journal of English Linguistics* 42 (3): 185–217.

Leyk, A. and J. Wawrzyniak (2020) *Cięcia: Mówiona Historia Transformacji*, Warszawa: Wydawnictwo Krytyki Politycznej. Seria Historyczna [38].

Li, Wei (2018) 'Translanguaging as a Practical Theory of Language', *Applied Linguistics* 39: 9–30.

Li, Wei and Zhu Hua (2013) 'Translanguaging Identities and Ideologies: Creating Transnational Space Through Flexible Multilingual Practices Amongst Chinese University Students in the UK', *Applied Linguistics* 34 (5): 516–35.

Lisker, L. and A. Abramson (1964) 'A Cross Language Study of Voicing in Initial Stops: Acoustic Measurements', *Word* 20: 384–422.

Lisker, L. and A. Abramson (1967a) 'Some Effects of Context on Voice Onset Time in English Stops', *Language and Speech* 10: 1–28.

Lisker, L., and A. Abramson (1967b) 'A Cross Language Study of Voicing in Initial Stops: Acoustic Measurements', *Word* 20: 384–422.

Local, J. (1992) 'Continuing and Restarting', in P. Auer and A. di Luzio (eds), *Contextualization of Language*, 272–96, Amsterdam: John Benjamins.

Lubaś, W. (1996) 'Polszczyzna Wobec Najnowszych Przemian Społecznych. O Zagrożeniach i Bogactwie Polszczyzny', *Forum Kultury Słowa*, 153–61.

Luczak, C. (1984) 'Displacement of People During the Second World War', in A. Pilch (ed.), *Emigration from Polish Lands in Modern and Recent Times*, Warsaw: Polish Scientific Publishers.

Macaulay, R. (1977) *Language, Social Class and Education: A Glasgow Study*, Edinburgh: University of Edinburgh Press.

Mackiewicz-Krassowska, H. (1973) 'Intonation of English and Polish Declarative Sentences', *Psicl* II: 137–44.

Maddieson, I. (1997) 'Phonetic Universals', in Hardcastle, W. and J. Laver (eds), *The Handbook of Phonetic Science*, 619–39, Oxford: Blackwell Publishing.

Mahmood, S. (2005) *Politics of Piety: The Islamic Revival and the Feminist Subject*, Princeton, NJ: Princeton University Press.

Major, R. (1992) 'Losing English as a First Language', *Modern Language Journal* 76: 190–208.

Makoni, S. and A. Pennycook (2007) *Disinventing and Reconstituting Languages*, Clevedon: Multilingual Matters.

Massey, Doreen (2007) *World City*, Cambridge: Polity Press.

Maternik, E. (2003) 'Polsko-angielski Pidgin w Dziedzinie Logistyki', in W. Krzeminska and P.Nowak (eds), *Studia nad Językiem, Informacją i Komunikacją*, Poznań: Sorus.

McLemore, C. (1991) *The Pragmatic Interpretation of English Declarative Intonation*, PhD, University of Texas.

McRobbie, A. (2009) *The Aftermath of Feminism: Gender, Culture and Social Change*, London: SAGE.

Mendoza-Denton, N. (2008) *Homegirls: Language and Cultural Practice Among Latina Youth Gangs*, Oxford: Blackwell Publishing.

Meyerhoff, M. and E. Schleef (2012) 'Variation, Contact and Social Indexicality in the Acquisition of (ing) by Teenage Migrants', *Journal of Sociolinguistics* 16 (3): 398–416.

Mignolo, W. (2020) 'Colonial Semiosis and Decolonial Reconstitutions', *Echo* 2: 8–15.

Mignolo, W. and C. Walsh (2018) *On Decoloniality: Concepts, Analytics, Praxis*, Durham, NC: Duke University Press [e-book].

Milroy, L. and J. Milroy (1992) 'Social Network and Social Class: Toward an Integrated Sociolinguistic Model', *Language in Society* 21 (1): 1–26.

Milroy, James and Lesley Milroy (2012) *Authority in Language: Investigating Standard English*, Abingdon: Routledge.

Ministerstwo Pracy i Polityki Społecznej Departament Rynku Pracy Wydział Analiz i Statystyki (2013) 'Sytuacja Na Rynku Pracy Osób Młodych w 2013 Roku', https://www.mpips.gov.pl/download/gfx/mpips/pl/defaultopisy/8666/1/1/SYTUACJA%20NA%20RYNKU%20PRACY%20OSOB%20MLODYCH%20W%202013.pdf, accessed March 2014.

Miodunka, W. (2003) *Bilingwizm polsko-portugalski w Brazylii. [Polish-Portuguese Bilingualism in Brazil.]*, Kraków: Universitas.

Moore, M. and G. Ramsay (2017) 'UK Media Coverage of the 2016 EU Referendum Campaign, King's College London, Centre for the Study of Media, Communication and Power', https://www.kcl.ac.uk/policy-institute/assets/cmcp/uk-media-coverage-of-the-2016-eureferendum-campaign.pdf.

Mufwene, S. (2010) 'Globalization: Global English, and World English(es): Myths and Facts', in N. Coupland (ed) *The Handbook of Language and Globalization*, 50–75.

Mufwene, S. (2020) 'Decolonial Linguistics as Paradigm Shift. A Commentary', in A. Deumert, A. Storch, and N. Shepherd (eds), *Colonial and Decolonial Linguistics: Knowledges and Epistemes*, 289–300, Oxford Scholarship Online.

Munn, N. (1992) 'The Cultural Anthropology of Time: A Critical Essay', *Annual Review of Anthropology* 21: 93–123.

Nagy, N. and A. Kochetov (2013) 'VOT Across the Generations: A Cross-linguistic Study of Contact-induced Change', in M. Schultz and P.Siemund (eds), *Multilingualism and Language Contact in Urban Areas: Acquisition-development-teaching -communication*, 19–38, Amsterdam: John Benjamins.

Ndikung, B. (2021) *The Delusions of Care*, Berlin: Archive Books.

Neiman, G., R. Klich, and E. Shuey (1983) 'Voice Onset Time in Young and 70-year-old Women', *Journal of Speech and Hearing Research* 26 (1), 118–23.

Newlin-Łukowicz, L. (2014) 'From Interference to Transfer in Language Contact: Variation in Voice Onset Time', *Language Variation and Change* 26: 359–85.

Nichols, P. (1983) 'Linguistic Options and Choices for Black Women in the Rural South', in B. Thome, C. Kramarae, and N. Henley (eds), *Language, Gender and Society*, 54–68, Rowley, MA: Newbury House.

Nowicka McLees, B. (2010) 'Polish in the USA', in K. Potowski (ed.), *Language Diversity in the USA*, 238–54, Cambridge: Cambridge University Press.

Ochs, E. (1992) 'Indexing Gender', in A. Duranti and C. Goodwin (eds), *Rethinking Context*, 335–58, Cambridge: Cambridge University Press.

Ochs, E. and L. Capps (2001) *Living Narrative: Creating Lives in Everyday Storytelling*, Cambridge, MA: Harvard University Press.

Office for National Statistics (2011) 'Detailed Country of Birth and Nationality Analysis From the 2011 Census of England and Wales', www.ons.gov.uk/ons/rel/census/2011-census/detailed-characteristics-for-localauthorities-in-england-and-wales/country-of-birth---rpt.html, accessed March 2015.

Ohala, J. (1981) 'Articulatory Constraints on the Cognitive Representation of Speech', in Myers, T. et al. (eds), *The Cognitive Representation of Speech*, 111–22, Amsterdam: North Holland.

Okólski, M. (1999) *'Poland's Migration: Growing Diversity of Flows and People.' Prace Migracyjne nr 29*. Warszawa: Instytut Studiów Społecznych Uniwersytet Warszawski.

Okólski, M. and J. Salt (2014) 'Polish Emigration to the UK After 2004: Why Did So Many Come?', *Central and Eastern European Migration Review*, 3 (2): 1–27.

Oliveros, P. (2022) *Quantum Listening*, United Kingdom: TJ Books Limited.

Orbist, H. (2014) *Ways of Curating*, London: Penguin Random House UK.

Otwinowska-Kasztelanic, A. (2000) *A Study of the Lexico-Semantic and Grammatical Influence of English on the Polish of the Younger Generation of Poles*, Warsaw: Dialog.

Pakuła, Ł. (ed.) (2021) *Linguistic Perspectives on Sexuality in Education: Representations, Constructions and Negotiations*, Palgrave Studies in Language, Gender and Sexuality (e-book).

Pańków, M. (2012) 'Młodzi Na Rynku Pracy: Raport z Badania', Warszawa, http://www.isp.org.pl/uploads/pdf/302561875.pdf, accessed May 2016.

Parcello, T., L. Meintjes, A. Ochoa, and D. Samuels (2010) 'The Reorganization of the Sensory World', *Annual Review of Anthropology* 39: 51–66.

Parutis, V. (2011) 'White, European, and Hardworking: East European Migrants' Relationships With Other Communities in London', *Journal of Baltic Studies* 42 (2): 263–88.

Patel, I. (2021) *We're Here Because You Were There: Immigration and the End of Empire*, London: Verso.

Peirce, C. (1931–1958) *The Collected Papers of Charles Sanders Peirce* (8 vols.), Cambridge, MA: Harvard University Press.

Peteri, G., (2010) *Imagining the West in Eastern Europe and the Soviet Union*, Pittsburgh: University of Pittsburgh Press.

Petrosino, L., R. Colcord, K. Kurcz, and R. Yonker (1993) 'Voice Onset Time of Velar Stop Productions in Aged Speakers', *Perceptual and Motor Skills* 76 (1): 83–8.

Pilkington, M. (2021) 'How to Believe Weird Things', in J. Sutcliffe (ed.), *Magic*, 63–70, London: Whitechapel Gallery and The MIT Press.
Pinheiro, J., D. Bates, S. DebRoy, D. Sarkar, R. Core Team (2015) *nlme: Linear and Nonlinear Mixed Effects Models*, http://CRAN.R-project.org/package.nlme, accessed April 2015.
Pink, S. (2006) *The Future of Visual Anthropology: Engaging the Senses*, New York: Routledge.
Podesva, R. (2006) 'Intonational Variation and Social Meaning: Categorical and Phonetic Aspects', *U. Penn Working Papers in Linguistics* 12 (2): 189–202.
Podesva, R. (2007) 'Phonation Type as a Stylistic Variable: The Use of Falsetto in Constructing a Persona', *Journal of Sociolinguistics* 11 (4): 478–504.
Podesva, R. (2016) 'Stance as a Window Into the Language-race Connection: Evidence From African American and White Speakers in Washington, DC', in H. S. Alim, J. Rickford, and A. Ball (eds), *Raciolinguistics: How Language Shapes Our Ideas About Race*, 203–19, Oxford Academic [online].
Pyzik, A. (2016) '"On the One Hand the State Is Funding You and Enabling Your Existence, on the Other, Your Whole Shtick Is to Rebel Against It": Post-Punk and Poland', in G. But et al. (eds), *Post Punk: Then and Now*, 84–97, London: Repeater Books.
Quijano, A. (2000) 'Coloniality of Power, Eurocentrism and Latin America'. *International Sociology* 15 (2): 215–32.
R Development Core Team, (2009) *R: A Language and Environment for Statistical Computing*. Vienna, Austria: R Foundation for Statistical Computing.
Ramaswamy, S. (1997) *Passions of the Tongue: Language Devotion in Tamil India, 1891–1970*, Berkeley: University of California Press.
Rancière, J. (2013) *The Politics of Aesthetics*, trans. Gabriel Rockhill, London: Continuum. [ebook].
Repp, B. and H.-B. Lin (1989) 'Effects of Preceding Context on Discrimination of Voice Onset Times', *Perception & Psychophysics* 45: 323–32.
Repp, B. and H.-B. Lin (1990) 'Effects of Preceding Context on the Voice-onset-time Category Boundary', *Journal of Experimental Psychology Human Perception* 17: 289–302.
Rickford, J. and S. King (2016) 'Language and Linguistics on Trial: Hearing Rachel Jeantel (and Other Vernacular Speakers) in the Courtroom and Beyond', https://www.linguisticsociety.org/sites/default/files/Rickford_92_4.pdf.
Rocławski, B. (1981) *System fonostatystyczny współczesnego języka polskiego*, Wrocław.
Rojczyk, A. (2009) 'Parametr VOT w Języku Polskim i Angielskim. Badanie percepcji', *Lingvaria* 1 (7): 29–47.
Romaine, S. (1994) *Language in Society: An Introduction to Sociolinguistics*, Oxford: Oxford University Press.
Ropa, A. (1981) *Intonacja Języka Polskiego. Z Problematyki Opisu i Nauczania*, Kraków: Instytut Badań Polonijnych.
Rosa, J. (2016) 'Standardization, Racialization, Languagelessness: Raciolinguistic Ideologies Across Communicative Contexts', *Journal of Linguistic Anthropology* 26 (2): 162–83.

Rosa, J. and N. Flores (2017) 'Unsettling Race and Language: Towards a Raciolinguistic Perspective', *Language in Society* 46 (5): 1–27.

Ross. E. (1914) 'The old world in the new: The significance of past and present immigration to the American people'. https://www.gutenberg.org/files/47954/47954-h/47954-h.htm#Page_120.

Rubach, J. (1974) 'Some Remarks on Aspiration in Received Pronunciation With Reference to Polish', *Psicl* 2: 97–103.

Ruszkiewicz, P. (1990) 'Aspiration in English and Polish: An Overview', *Papers and Studies in Contrastive Linguistics* 25: 147–61.

Ryalls, J., A. Zipprer, and B. Penelope (1997) 'A Preliminary Investigation of the Effects of Gender and Race on Voice Onset Time', *Journal of Speech and Hearing Research* 40 (3): 642–45.

Ryan, K. (2005) 'Getting all files', http://www.linguistics.ucla.edu/faciliti/facilities/acoustic/get-files.praat, accessed December 2014.

Ryan, L. (2007) 'Who do You Think You are? Irish Nurses Encountering Ethnicity and Constructing Identity in Britain', *Ethnic and Racial Studies* 30 (3): 416–38.

Ryan, L., R. Sales, M. Tilki, and B. Siara (2009) 'Family Strategies and Transnational Migration: Recent Polish Migrants in London', *Journal of Ethnic and Migration Studies* 35 (1): 61–77.

Rzepnikowska, A. (2018) 'Racism and Xenophobia Experienced by Polish Migrants in the UK Before and After Brexit Vote', *Journal of Ethnic and Migration Studies* 45 (1): 61–77.

Sales, R., L. Ryan, M. Rodriguez, and A. D'Angelo (2008) 'Polish Pupils in London Schools: Opportunities and Challenges'. https://eprints.mdx.ac.uk/6326/1/%5DPolish_pupils_in_London_schools.pdf

Salt, J. (2011) 'Migration to and From the UK', in T. Modoodand and J. Salt (eds), *Global Migration, Ethnicity and Britishness*, 14–39, Basingstoke: Palgrave Macmillan.

Sansi, R. (2018) 'The Recursivity of the Gift in Art and Anthropology', in G. Bakke and M. Peterson (eds), *Between Matter and Method: Encounters in Anthropology and Art*, 117–30, London: Bloomsbury.

Sansi, R. (2020) 'Introduction: Anthropology and Curation Through the Looking Glass', in R. Sansi (ed.), *Anthropologist as Curator*, 1–17, London: Bloomsbury Academic.

Schleef, Erik (2017) 'Developmental Sociolinguistics and the Acquisition of T-glottalling by Immigrant Teenagers in London', in G. de Vogelaer and M. Katerbow (eds), *Acquiring Sociolinguistic Variation*, 305–41, Amsterdam: John Benjamins.

Schulte, L. (2021) *Learning to Integrate, Waiting to Belong: Language, Time and Uncertainty Among Newcomers in Germany*, DPhil thesis, University of Oxford.

Selkirk, E. (1986) 'On Derived Domains in Sentence Phonology', *Phonology Yearbook* 3 (37): 1–405.

Shankar, S. (2016) 'Coming in First: Sound and Embodiment in Spelling Bees', *Journal of Linguistic Anthropology* 26 (2): 119–40.
Sharifi, K. (2021) 'Manchester, Music and Multiethnolects: A Sociolinguistic Analysis of an Interview With Rapper Aitch', MSt thesis, University of Oxford.
Sharma, D. (2011) 'Style Repertoire and Social Change in British Asian English', *Journal of Sociolinguistics* 15 (4): 464–92.
Sharma, D. and B. Rampton (2015) 'Lectal Focusing in Interaction: A New Methodology for the Study of Style Variation', *Journal of English Linguistics* 43 (1): 3–35.
Sheller, M. (2018) *Mobility Justice: The Politics of Movement in an Age of Extremes*, London: Verso.
Shobbrook, K. and J. House (2003) *High Rising Tones in Southern British English*, Paper presented at 15th ICPh5, Barcelona.
Silverstein, M. (1985) 'Language and the Culture of Gender: At the Intersection of Structure, Usage, and Ideology', in E. Mertz and R. Parmentier (eds), *Semiotic Mediation: Sociocultural and Psychological Perspectives*, 219–59, Orlando, FL: Academic Press.
Silverstein, M. (1992) 'The Indeterminacy of Contextualization: When is Enough Enough?', in P. Auer and A. di Luzio (eds), *The Contextualization of Language*, 55–76, Amsterdam: John Benjamins Publishing.
Silverstein, M. (2003) 'Indexical Order and the Dialectics of Sociolinguistic Life', *Language and Communication* 23: 193–229.
Silverstein, M. (2016) 'The "Push" of Lautgesetze, the "Pull" of Enregisterment', in N. Coupland (ed.), *Sociolinguistics: Theoretical Debates*, 37–67, Cambridge: Cambridge University Press.
SimilarWeb (2017) https://www.similarweb.com/corp/blog/uk-media-publications-rankingfebruary-2017, accessed 20 March 2021.
Skeggs, B (1997) *Formations of Class and Gender*, London: SAGE.
Skeggs, B. (2016) 'Class: Disidentification, Singular Selves and Person-Value (Published in Portuguese as Classe; Disidenificacao, Selves Singulars E Valor Da Pessoa)', in B Sallum Jnr; L. M. Schwarcz; D Vidal, and A Catani (eds), *Identidades*, 145–73, Sao Paulo: Universidade De Sao Paulo.
Słabek, H. (2009) *O Społecznej Historii Polski 1945–89*. S.68, Książka i Wiedza.
Small, M. (2009) '"How Many Cases Do I Need?" On Science and the Logic of Case Selection in Field-Based Research', *Ethnography* 10 (1): 5–38.
Spencer, I. (1997) *British Immigration Policy Since 1939: The Making of Multi-racial Britain*, London: Routledge.
Spigelman, A. (2013) 'The Depiction of Polish Migrants in the United Kingdom by the British Press After Poland's Accession to the European Union', *International Journal of Sociology and Social Policy* 30 (1/2): 98–113.
Spivak, G. (1988) 'Can the Subaltern Speak?', in C. Nelson and L. Grossberg (eds), *Marxism and the Interpretation of Culture*, 271–316, Urbana: University of Illinois Press.

Środa, M. (2012) *Kobiety i Władza*, Warszawa: Wydawnictwo W.A.B.
Stavrides, S. (2016) *Common Space: The City as Commons*, London: Zed Books.
Strathern, M. (1992) *After Nature: English Kinship in the Late Twentieth Century*, Cambridge: Cambridge University Press
Stroud, C. (2001) 'African Mother Tongue Programs and the Politics of Language: Linguistic Citizenship Versus Linguistic Human Rights', *Journal of Multilingual and Multicultural Development* 22 (4): 339–55.
Stroud, C. (2009) 'A Postliberal Critique of Language Rights: Toward a Politics of Language for a Linguistics of Contact', in J. Petrovic (ed.), *International Perspectives on Bilingual Education: Policy, Practice and Controversy*, 191–218, Charlotte: Information Age Publishing.
Stroud, C. (2018) 'Linguistic Citizenship', in L. Lim, Ch. Stroud and L. Wee (eds), *The Multilingual Citizen: Towards a Politics of Language for Agency and Change*, Bristol: Multilingual Matters [online].
Stuart-Smith, J., M. Sonderegger, T. Rathcke, and M. Rachel (2015) 'The Private Life of Stops: VOT in a Real-time Corpus of Spontaneous Glaswegian', *Laboratory Phonology* 6: 3–4.
Sword, K. (1994) *Community in Flux*, London: SSEES UCL.
Syrdal, A. (1996) 'Acoustic Variability in Spontaneous Conversational Speech of American English Talkers', Paper presented at ICSLP 96 (Fourth International Conference on Spoken Language Processing), Philadelphia, October 3–6, www.asel.udel.edu/icslp/cdrom/voll/582/a582/pdf, accessed March 2015.
Szpakowska, M. (2003) *Chcieć i Mieć. Samowiedza Obyczajowa w Polsce Czasu Przemian*, Warszawa: Wydawnictwo W.A.B.
Sztencel, M. (2009) 'Boundaries Crossed: The Influence of English on Modern Polish', https://research.ncl.ac.uk/e-pisteme/issues/issue02/contents/e-pisteme%20Vol.2(1)%20-%20Magdalena%20Sztencel.pdf, accessed in 2019.
Tabili, L. (1994) *'We Ask for British Justice': Workers and Racial Difference in Late Imperial Britain*, Ithaca, NY: Cornell University Press.
Tannahill, J. (1958) *European Volunteer Workers in Britain*, Manchester: Manchester University Press.
Thibault, P. (2017) 'The Reflexivity of Human Languaging and Nigel Love's Two Orders of Language', *Language Sciences* 61: 74–85.
Thomas, W. and F. Znaniecki (1918) *The Polish Peasant in Europe and America*, Boston: Badger.
Thompson, E. (2015 [2002]) 'Sound, Modernity and History', in C. Kelly (ed) *Sound*, 117–20, London: Whitechapel Gallery.
Tinius, J. and S. Macdonald (2020) 'The Recursivity of the Curatorial', in R. Sansi (ed.), *The Anthropologist as Curator*, 35–58, London: Bloomsbury Academic.
Triandafyllidou, A. (2006) *Contemporary Polish Migration in Europe: Complex Patterns of Movement and Settlement*, Lewiston, NY: The Edwin Mellen Press.

Trudgill, P. (1974) *The Social Stratification of English in Norwich*, Cambridge: Cambridge University Press.
Tsing, A. (2015) *The Mushroom at the End of the World*, Princeton, NJ: Princeton University Press.
Urbańczyk, S. and M. Kucała (1999) *Encyklopedia Języka Polskiego*, Wrocław: Zakład Narodowy im. Ossolińskich.
Urla, J. (1993) 'Cultural Politics in an Age of Statistics: Numbers, Nations and the Making of Basque Identity', *American Ethnologist* 20 (4): 818–43.
Wagner, A. (2009) *A Comprehensive Model of Intonation for Application in Speech Synthesis*, PhD, Uniwersytet im. Adama Mickiewicza w Poznaniu.
Walczak, B. (2012) 'Kontakty polszczyzny z językami niesłowiańskimi', in Jerzy Bartmiński (ed.), *Współczesny język polski. Wydanie IV*, 527–41, Lublin: Wydawnictwo Uniwersytetu Marii Curie-Skłodowskiej.
Waniek-Klimczak, E. (2009) *Socio-Psychological Conditioning in ESL Pronunciation Consonant Voicing in English Spoken by Polish Immigrants to Britain*, Włocławek: Redakcja Wydawnictwa Państwowej Wyższej Szkoły Zawodowej.
Waniek-Klimczak, E., (2011) 'Aspiration in Polish: Sound Change in Progress?', in M. Pawlak and M. Bielak (eds), *New Perspectives in Language, Discourse and Translation Studies*, 3–13, Berlin: Springer-Verlag.
Warren, P (2005) 'Patterns of Late Rising in New Zealand English: Intonational Variation or Intonational Change?' *Language Variation and Change* 17: 209–30.
Weinreich, U., W. Labov, and M. Herzog (1968) 'Empirical Foundations of a Theory of Language Change', in W. Lehman and Y. Malkiel (eds), *Directions for Historical Linguistics*, 97–195, Austin: University of Texas Press.
Wells, J. (2006) *English Intonation: An Introduction*, Cambridge: Cambridge University Press.
White, A. (2011) *Polish Families and Migration since EU Accession*, Bristol: The Policy Press.
White, A. (2016) Paper at Gender, Identity and Migration seminar, King's College London.
White, A., I. Grabowska, P. Kaczmarczyk, and K. Slany (2018) *The Impact of Migration on Poland: EU Mobility and Social Change*, London: UCL Press.
Whiteside, S. and C. Irving (1998) 'Speakers' Sex Differences in Voice Onset Time: A Study of Isolated Word Production', *Percept. Mot. Skills* 86 (2), 651–4.
Wierzchowska, B. (1971) *Wymowa Polska*, Warszawa: Państwowe Zakłady Wydawnictw Szkolnych.
Williams, R. (1977) *Marxism and Literature*, Oxford.
Williams, Q. (2016) 'Ethnicity and Extreme Locality in South Africa's Multilingual Hip Hop Ciphas', in H. Alim, J. Rickford, and A. Ball (eds), *Raciolinguistics: How Language Shapes Our Ideas About Race*, 113–34, Oxford Academic [online].
Williams, Q. and C. Stroud (2015) 'Linguistic Citizenship: Language and Politics in Postnational Modernities', *Journal of Language and Politics* 14 (3): 406–30.

Wittenburg, P., H. Brugman, A. Russel, A. Klassmann, and H. Sloetjes, (2006) *ELAN: A Professional Framework for Multimodality Research*. accessed from 2012 onwards.

Wodarz, H. (1962) 'Zur Satzintonation Des Polnischen', *Phonetica* VIII: 128–46.

Wojnicka, K. (2011) '(Re)constructing Masculinity à la Polonaise', in E. Ruspini et al (eds), *Men and Masculinities Around the World: Transforming Men's Practices*, 71–83, SpringerLink, https://link.springer.com/book/10.1057/9780230338005#about-this-book.

Wolfram, W. (1969) *A Linguistic Description of Detroit Negro Speech*, Washington, DC: Center for Applied Linguistics.

Woolard, K. (1998) 'Introduction: Language Ideology as a Field of Inquiry', in B. Schieffelin, K. Woolard, and P. Kroskrity (eds), *Language Ideologies: Practice and Theory*, 3–51, Oxford: Oxford University Press.

Woolard, K. (2008) 'Why Dat Now?: Linguistic-anthropological Contributions to the Explanation of Sociolinguistic Icons and Change', *Journal of Sociolinguistics* 12 (4): 432–52.

Woolard, K. (2013) 'Is the Personal Political? Chronotopes and Changing Stances Toward Catalan Language and Identity', *International Journal of Bilingual Education and Bilingualism* 16 (2): 210–24.

Woolard, K. (2016) *Singular and Plural: Ideologies of Linguistic Authority in 21st Century Catalonia*, New York: Oxford University Press.

Yao, Y. (2007) 'Closure Duration and VOT of Word-initial Voiceless Plosives in English Spontaneous Connected Speech', *UC Berkeley Phonology Lab Annual Report*, 183–225.

Young, S. (2018) *The Construction of Ethno-linguistic Identity Amongst Polish-born Adolescents Living in the UK*, PhD thesis, UCL.

Zentella, A. (1997) *Growing Up Bilingual: Puerto Rican Children in New York*, Oxford: Blackwell Publishing.

Zhang, Q. (2005) 'A Chinese Yuppie in Beijing: Phonological Variation and the Construction of a New Professional Identity', *Language in Society* 34 (3): 431–66.

Zhu, Hua (2008) 'Duelling Languages, Duelling Values: Codeswitching in Bilingual Intergenerational Conflict Talk in Diasporic Families', *Journal of Pragmatics* 40: 1799–816.

Zhu, Hua and Li Wei (2019) 'Imagination as a Key Factor in LMLS in Transnational Families', *International Journal of Sociology of Language* 255: 73–107.

Zhu, Hua and Li Wei (2021) 'Translation as Translanguaging: Acts of Distinction in Multilingual Karate Clubs in London', in Tong King Lee (ed.), *The Routledge Handbook of Translation and the City*, London: Routledge.

Zubrzycki, J. (1956) *Polish Immigrants in Britain: A Study of Adjustment*, The Hague: Martinus Nijhoff.

Zukowski, T. and M. Theiss (2014) 'Islands of Civic Engagement', *International Journal of Sociology* 39 (4): 65–87.

Index

acoustic social becoming   80
aesthetics, aesthetic, aesthetic judgments   88, 92, 96, 180, 191
affective   14, 50, 105, 191
affordances   77, 79, 124, 126, 181, 187
Africa and African linguistics   37, 46, 60, 69, 189–90
African American English   49, 65
agency   71, 98, 189
Agha, Asif   13, 53–5, 66, 70–2, 74, 113
alignment   91, 119–76, 182, 184
anonymity   73, 151, 184
art, artistic   11, 68, 70, 191–2
aspiration, aspirated   63, 105, 107–9, 111, 120–1
assemblage and reassemblage   70, 72, 78
audiovisual   77, 101
authentic, authenticity   1, 49, 51, 55, 64–5, 73, 127, 130, 140, 181, 188, 194

Bakhtin, Mikhail   44, 69, 71, 179
becoming   69, 80
black, blackness   11, 27, 34, 37, 57, 67, 98, 115
Black Asian and Minority Ethnic (BAME)   33
Blommaert, Jan   49, 72–4, 98
bodies in process   179
bodily hexis   76
borderland thinking, borderlands   68
boundaries, boundary projects   35, 62, 120, 181, 187, 189
Bourdieu, P.   16, 58, 62, 66
Brexit vote   28–9, 32–3, 35, 183
Britain, British   4–8, 14–17, 22, 26–7, 31–4, 55, 94, 96, 103, 115
British Asian English   63
British Empire   5, 31–2, 34–5
British youth subcultures   62

Bucholtz, Mary and Kira Hall   51, 64, 78, 80, 126, 181
Butler, Judith   60–1

Cameron, Deborah   26, 103
capitalist, capitalism   14, 16, 18–19, 24, 37, 39, 45, 72, 185
care, caring   28, 81, 185, 192
categorization   61, 190
chronotope   41, 65, 71, 73, 74, 99, 126, 179–80, 189
citizenship   31, 69, 184, 189
class   15–20, 34, 57, 96–7, 148–55, 166–71, 178, 180
close listening   80, 105
coalition-building   192
collective, collective image   13, 62, 105, 126, 179, 183
collective memory   42, 83, 95–6, 104, 178, 192
Collins, Patricia   14, 39, 68, 98, 119, 185–6
colonialism   31–2, 69, 190
colonial linguistics   46–8
colonial matrices of power   192
communicability   1, 13, 74, 99, 178
communication   1, 41, 57, 77–9, 186
communication technologies; digital technologies   55, 76–8, 85, 89, 100, 121, 186
communism, communist modernity   5, 19, 24, 37, 84, 152
communities of movement   11, 182
community of practice   11
comparison and units of comparison   62, 72, 98, 127, 134, 158, 160, 179
conjunctures   119, 185, 188
consciousness   17, 52, 54, 69, 71, 76, 98, 101, 186–7, 192
context   13, 41, 44, 50, 53, 56, 59, 71, 102, 115, 180–1, 183–4

contingent, indeterminate   13, 68, 74
contrast   72–3, 127, 131, 143, 180
conversation analysis   113, 125
cosmopolitan   13, 119–27, 140–60
creoles   47–8
crisis of care   185
culture of listening   80
curator, curatorial authority, curatorship   191

decolonial   36, 68–9
dialectic of positionality   190
dialectics, dialectical   56–7, 191
dialectology   51
diaspora, diasporic   6, 8, 11, 38, 67, 72–4, 76–9, 89, 99–100, 178
discourse analysis   77, 102, 119
discourse and materiality dichotomy   61, 78
discourses of normality   179
distinction   61–2
distribution of the sensible   2, 92
dominant   60, 70–1, 83, 126, 175, 178, 179
domination   61, 78, 106, 119, 181, 185, 191

Eastern European   6, 14, 27, 29–30, 32–7, 59
Eckert, Penelope   58–9
economies of attention   182
embodied, embodiment   75, 77–8, 183, 191
embodied cognitive science   126
embodied knowledge production   181
embodied material practice   106
embodied memory   1, 71
emergent   13, 60–1
emerging networks   76
enactment, including material enactment   14, 61, 68, 71, 98, 106, 126, 175, 184
enregister, enregistered   70, 189–90
enregisterment   53, 55, 105
epistemic and ontological borders   116
epistemic violence   12, 47
epistemologies of purification   13, 176
epistemology of partial perspectives   191
erasure   48, 60–1, 68, 81
ethnicity, including new ethnicities   14, 51, 63–4, 67, 98–9, 131, 190

ethnographic   1, 7–8, 11, 57–8, 74, 91–2, 101, 177, 183, 184
European citizenship   17, 28, 101
Europe and European Union   5, 8, 10, 15–17, 20–1, 24–7, 29, 32–9, 44, 46–8, 73, 99, 139–40, 145–8, 162–3
exchange   181
exclusion and exclusionary   37–8, 48, 69, 73–4, 177, 189
expert   46, 71, 95–6, 177
expressive forms   62, 79, 106, 187

falling, the fall   124, 124–76
fall-rise, falling-rising intonation   105, 107, 112–15, 120, 124–5, 124–76
figuration   177, 182
floor control mechanism   105, 116, 120
flows of energies   79
fractal recursivity   60–1, 94, 136
fragment, fragmentary   11, 62, 179

Gal, Susan   60, 72, 74, 78, 98, 187, 191
gender, gendered   57–8, 97, 135, 154, 156, 157, 171, 180

Hall, Stuart   60
Haraway, Donna   12–13, 81, 178, 181
healing   185, 191–2
hegemonic   25, 42, 48, 58, 66, 71, 190
heteroglossia, heteroglossic   76, 179
heterosexual market   58
high rising terminal   115
historicity, historicities   57, 65, 72, 189
homogeneity, homogenization   85
hooks, bell   14, 184

iconization   60–1
icons   56
ideological   57, 60, 96, 98, 106, 130, 184
images of masculinity   65
images of normality   41, 55, 60, 126, 177–8
imperfection   40, 182
imperialism, imperialist   30–1, 36, 81
inauthenticity   188
in-betweenness   13, 165, 119–27, 160–76
inclusion   48, 74
index, indexes of subjectivity   56, 183, 188
indexical, indexicality   13, 55, 76, 88, 92, 107, 113, 160

indigenous, indigeneity   28, 37, 47, 69–70, 191
Inoue, Miyako   189
insider/outsider   27
institutional contexts, institutionalized processes   49–50, 67
interactional prosody studies   102, 113
intersectional, intersectionality   14, 39, 67, 68, 97
intersubjectively   74
interview   98, 101–3, 105
intonation   113, 119–76
intonational contour   102, 118
intonational phrase   102, 113–15
Irvine, Judith   60, 72, 74, 78, 98, 187, 191

Jacquemet, Marco   76
Johnstone, Barbara   54. *See also* Pittsburghese

knowledge production   1, 14, 47, 52, 71, 95, 98, 101, 106, 124, 127, 177, 181, 186, 191
kosmopolitanizm   99

LaBelle, Brandon   13, 80, 105, 180, 183, 188
language and nation   44–6
language ideologies   45, 60, 67, 70, 100
language labels   42
language norms   84–6, 185
LGBTQ+ citizens in Poland   25
linguistic authenticity and legitimacy   67, 73
linguistic habitus   66
linguistic landscape   86
linguistic market   58
linguistic profiling   49
linguistic representation   42–4, 46, 83
listening (politics of)   57, 79, 83, 181, 185, 188, 190
literacy of listening   57
London   2–11, 17, 22, 28, 63, 66–7, 77, 90–1, 96–7, 115, 131, 148, 184

marginal   190
materiality, materialization   2, 75, 77–80, 126, 181, 186–7
material-semiotic   103, 111

matter energies   80, 106
medium   77
metadiscursive regimes   48
metaphors   79, 119, 126–7, 179–84, 187
metapragmatic awareness   189
metric standards   188
Mignolo, Walter   29, 39, 118, 187, 192
'migrant crisis'   29
migration, migrants, immigration   2, 4–8, 11, 29–33, 35, 38, 54, 66, 68, 74, 79–80, 89
mixed modelling   111, 120
mobility (social, geographical, linguistic)   19, 23, 29–30, 52–3, 72–3, 76, 170, 190
modern, modernity/coloniality, modernities, including Western modernity   178, 180, 187–9
modern/colonial power differentials   29
modes   77–8, 183, 187
modes of transformation   1, 106, 177
moments, momentary   95, 183, 187, 189
Multicultural London English   66
multilingual   68–70, 77–8
multimodal analysis   75
multiple colonialisms   36
multipresence   55, 78, 177, 192
multisensory   78, 103

nationalism   39, 45, 99, 180
nation-state   14, 24, 30, 45, 50, 52, 68, 72–3, 118, 130–1
Nazi, Nazism   35–7
nesting orientalism   36
networks   57, 156
new mobilities   73
non-dominant   66, 70, 189
nonheteronormative   131
nuclear accent   111, 113

orders of indexicality   56
othering and antimigration sentiments   34–5, 148–50, 163, 167, 176, 180
other White   27, 33

participation framework   76, 79, 183
Peirce, Charles   56
perception and perceptual knowledge   2, 55, 64, 66, 80–1, 96, 127, 188, 192

performance   1–2, 13, 43, 59, 62, 67, 69, 71, 95, 103, 182, 187–9
perspectives   11–13, 68, 75, 97–8, 142, 179, 182, 188, 191
Pittsburghese   54
Poland   3–6, 9–11, 16–27, 35–9, 97
Polish diaspora   38
Polish Pole   13, 119–27, 127–40
politics   42, 46, 57, 71, 73, 83, 91, 183–6, 188–90; see also listening
politics of radical compassion, care and sharing   81, 182
polycentricity   179
Ponglish   89–90
post-apartheid   189–90
Post-EU Polish migration   6–10
Post-war Polish migration   3–6
power   2, 14, 18, 29, 46–7, 54, 59–60, 68, 71, 92, 96, 101, 165, 184, 188–92
public subjectivities and political subjectivities   12, 178, 183
purification, pure, purity   8, 13, 37, 48, 50, 57, 72, 91, 133–4, 136, 176, 180

qualities   52, 60, 167–8, 187
quantitative analysis, statistical analysis   119–24

race, racial, racialized and racialization   31, 34, 64, 66–7, 131, 183, 190
radically caring societies   185
radical openness   13, 185
Rancière, Jacques   1–2, 79, 83, 192
realness   130–2; see also authentic, authenticity
Received Pronunciation   55
recontextualization   77, 180
recursivity   78, 187
register   53–5, 61, 64, 70, 178, 189
relation, relationality   120, 126, 145, 165, 182, 186, 191
resemioticization   54
rhythms, rhythming   83, 102, 105, 119, 126, 119–76, 179, 184, 186–90
rising, the rise   124–76
Russian Empire   35–6

scale, scalar, scale-making   74–5, 79, 80–1, 98–100, 119–20, 126–7, 179–82, 185–6, 189–91, 127–76

semiotic-material   13, 70, 90
senses and sensing, including senses of scale   75, 78, 92, 105, 181, 184, 186–7, 189–92
sensorial-linguistic   106
sensorial matter   188
sensorial mode   75, 83, 118, 177, 183
sensorium   2, 41–2, 78, 177
sensory, sensory experience   79–81, 119, 127, 176, 186–8
signs   1–2, 41–3, 53–8, 60–1, 64, 75–6, 80–3, 90, 105–6, 113, 118, 126, 164, 181, 183, 187, 191
silence, silenced   80, 96, 188
Silverstein, Michael   52–3, 56, 57, 60–1
situated knowledges   13–14, 119
situatedness   63
social justice   39, 68
sociolinguistic listening   189–92; see also listening
sociolinguistics of variation   51, 67
sonic, sonic materiality   52, 57, 79, 80, 105, 119, 141, 181
sound, soundings, sounded experiences, sounded perspective   1–3, 10–14, 41–4, 51, 67, 77, 79–83, 104, 181–3, 187–92
sound systems   105–6
Soviet and Soviet Union   4, 7, 17–18, 23, 30, 35–7, 100
space of appearance   79
spaces of care   192
stance, stance act, stance-taking   64–5, 103, 113, 119, 126, 142, 127–76, 182, 191
Standard British English   55, 63
standard language, standardization   14, 49, 53, 55, 57–8, 61, 84, 91
'standard' Polish   86, 126
stereotype   24, 35, 49, 54, 59, 130, 152–3, 157, 169, 171, 173, 190
stops   107–11, 120–4, 127–76, 120–2
style   52, 54, 59, 62–3
stylistic aesthetics   61
subaltern   68
symbols   56

time- and place-making processes   1, 105, 177
time-space-personhood images   119, 186
togetherness   40, 183
Transformation of Eastern Europe   19–21

translanguaging   71
transracial   184

UK Polish organizations   3–5, 7–10
underheard   188
uptake   189

value and values   2, 7, 8, 15, 17, 24, 25, 30, 53–7, 59, 61–2, 65, 69–70, 72, 74, 77, 88–9, 135, 142, 184–5, 187
visual semiotics   182
Voice Onset Time (VOT)   105, 108–11, 121, 124, 120–4, 127–76

weirdness   186
white, whiteness   27, 32–7, 58, 190

Williams, Raymond   52
Wolof styles   61, 72
women in Britain   26–7
women in Poland   21–5
Woolard, Kathryn   60, 71–3, 107, 183–4
World Englishes   89

xenoracism   33–4

Young in Poland and economic crisis of 2008   21

Zhu Hua and Li Wei   71; Li Wei   77–8, 191
zones of encounters   189

www.ingramcontent.com/pod-product-compliance
Lightning Source LLC
Chambersburg PA
CBHW052107300426
44116CB00010B/1561